My Army

My Army Daze

By

<u>Andrew Wishart</u>

MY ARMY DAZE
by
ANDREW WISHART

Military memoirs and whimsical musings of a private soldier on active service with a Scottish Infantry Regiment in the jungles of Malaya during the 1950's.

© 2012 ANDREW WISHART

Andrew Wishart has asserted his rights in accordance with the Copyright, Designs and Patents Act 1988 to be identified as the author of this work.

Published by Andrew Wishart

First published in eBook format in 2012

Paperback format in 2020

All rights reserved under International and Pan-American Copyright Conventions. By payment of the required fees, you have been granted the non-exclusive, non-transferable right to access and read the text of this e-book on-screen. No part of this text may be reproduced, transmitted, downloaded, decompiled, reverse-engineered, or stored in or introduced into any information storage and retrieval system, in any form or by any means, whether electronic or mechanical, now known or hereinafter invented, without the express written permission of the Publisher.

Ebook Conversion by www.ebookpartnership.com

My Army Daze

'My Army Daze by Andrew Wishart', chronicles the impressions of an eighteen year old teenager. He is suddenly propelled from civilian life into the puzzling discipline of a Scottish Infantry Regiment where he serves his compulsory National Service and experiences an abrupt transfer from former Boy Scout to Infantry Soldier during the fading days of the British Empire during the 1950's.

Funny and Serious

By John Handling MSc CMgr FCMI FICPEM.

Format:Kindle Edition|Amazon Verified Purchase

I don't normally read personal accounts but this appealed to me as it was written by an ordinary soldier called up to do his national service as opposed to a self certified all action hero. Andrew has told the story very well. I was both fascinated and in awe of the things he and his comrades had to endure and was really pleased that there was no glorification or embellishment with unrealistic action scenes like most books of this nature. I read it with a smile on my face as he turned it into light-hearted banter even in difficult circumstances. A truly down to earth, realistic account told as it was. Well done Andrew.

Table of Contents

1   THE JUNGLE, JOHORE STATE, MALAYA, 1955.
2   INVITATION FROM THE QUEEN OF ENGLAND
3   I JOIN THE REGIMENT
4   BROWN BOOTS! I ASK YOU, BROWN BOOTS?
5   THE BOOGIE WOOGIE BUGLE BOY
6   NEW MATES
7   BASIC INFANTRY TRAINING
8   THE GREAT ROUTE MARCH
9   THE MUCH FEARED INNOCULATION INJECTION.
10   THE GREAT McBAIN
11   THE BLESSED BIBLE BASHER
12   THEN THERE WAS DREW
13   THE DREADED KIT LAYOUT INSPECTION
14   MR 'LETS GET ORGANISED' HAS ANOTHER BRIGHT IDEA
15   THE MYSTERIOUS POLE SCRAPING CEREMONY
16   SCRUFFY SOLDIER
17   PLAN' B' WILL SEE US THROUGH.
18   PISSED UP PERFECT PASSING OUT PERFORMANCE
19   THE NATIVES ARE GETTING RESTLESS.
20   EMBARKATION LEAVE- PENICUIK, SCOTLAND.
21   WE HEAD BACK TO BERWICK ON TWEED
22   THE BROOMIELAW QUAY, GLASGOW.
23   I VENTURE INTO INDIAN COUNTRY-SCOTTISH STYLE

24 BALLYKINLER ARMY CAMP, NORTHERN IRELAND
25 SETTLING IN
26 WE SHIP FOR THE FAR EAST. (Ahoy there)
27 I SAIL FOR THE FAR EAST.
28 TERROR ON THE HIGH SEAS!
29 PORRIDGE
30 THE MEDITERANIAN
31 SUEZ CANAL
32 ADEN
34 CEYLON
35 ARRIVAL in SINGAPORE
36 CHINATOWN IN SINGAPORE ISLAND IN THE 1950'S
37 WEE SPOT OF EGYPTIAN P.T. (BRITISH ARMY STYLE).
38 JUNGLE FEET
39 GUARD MOUNTING
40 WRITING LETTERS BACK HOME
41 SPIKE.
42 STRANGE HAPPENING.
43 I DECIDE TO VOLOUNTEER FOR THE S.A.S.
44 GUILTY AS CHARGED.
45 IS YOU IS, OR IS YOU AINT ?
46 A FLATUENT WHORE IN SINGAPORE
47 GOODBYE VIRGINITY.
48 I HIT THE NEWSPAPER HEADLINES, AT LAST!
49 THE FIJI REGIMENT HAND OVER TO THE K.O.S.B.
50 MARCHING ORDERS

51 PIPES AND DRUMS.

52 SETTLING IN

53 AMBUSH !

54 SUBLIME TO RIDICULOUS

55 CHARACTERS AND HARD MEN IN THE REGIMENT

56 SPOT OF PIG SHOOTING

57 McNICOLLS TRIES TO WORK HIS TICKET!

58 JUNGLE SOLDIERS

59 THE SECURITY TIDE TURNS A WEE BIT

60 OH - AN ACTORS LIFE FOR ME.

61 WEE SPOT OF LEAVE

62 IT'S SATURDAY NIGHT AND I JUST GOT PAID.

63 THE UNION JACK CLUB, SINGAPORE. 1956.

64 MERDEKA

65   BRAVO COMPANY COMPOUND (DESERTED). JOHORE STATE, MALAYA .

66 THE TATTOOED HEAD HUNTERS FROM SARAWAK

67 HOGMANAY 1956.

68 NEW YEAR'S DAY 1956. FRIENDLY FOOTBALL GAME.

69 THE POINT OF NO RETURN

70 NEWS FLASH

71 HOMEWARD BOUND

72 THE BALLROOM DANCER.

73 I AUDITION FOR A DANCE BAND AT SEA.

74 NO ENTRY FOR OTHER RANKS BEYOND THIS POINT

75 BIG PARTY NIGHT

76 SRI LANKA (CEYLON - AS WAS).

77 THE NIGHT TIME IS THE RIGHT TIME.

78 WE CROSS THE EQUATOR - AND YOU KNOW WHAT SAILORS ARE

79 CAPETOWN, SOUTH AFRICA.

80 BRIEF VISIT TO DAKAR, SENEGAL

81 LAST DANCE, GENTLEMEN, PLEASE.

82 SOUTHAMPTON, ENGLAND.

83 HAME AGAIN

Thanks to:

1 THE JUNGLE, JOHORE STATE, MALAYA, 1955.

There was a hell of a bang from the huge swamp nearby, hidden by the dense Malayan jungle. Our mortar platoon had started to bombard the nest of heavily armed Communist Terrorists reported to have taken refuge there.

Never volunteer for ANYTHING!! Guess I had already forgotten this good advice that had been drummed into my thick, Scottish head during my very recent basic infantry training back in the U.K. How else could I explain why Charlie Jeffrey and I were clanking along, festooned like bloody mobile Christmas trees, adorned with lots of empty, noisy, aluminium water bottles. We were walking alone on this lonely path through the edge of a rubber plantation situated right next to dense secondary jungle which reared its prehensile growth straight upwards seeking the open sky above.

I was following Charlie, staring at the bad haircut just peeping out from under his floppy jungle hat when I saw him jump as the shelling started. *'Stupid bugger'*, flashed through my head. The *stupid* part actually applied to both of us for putting ourselves in this dangerous situation in the first place but my stupid head was now also multi-tasking by urgently signalling *Duck and Run!*

I should have had this bloody thought about fifteen minutes ago when we were still safely with the rest of our well-armed and situated mates in their secure ambush position. My alarm was not triggered by the bombing from our mortar platoon, we were used to that. The enemy reaction to our shelling attack could really put Charlie and me into a wee bit of bother, isolated from our platoon by our stupid water fetching idea. There could now be a whole gang of armed and desperate C.T's making a break for it, heading through the dense jungle directly towards our lonely little piece of the neighbouring rubber plantation.

Our platoon had been in position since dusk the previous day and each water bottle was now either empty or dangerously low. Charlie had probably been a bit bored. The wild excitement generated by slapping ineffectually at the ravenous biting mosquitoes had eventually lost its attraction for him. That was when he volunteered to gather up all our water bottles and head for a stream about half a mile away which we had crossed on our way to take up our positions on the fringe of the rubber plantation late yesterday afternoon. Stupidly, (I mean that sincerely folks), I had offered to accompany him, temporarily forgetting my usual attitude to the volunteering thingy.

The loud bang alerted us to our plight. Our regiment was strung out for miles around a huge swamp area in dense jungle where we had reports of a heavy concentration of communist terrorists. The exploding carpet bombing mortar shells in the swamp was designed hopefully to flush them out, tempting them to make their escape through the neighbouring rubber plantation where we would be waiting to strike. Well, as my Irish friend Kevin might say with tongue in cheek, 'Dat's de teory of de ting'.

It was grand as theory goes, and, as is the way with grand theories, it went. Unfortunately, the theory had not made any allowance for the stupidity of both Charlie and me when we jumped to our feet, full of overgrown Boy Scout zeal, volunteering to skip on our merry, innocent way to fetch a pail of water. More correctly, to festoon ourselves with all available empty, noisy, clanging aluminium water bottles before heading off down the track. We were now alone, only lightly armed, our empty water bottles banging against each other, noisily advertising our location to any interested party. Good thinking Batman!!

'Oh we're going down the track, and will never come back.

Sergeant Harrigan is our leader,

Oh we know he's true, but he doesn't have a clue,

Away, down in the green hell, yes – the green hell.'

The above lines are from a popular army ditty of the time which now started to repeat over and over rather ominously in my head.

The thirsty corporal who was the leader in charge of our platoon must not have thought things through when he nodded approval for Charlie and me to bugger off and replenish water supplies for the whole platoon. We were all a bit new to this jungle game, the regiment had only moved away from our safe barracks on Singapore Island a few days previously to take up our active service posting in the dense, dangerous jungle country of terrorist ridden Malaya.

This recent move into Malaya for active service had been planned for months. We had all been through the very realistic jungle training course. However, this was the real thing, it would take some time till we adjusted properly and time was now in short supply. Just like Pronto, we would have to adjust fast, or else.

It was at this point that Charlie and I were forced to adjust a lot bloody quicker than Pronto. An entire section of the bushes near the edge of the jungle was suddenly, noisily and violently, disturbed, something or some bodies were crashing through the undergrowth towards us!

It's amazing what goes through your head when the adrenalin starts to flow through the endangered body. Apart from the repetitive Green Hell tune, my immediate, rather detached thought was, *"What the fuck am I doing here?"*

That thought should lead to the real beginning of my story starting with the invitation from The Queen of England, requesting my presence in this strange part of the world. But I am still mentally standing on the edge of a rubber plantation in Malaya in 1955, frozen stiff with fear, facing some violently disturbed bushes in the dense jungle only a few yards away but getting ominously closer.

With only the regular plantation lines of skinny young rubber trees around, we had little cover. There was nothing for it but to stand and wait for God knows what to emerge. My sweaty thumb was rapidly pushing the rifle safety catch forward to the 'off' position.

I seem to be a wee bit frozen in time here. You will just have to carry on without me for a minute. Just get to the start bit all by yourself and read on, I should catch up with you fairly soon…..

2 INVITATION FROM THE QUEEN OF ENGLAND

The brown, official, 'On Her Majesties Service' envelope came through our letter box one spring morning in Scotland just after my eighteenth birthday. It contained an invitation from Her Majesty Queen Elizabeth II to join her armed service forces at the depot of The Kings Own Scottish Borderers Regiment. The destination was their H.Q. in Berwick upon Tweed on 12th May 1955. I recall the wording towards the end of the invitation mentioned, 'and fail not to appear'.

This could have also been applied to the invitation from a former Queen of England, Elizabeth 1. As the Protestant Queen of England, the earlier Elizabeth had been aware that Catholic Queen Mary of Scotland could be a strong threat, a possible contender for the English throne and more than capable of possibly dislodging her from that position. Queen Liz was no fool. She promptly offered a hand of friendship to her cousin Mary, Queen of Scots who was experiencing a wee bit of bother in her own country of Scotland north of the border. Queen Mary had recently been engaged in pursuing the old Scottish custom of 'hide the sausage' with great enthusiasm, this activity had caused a great deal of concern among some of her subjects and led to the above mentioned 'wee bit of bother'. She eagerly grasped the hand of friendship when her cousin invited her to flee south of the border to England and take advantage of the thinly disguised invitation to join in the old, traditional English ceremony called,

How to get rid of the competition. This would lead to imprisonment and, eventually, to have her head chopped off.

I had a visit in late April from my friend Dave Abernethy who lived in my home town. He had also received an invite from Her Majesty requesting his presence in Berwick upon Tweed, although there was no small print about possible head chopping. I was pleased to see Dave. This meant I had company for the journey which was to be our first step into a world of action, travel, companionship and adventure. Not to mention a chance to wear a pair of Leslie tartan trews. These pants to be offset by a pair of sparkling white spats, worn over a pair of gleaming, black brogues, a fairly big step into the world of men's fashion for both of us.

Dave produced his army travel warrant for his trip by train from nearby Edinburgh to Berwick upon Tweed, and I was about to have my first *Army Daze* experience. My travel warrant from the same source, for exactly the same day and purpose, was to jump onto a Scottish Motor Traction bus when it travelled through my hometown of Penicuik, heading for Galashiels in the Scottish Borders! I was to change buses there and wander off across the southern Scottish countryside, eventually winding up just across the Scottish Border at the bus depot of Berwick in England. No efficient and quick rail trip for this child: I had been chosen for the panoramic tour. Lucky me! How the hell had the British Army managed to send two entirely different travel warrants to the only two guys from our small home town who were to travel to Berwick on the same day on 12th May? I guessed it might be an intelligence test to see if I was possible officer material. If this was indeed the case, I was about to fail the test within the first hour of my journey.

Our invitation to enlist into the army and serve Queen and Country for the next two years was the compulsory conscript obligation of National Service in Great Britain during the nineteen fifties. It applied to all young men on reaching the age of eighteen, provided they were healthy and reasonably fit. This also seemed to include the lame, sick and slightly batty if my, soon to be companions, were anything to go by.

I had been seriously considering applying to join the Seaforth Highlanders as a regular soldier, the regiment my grandfather had served and died with. My uncle had also been killed in action with the Seaforth Highlanders regiment when on active service in Anzio, Italy during World War II. I had carelessly brushed aside the prospect that a long and happy life serving with The Seaforths might seem a wee bit remote for members of my family. I would optimistically brush up my Celtic heritage, wear the kilt with pride and travel to foreign places.

Fortunately, I was advised by a friend against my impulsive intention to 'sign on the dotted line' and join the regular army. My advisor had recently completed his own National Service with the Royal Scots regiment where he had spent some time in Korea.

My wise twenty year old friend suggested I wait to see whether my seventeen year old body would be passed as fit, then wait to be called up for National Service to make sure I liked it. I could then sign and transfer to the regular army at any time after being called for conscript service, I could then also specify which Regiment I wanted to join. My experienced friend must have guessed the basic infantry training ordeal would probably push aside any daft thoughts of mine about signing on to be a regular army soldier. He had also guessed correctly that my ideas of military derring do and romantic army service in the old British Empire would soon evaporate.

I caught the bus on the appointed day as it passed through my home town of Penicuik, changing at Galashiels and aiming for Berwick upon Tweed as directed on my travel warrant. Galashiels is not exactly a humming hub of activity. It's just a wee Scottish border town, nice to visit on a day out. There were only two buses at the small depot when I arrived, one of which was actually edging slowly out of the bus station. I decided to board the remaining bus and settled down to watch as the world went past when we left Gala. This is the point where I would have failed any intelligence test.

I had my travel warrant ready to hand to the conductor as he worked his way through the other passengers before reaching me. The guy looked puzzled then handed my warrant back to me,"*Yer oan the wrang bus*", (the conductor spoke with a strange accent- he was a South Lanarkshire man). It was time for panic stations accompanied by red face. What to do? The resourceful conductor with the accent saved the day. He would talk to our driver to ask if he could possibly catch up with the correct bus, the one which was leaving the depot just as I had arrived in Galashiels. He could then try to overtake the other bus and head it off at the pass to arrange the handover of the stupid wee bugger who was on the wrong bus!

So, as they say, it came to pass. Our driver revved up to achieve a dizzy 50 miles per hour, managed to overtake the other vehicle, now being steered by a very puzzled driver, looking anxiously at our unscheduled approach in his rear mirror. He was about to reach the point where his bus was due to veer off in a different direction but, just in time, our driver managed to overtake and flagged the other bus to stop.

Our guy explained the situation about the stupid wee prat being found on the wrong bus. I was then safely transferred, still with red face, onto the correct bus for Berwick, viewed by the interested but puzzled looks from passengers in both the receiving and sending vehicles. I can't recall any further incidents for the rest of that journey as I had buried my red face into a book to escape further attention.

I duly arrived at the Berwick on Tweed bus depot where it seemed I was the only new guy arriving by bus to join the army that day. I later found out all the other recruits, including my friend Dave from Penicuik, had already arrived by train that morning. The military authorities were at the point of announcing me 'absent without leave'. This army crime, I soon learned, was a punishable offence. Here was I, not even started with the army, but already committing a bloody offence which was actually the fault of some travel clerk who had sent me by road, instead of rail, like all the other soldier boys that day. To be fair, the dumb, anonymous clerk who arranged my travel warrant probably had failed to anticipate my boarding the wrong bus in Galashiels, but it was too late, the word Daze had already formed in my head.

Actually, there was one other guy named McDow, already waiting at the bus depot. He was wearing an army battle dress tunic with the coveted tartan trews but minus the swanky, white, spats. He had been sent to the bus depot in case I arrived there. It seemed McDow was also a new arrival, but had reached the army depot a couple of days earlier. Unlike the rest of us, McDow was the only regular army volunteer among our intake of National Service conscripts, having signed for three years' regular service with Her Majesty which qualified him to receive a few shillings higher pay (remember shillings?). He was also allowed to join the Regiment a couple of days earlier than us.

This probably earned him the precious perk like jumping the queue to attend the regimental barber before the rest of us arrived. His line jumping had obviously been rewarded by receiving a bloody awful drastic army haircut, badly constructed by the regimental barber armed only with old fashioned manual hair clippers. The haircut damage to his already strange looking skull was now partly concealed by his T.O.S. (Tam 'o' Shanter), army bonnet, also badly constructed by some anonymous army clothing supplier with no eye for style. It was just the same shapeless piece of shit hat which would be issued to my, soon to be shorn, head.

He seemed very important as he marched towards me, full of purpose, shit and vinegar. Just then, a distraction caught his easily distracted eye, he stopped and pointed to a vehicle parked in the bus station. The van was painted in army khaki colour with a huge red cross on the side. For a moment, I feared I would be transported to a secure location in this vehicle but it was not to be. *"That's an ambulance, that's for sick people"*, Private McDow proudly informed me. This man should go far, I thought, as far away from me as possible.

The effort of having imparted this vital information made him almost visibly swell with pride and importance, it had also probably tired him out quite a bit. With no further communication, this loony marched off smartly round a corner to board a concealed army truck complete with driver. Could this be my chance to correct my great travel blunder and pass the intelligence test after all? I managed to put two and two together all by myself. No other communication was forthcoming from our soldier boy. This vehicle was probably my transport to the army depot and I merely followed Private McDow with a sinking feeling.

If this loony man, who had a face like a dog's bum with a hat on, was to set the standard for my future companions, it did not fill me with a great deal of hope for the future two years' service to which I had been invited. I did not seem to have much to look forward to.

(Photo taken by D.M. Smith. Photo News Service. Berwick-upon-Tweed).

My squad of soon to be, ex civilian recruits pictured on reception day at the Army Depot. 12th May 1955. Why should Britain tremble? I am seated in front row, second from left and wearing an unfortunate tie, more of this tie later. My new friend Robbie from Glasgow is seated on my left. Big Ray is fourth from left, middle row.

3 I JOIN THE REGIMENT

My disappointment increased when I realised I would be separated from my old friend Dave Abernethy. The alphabetic system applied to everything in the army, Dave was assigned to join 'A' training squad while I was sent to 'B' squad. There existed a rather home made sense of rivalry deliberately engendered between the two training companies. I guess this was intended to make us try really hard to aspire to be the eventual winners of an imaginary competition which was to be tantalizingly announced at the conclusion of our training. I remember making a silent baaing sheep noise in my head (I was too scared to do it aloud). Imagine them thinking we would fall for an obvious con like this competition nonsense. Of course we all *did* fall for it, spending the next three months trying to prove how smartly we drilled, how fast we could run, how we could survive personal insults, ignore verbal questions regarding the legitimacy of our birth and all the other daft activities the 1950's British Army offered us. I guess we were all too busy running about all over the place that nobody noticed there was no announcement of any winner of the competition when the training was completed.

Queen Elizabeth seemingly needed our regiment to be sent out to Malaya in the Far East where some ungrateful Communist terrorists were objecting to being part of the British Empire. Their objections took the form of total war, attacking the profitable rubber tree planting estates and rich tin mining locations. They were busy ambushing and killing anything that moved on the Malayan roads or railways, their main targets were the British Army and any Imperial British targets like owners of rubber estates. These owners were temporarily displaced by the Japanese during the Second World War but now the Brits were back in Malaya to take over again. The terrorists also wanted to be rid of the British Army altogether which is where my mates and I enter the story.

The communists waged war indiscriminately. One of their favourite methods was to derail the passenger trains as they steamed through the perilous thick jungle covered mountain railroads. The now stationary trains would then be raked with machine gun fire from a previously selected ambush position. These positions were usually situated on a slope above the railway line and anything else that still moved could then be picked off with rifle fire from above. This attack method was very effective but unfortunately did not discriminate in any way and often included women and children and anybody else that got in the way.

The British government referred to the general slaughter and mayhem as 'The Emergency'. This made the problem sound as if it could be solved by arranging a social visit from a friendly, local, good old British style police inspector to have a chat with the troublesome Communist Terrorists and explain the situation to them. He could even give the C.T's, as they were known, a stern talking to. This would probably sort things out. If the visit from the local cop had little effect then maybe, just maybe, the government could send a gunboat up the nearest big river, that would do the trick, just like the good old colonial days. I privately thought it had not worked in the United States during their revolution and I feared it would not help much in Malaya either, but what would I know. I was just a wee thick bugger from Penicuik in Scotland.

The real ugly side of the Emergency system would be revealed to us when we actually arrived in Malaya but that still seemed to be somewhere in a faraway place. Actually it really *was* somewhere in a faraway place, about 10,000 miles from home as the crow flies. Even sailing to Singapore in our troopship would take about four weeks from Belfast via the Atlantic through the Bay of Biscay to the Mediterranean, then into the Suez Canal, the Red Sea, the Gulf and the Indian Ocean all the way to the South China Sea. It was even longer if you have to walk.

At this stage in the Army Game we were more concerned with trying to get used to our very uncomfortable army issue scratchy shirts while trying to master unfamiliar army drill movements and new rules and regulations. All the while we tried to keep clear of any of the yelling and shouting authority figures. They frightened the shit out of us.

4   BROWN BOOTS! I ASK YOU, BROWN BOOTS?

The alphabet method seemed to be applied to all the military systems. It was the same story when kit was being issued. By the time the issuing quartermaster reached surnames beginning with 'W', he had run out of boots, black, army, size 8, (other ranks for the use of.) SHOCK – HORROR! No black army boots available for Private Wishart.A. This could hold up the entire war effort for weeks. What to do?

Some high level discussion took place when the kit issuing store man popped his head round the door to the next room. Having run out of black boots in my size he had to ask the corporal in charge what to do now? Of course I was still wearing my nice civilian shoes but we had all been issued with sheets of brown wrapping paper and a long piece of string to make a parcel of our civilian clothing to be sent home. It would be strictly army uniform from now on. This was an emergency. The war effort could be held up if Private Wishart.A had no boots to wear. It was decided that I should be given special official permission to be issued with nice, supple, smooth, comfortable, BROWN, size eight, leather boots, intended for issue to Officers only. These boots were only a distant cousin to the heavily marbled, stiff, unyielding, black army leather boots for issue to the Other Ranks. It seemed my luck was turning. There was only one problem, I soon had to get these nice, soft leather but bloody brown boots disguised to a black colour to blend in with the other guys.

I was sent to the N.A.A.F.I. (Navy Army and Air Force Institute) canteen, located inside the depot, to purchase a bottle of black dye and applicator brush (bought with my own money, of course). I was soon able to change my new brown boots to an acceptable black colour, just like the others. Applying the dye was a very small inconvenient price to pay. My new boots were comfortable from day one.

The black boots issued to the others were a different kettle of fish altogether. The heavily marbled leather surface on the regular issue boots had to be smoothed out by applying, I think, the heated end of a metal spoon covered with black boot polish and a great deal of elbow grease. It all looked a really messy business to me, involving heating the handle end of the spoon over a lighted candle before it was applied hot to the boot surface, then rubbed vigorously over the surface again, again, and again. Quite often this surface smoothing exercise extended well past lights out time in order to be ready for first parade in the morning. I remember seeing the other guys toiling away at their boots by candlelight as I slipped into dreamland.

My comfortable boots were obviously intended for a higher class of military man. I was easily able to achieve a dazzling type of shine on my officer class brown boots with a nice smooth leather finish, now black, by applying a soft, yellow duster with some black polish plus the merest amount of spittle which soon displayed the desired 'spit and polish' mirror finish desired. I was beginning to think I might be destined for greater things after all. Perhaps the boots were an indication that my intelligence test was still in progress, a sign that I was ascending the promotion ladder, so to speak. It did cross my mind at the time that perhaps I should suggest to the army authorities that it might be a good idea for the army to supply smooth, comfortable, black boots to the other ranks just like my officer class brown boots. This would cut out the laborious smoothing of the stiff leather boot material which took up so much time for the new army recruits. Army Daze had, of course, made another mental appearance to me to suggest the leather smoothing might just be some secret army training in discipline for the young, conscript soldiers. After all, I had nice officer quality boots. The time consuming smoothing of black leather boots was not my problem. Perhaps the best policy for me was to remain silent. I took my own advice.

5   THE BOOGIE WOOGIE BUGLE BOY

Reveille was always sounded at six o'clock. There was a true story about the bugler based with us at the depot who occupied a small ground floor room all to himself. His was a lonely life as he was one of the very few regular army soldiers actually based at the depot, the rest of us were all conscripts and not allowed out of barracks until the conclusion of our basic training. No beer swilling for us till the end of basic training. The lonely bugler at the barracks had spent most of the previous evening, drinking solitary beers at a local pub and returned late, 'well fortified', as they say. Next morning when he gradually and reluctantly awoke, he realised it was only a few seconds away from reveille which was his regular bugling duty time and he was still in bed. *Shock, horror!*

He saved the day by scrambling naked from his bed, grabbed his bugle then threw the window wide open, pointed his bugle outwards and put his lips to the instrument just in time to sound the traditional reveille, as required. The bugle blowing legend grew some more during our time at the depot. Last I heard was the beer swilling bugler had realised he could always have extra time in bed *and* lead a healthy lifestyle.

From that day onwards he would open his window **before** proceeding for his evening solitary drinking session. On his wobbly arrival back to the depot he could crash into his bed, sleep healthily each night with fresh, seaside air blowing in through the wide open window.

When morning arrived, he only needed to prop himself up in bed, reach for his trusty bugle and blow a merry tootle through the open window to arouse the young, captive, draftee soldiers in time for them to start another busy day. Our still half-pissed bugler could then roll over in bed and enjoy another couple of hours relaxing before it was time for his next, not too strenuous, duties. How he handled the freezing cold winter nights on the East coast of Britain with a winters gale from the North Sea blowing through an open window, was not mentioned in the story.

6 NEW MATES

I soon made new friends with some of the guys who, like me had been conscripted from all parts of Scotland. It seemed we were now living in what we were informed was the oldest occupied army barracks in the country, although why a Scottish Infantry regiment had its H.Q. situated just over the border into England was never actually made clear to me. Heavily fought over between both England and Scotland, Berwick upon Tweed had been claimed, changed hands and controlled by both nations over many years which gave the natives an accent which was not quite the same as northern English Geordie but not quite like the Scottish Border lilt either. I guessed our Scottish regiment had been beached there after the last English takeover then overlooked at some point and, *everybody has to be somewhere.*

The local football team, although technically English were closer geographically to soccer activities in the north of the country, the local team played in the Scottish football league.

Two of my new mates were Ray Reid from Jedburgh in the Scottish Borders and Robbie Robertson from a tough part of Glasgow. We soon bonded together as some sort of defence against this strange new world in which we now found ourselves.

Robbie and I shared a room, there was another guy there called Drew, also from Glasgow. Drew and Robbie were actually neighbours who lived in the same neck of the woods in Glasgow's Gorbals District but had never set eyes on each other. Robbie told me he belonged to the Hammer gang back home in Glasgow. Drew, who lived in the next street but either because of religious difference or even a slightly different territory, belonged to another gang in the same area.

Strange, I thought I knew every guy who lived in my small country town of Penicuik. I guess I still had a lot to learn about religious differences in parts of my own country. There was also a rather odd religious guy from Hamilton in Lanarkshire in our room, more of him later. Ray, my soon to be jazz fan mate from Jedburgh in the Scottish Borders was in the next room, just over the landing. In the group intake picture, I am seated second from left in the front row with Robbie seated on my left. I am the good looking one but wearing an unfortunate tie as I did not wish to join the army wearing my best gear. I suspected they might actually start training us in the mud before issuing us with proper uniforms.

This advice was given by my mother, bless her, before I left home, she was probably more familiar with stories of the Home Guard when my father was a Sergeant during World War II. The original Dad's Army had to wear their own clothes at the beginning of the war as uniforms were in short supply. My mother also advised me to make sure my underwear was freshly laundered in case I should be involved in any road accident on my way to start what was probably the greatest adventure of my young life.

My mother was perhaps giving me more advice than necessary. However, she was not even close to going as far overboard with her sensitive son than was Mrs.Aikman who was a neighbour of ours.

Every school day, eight year old Arthur Aikman would leave home on his way to school at around eight o'clock. Mrs. Aikman would follow him from the house, watching to make sure he made it to the other side of the street safely. Don't know why she bothered really, we lived in a cul de sac, a dead end street where nobody yet owned a car. At this point, every morning, she would call out in a loud voice *"Boy…, Boy…! Have you piddled"?* Poor Arthur, highly embarrassed in front of the neighbours would give a hurried nod of his head before quickly escaping out of sight round the corner.

7 BASIC INFANTRY TRAINING

Our training squad had Sergeant Fleming in charge, assisted by a Corporal Duckett and two Lance Corporals. These guys kept us on the move for everything. I had to shelve my normal slow shuffle which I thought was rather cool and now ran everywhere, even for meals which, as far as I remember, were not worth crossing the street for. We were all young, about to become very fit and burning lots and lots of energy which gave us enormous appetites so that even the disgusting food was quickly demolished daily.

I also started to swallow large quantities of peculiar army tea with every meal, even although ugly rumours were circulating claiming the tea was loaded with bromide which was supposed to curb our sexual appetite and probable conserve our energy. This conservation would enable us to burn the saved energy on the other manly pursuits like marching and running everywhere.

I loaded my tea with large quantities of sugar which was available from a big can in the mess hall, trying to make the drink more palatable. The possible bromide was not a problem for us, there was no possibility of sexual intercourse around here but the sugar possibly helped to maintain my energy level to cope with the extra physical effort during training.

8 THE GREAT ROUTE MARCH

It was at this early stage of basic training that the dreaded route march was announced and more rumours broke out. These were the usual brand of *'Shithouse rumours',* so called because no one ever knew who started these far-fetched stories, but it was murmured they all got their start in life in our ablutions area. The only route march any of us had ever seen would have been in a cinema. The film that comes to my mind is the movie that featured Laurel and Hardy apparently marching with a Scottish regiment in Afghanistan. You would think we might have learned our lesson about that region the first time round. Apparently not, we are still sending soldiers over there as I write this.

The actual route march was not really too bad, about ten miles distance, as I recall. The instructors were marching with us instead of sitting comfortably in an army truck and merely observing, that really encouraged us a lot.

I had been very active in the Boy Scouts for years. On one of our organized hiking trips we took the train from Edinburgh to the West Highlands area to start our hiking trip. We had scorned the local service bus which would have taken us into the city where we could catch the last train for the Scottish Highlands that day. Instead, full of bullshit, we marched the 10 miles from Penicuik into Edinburgh one evening in the early spring of this same year. Unfortunately, thanks to our devotion to the scorning bullshit, we had to carry all the required hiking gear on our backs instead of dumping our kit on the bus where we could have sat in comfort. I think I was already beginning to question all this Boy Scout enthusiastic nonsense just before being called up for the army. We entered the City of Edinburgh in fairly ragged style. There we boarded a steam train (remember the old steam trains?) bound for the West Highlands.

We used to do a bit of smart marching in the Boy Scouts. All of us keeping in step by singing daft songs as we marched along, this current army activity seemed much the same to me, except there was no singing.

I decided to show the novice soldiers how. Unbidden, I started to sing the well-known marching song. The one we are all familiar with, *'The Lassie wi' the wee snub nose'*, complete with a frequent chorus which, I was surprised to learn, none of the others seemed to know. I was sure everybody would know it. The song goes:

'Ooooooooooooh, the lassie wi' the wee snub nose,

nobody knows, nobody knows,

and my heart like a big steam engine goes,

for the lassie in the biscuit factory'.

Chorus

Oompa, oompa, tiddley om pom,

Oompa, oompa, tiddley om pom,

for the lassie in the biscuit factory.

Second verse

Oooooooooooh, the lassie wi' the wee snub nose,'

she wears pink hose, everybody knows

and ma heart is bustin' thru ma clothes

for the lassie in the biscuit factory.

Chorus.

Oh the lassie wi' the wee snub nose

I'm daft for her, everybody knows

I'd be hame fae work early, I'd propose,

tae the lassie in the biscuit factory.

Chorus.

The trick I employed to make this one of the best marching songs ever was to sing the beginning *Ooooooooooh* part, dragging it out till you come to *'the lassie'* part when you stamp your left foot in time with *'lassie'*. This really gets the marching rhythm going and the whole hike goes with a swing.

Unfortunately, none of the other guys seemed to know this song. I had to sing the whole bloody thing by myself, including chorus. When I started to falter on my new solo career, Sergeant Fleming fell into step beside me, urging me to keep singing. I was really encouraged then and kept on singing solo for several more choruses, quite chuffed really.

Hindsight now tells me Sergeant Fleming was selecting me for the part of, *'daft laddie'*. I, of course, being a very young soldier, immediately fell for it. He had a good reason for doing this. During the first few days of being formed up as a marching squad on the barrack square, he had instructed us to chant out the drill movements in unison. This enabled us recent civilian duffers, unfamiliar with army movements, to do the drill movements together. He instructed all of us to chant 1-2-3, 2-2-3-etc when we followed the drill instructions being given, this effectively guided us to follow the basic movements.

When the basic 1-2-3 etc. had penetrated into our thick skulls, Sergeant Fleming ordered us to drop the loud unison drill shouting which could have been alarming the neighbours. He now needed only one man to do the time calling. This lone voice would not normally be audible to anyone else but our own drill squad.

I was certain our Sergeant had selected me as the very best man for the solo job. He was probably intrigued by my marching and singing medley. He decided I was to be the solo chanting voice, starting with first parade tomorrow morning, where I was buried out of sight right in the middle of the drill squad. Fame at last, thanks to my solo efforts at singing. I was also convinced I had probably been responsible for the successful progress of the dreaded route march. At what age do you get sense?

9 THE MUCH FEARED INNOCULATION INJECTION.

We would soon be ready to join the regiment in Ireland before sailing for the Far East. There was an announcement made that we were all to have something called a T.A.B. injection. This was a very powerful medication to protect us against beriberi, yellow fever, cholera, possible daftness and so many other exotic, Far Eastern diseases too numerous to mention.

This multiple injection was so potent that it was to be administered late Saturday morning which would (in theory) allow us to recover during the rest of Saturday followed by the entire day of Sunday. This break would enable us to survive from the effects of the awful injection and be fit for the running and drilling starting again on Monday.

Of course, the usual shit house rumours spread like wild-fire. We would all be confined to bed after the terrible injection. Wheel chairs would be supplied to wheel us to the NAAFI for complimentary beers to aid with the convalescence (this particular rumour was probably prompted by wishful thinking, we were not allowed strong drink at all during our training months). All these imaginings really came under the heading, 'Shit House Rumours', nobody was ever found to be guilty of spreading these stories but they surfaced all the time, answering to neither rhyme or reason.

The dreaded Saturday morning inoculation day arrived, we all gathered at the foot of the long wooden stairs which led up to the ancient room converted for the day into a medical ward (army style) where a couple of medical orderlies were stationed with sharp hypodermic needles, ready for business.

One of our guys, Rab Nesbit, was about my height but with barrel chest and built like a brick shithouse. He rolled up one sleeve to reveal his huge biceps, then pushed past the others all the way up the steep old wooden stairs to be first in line. There was no competition for the leading spot and Nesbit boasted all the way up that he wanted to get this ordeal over with and enquiring why we were all so scared of *'a little bit of a scratch'*. He strode right into the room just like a brave man leading the way for the rest of us.

A few seconds later there was a commotion at the top of the stairs and then Nesbit's inert and unconscious but still not inoculated body came slithering swiftly downwards being transferred from hand to hand overhead down the line. Our hard man Nesbit had passed out cold before the orderly could carry out the injection.

I do not recall seeing him again for the remaining basic training days, nor at any time after that morning. Another mysterious disappearance, I sometimes had to wonder what happened to guys like him.

10   THE GREAT McBAIN

Private McBain was a very interesting guy. He was a slight, nervous looking wee guy who seemed to suddenly appear in our midst as if by magic a few days after the rest of us arrived. Apparently he had been part of an earlier intake but had then been sent away for an intensive 'building up' physical training course as he seemed a bit frail for the strenuous basic training ahead. I have no idea what his building up course involved for he was still not a strong looking guy by the time he returned to join us.

However, his strength seemed to lie more in the business of entertaining. He enlivened our basic training with good stories although, whether his tales were true or not, we were never sure.

He claimed to have been on stage in his civilian life, performing as *The Great McBain*, hypnotist and conjurer, touring the country on the Moss Empire Theatre circuit.

Although our guys came mainly from the industrial centre of Scotland from Glasgow to Edinburgh, where both cities had well established *Empire* theatres, nobody could actually claim to have seen McBain perform. But this was not just any theatre. We were a captive audience starved for any sort of leisure activity. We had neither time, money, permission nor leisure for pleasure. We were, of course, confined to barracks for the duration of basic training.

Saturday afternoon was when McBain had his chance to shine and he grabbed it with both dexterous hands. We probably had spent the morning running around and also being drilled, drilled and drilled again so we were usually relieved to be told we had the afternoon off. This, of course, was just another shithouse rumour. In reality we had all our kit, boots, buckles etc. to be cleaned and polished, laundry to be organized, shirts and uniforms to be pressed and ironed. Our webbing had to be regularly scrubbed till it was almost white. I say almost because a snow like white was impossible to achieve with our heavy webbing but that did not discourage us from trying to achieve the impossible.

We sometimes exercised on the nearby sea shore doing healthy things like P.T. or sprinting on the hard sand. The North Sea was where I had another of my really bright ideas. I persuaded a bunch of my mates to immerse their webbing belts in the salty sea then spread them over some rocks to dry while we sprinted about doing the healthy things. My reasoning was the sea water would bleach our almost white webbing belts even whiter as they dried in the sun. Unfortunately, our scruffy soldier Alfie had failed to notice the returning tide was coming in, his belt was wheeched away for good.

Our big fat Northern Irish Quartermaster had a field day the following morning when Alfie reported the loss of his new army belt. The Q.M's loud Irish bellow echoed round the depot, ***"Deficient are ye, deficient! Al'l give ye deficient, and that's not all al'l give ye, ya scruffy wee bastard. Deficient ye say, ye scruffy wee Glasgow gobshite, al'l give ye deficient, ya wee black enamelled bastard."*** I think I should mention that Alfie's skin pigmentation, although it sometimes seemed to be a little grey, was exactly the same shade as the rest of us. The description is not racial in any way and is just a general term used in our part of the world to make the point that the individual thus addressed had somehow incurred your displeasure.

Now looking back at our activities on the white webbing front, I scratch my puzzled head at the futility of it all. When we eventually joined the regiment a few weeks later after spending day after day scrubbing our webbing belts, almost the first thing we heard was some Sergeant shouting, **"Get some blanco on these fuckin' belts"**! Sometimes you just can't win.

Normally we would gather in our rooms and shoot the shit on these late Saturday afternoons while using lots of boot polish and Brasso (reg. trade mark). This was the opportunity for *The Great McBain t*o seize the moment, shove his cleaning materials aside, stride confidently to centre stage and entertain the troops. Most of McBain's entertaining took place in my room where something was always happening. Most of our squad would crowd in there looking for some diversion, giving McBain a good audience to work with.

He would usually warm up the small crowd with a few, simple conjuring tricks involving disappearing coins. Not really much of a novelty for us poor recruits, no coins ever stayed in our poorly paid pockets for very long anyway.

His hypnotist act was most popular though, everybody loves to see somebody else being made to act foolishly. However, it was amazing how many of our guys were attracted from the nearby rooms to volunteer to be one of McBain's subjects. I guess most people think they are immune to this kind of rubbish but the dafties used to line up regularly to test whether McBain could, 'put them under'.

On any Saturday afternoon, it was not unusual to see one of our hard men from Glasgow, sitting cross legged on the floor just like a little girl, singing, **'*Somewhere over the rainbow*'**, in a high, falsetto voice. He would soon be followed by another guy hopping over the floor clucking like a hen or possibly taking an imagined bath with imaginary soap while sitting on the very real bare, uncomfortable wooden floor, all due to the hypnotic efforts of **The Great McBain.**

He even had one tough looking guy from Glasgow attempting to make love to an old broom handle. Lover man had even reached the stage of unbuttoning his pants as a prelude to his next romantic move when McBain realised where this act was going and gently brought the big guy back into the land of the living. One witness to the randy sex act show tried to explain to the unbelieving ex-lover exactly what had taken place with the broom handle and received a split lip from the disbelieving former porn star.

Our favourite event was when McBain whispered something to one of these guys just before snapping his fingers, bringing his subject back to what we regarded as normal.

The chosen guy, now apparently back to '*normal*', would have no idea what had been happening to him. He would sit, scratching his head or bum depending on his needs, asking us to describe exactly what antics he had been made to perform. Suddenly, without any knowledge or warning, he would raise his head and shout, **"Get your Durex here"**, before picking up his conversation again, exactly where he had left off.

Durex is a well-known brand of condom and was always good for a laugh. McBain would whisper something to the hypnotised guy just before he brought him round again, his whisper planted the trigger word in the guy's head. That was usually enough. McBain was sure to use the specified word at some time after the victim was back to normal, the recently hypnotised guy would then take it from there all by himself. This always got an immediate response and loud laughter.

I accidentally got McBain into trouble one afternoon when I asked if he could hypnotise me. Yes, I know what you are saying but I was only eighteen and as much of a daftie as anybody else.

I actually knew an amateur hypnotist back home. He had worked in the Glasgow sales office of our paper-making company during the last few years of World War II. Paper was so scarce by then that he soon sold his weekly paper allocation. Having time to kill and being a bit of a mystic himself, he appeared as a hypnotist and mystery man in the matinee performances at the Empire Theatre in Glasgow, much like McBain claimed to have done. Our paper salesman, come magician, had tried unsuccessfully, to put me under once during tea break when he was visiting our office where he sometimes gave short, entertaining impromptu shows. He eventually gave up and told me I was not suitable. Why I was unsuitable was never explained to me. Probably I was too bright for this nonsense. I was curious to see if the Great McBain could do it.

He agreed and kept trying for ages until the rest of the guys got fed up and headed for the NAAFI canteen to partake in the other late Saturday afternoon diversion of tea drinking leaving McBain and me to get on with the hypnotising by ourselves.

Once again, I proved to be an unsuccessful candidate so McBain decided to call it a day (he called it Saturday) and we followed the others to the NAAFI. However, on the way there, I thought I would play a joke on the guys by acting a bit daft when we joined them. Unfortunately, I decided to do this playacting without mentioning anything to McBain.

My acting effort playing, **Andy the Loony**, was so convincing that it backfired and I had to make a quick pretend recovery to move between Robbie and McBain and prevent the great hypnotist having his head kicked in by Robbie, my roommate. He was convinced I had been mentally damaged and nobody does that kind of thing to Robbie's mate!

I don't think McBain ever forgave me for overacting. Our passing out parade picture shows he completed our basic training. He is seated fourth from right, so he was still with us up to that point. Strange thing, I have no recollection or photographs of him after that, perhaps he did his greatest act ever and made himself disappear from the army.

11   THE BLESSED BIBLE BASHER

One of our roommates was a rather strange guy from Hamilton in Lanarkshire. He didn't join in with our usual telling of mostly imaginary stories about the various girls we had known, and stories of far-fetched sexual prowess, interspersed with blue jokes. He seemed to prefer spending any, very rare, spare time, lying on his bed reading the bible.

We started taking the piss by mocking his apparently earnest religious fixation but eventually we would get bored with our repetitive banter and let it drop. We more or less started to ignore him although he would still deliver little morality lessons from time to time as if trying to get us to see the light and lead a better and clean living life style by following his example. Instead following our live-and-let-live out-look, we rarely paid him much attention. That changed dramatically one afternoon.

We had dressed for P.T. and were gathering on the square outside our building when I realised I had forgotten something in my room. I ran quickly back up the stairs but now wearing soft, canvas P.T. plimsolls, not the normal heavy boots. I made very little noise and burst into our room where I surprised our goodie-two-shoes religious guy. He had his back to me with the window wide open.

The window in that part of the building overlooked a nice park often used by the locals for quiet walks and there were two attractive girls doing just that. Their walk was being interrupted by the shouting from our resident loony bible thumper. The startled girls were rooted to the spot, staring at the wild figure in the open window.

He was making obscene gestures at them and his blue language included some words that even I had not heard before, this religious zealot was raving and screaming to the girls about various sexual acts he would like to perform with them. He was standing on the wide inside window ledge with his P.T. shorts round his ankles, making obscene gestures at the astounded girls. He was so carried away that he did not notice me, I just grabbed my forgotten item and hurried back to the PT session. Our bible thumper quietly joined us for P.T. a couple of minutes later, looking as if butter would not melt, etc. Very strange.

We were kept very busy for the rest of the afternoon so I had no time or opportunity to tell the other guys what I had seen. The final scheduled training for the afternoon was bayonet practice, one I rather enjoyed.

Bayonet practice was a good way to let off steam when we could also show off as wild warriors to any holiday maker girls who happened to see us. Berwick was right in the middle of the holiday season or what passed for a holiday season in those days. Our daily drilling took place within the barracks but lack of suitable space meant we conducted all other exercises outside the depot on the grassy area beside the thick defensive old wall which encircled the older part of the town. The wall had been built in Elizabethan times to keep out the unruly Scots. Bit of a waste of time as far as this present group of unruly Scots was concerned.

Visitors would be strolling around the wall about this time in the afternoon, taking the air, looking out to sea and seeking out available divertissement. This was the normal thing for holiday makers in Berwick before tea was served at their wee hotels spread through the town. The local Punch and Judy man would have packed up by this time, and our warlike training exploits often attracted their attention.

It was now July and we were about half way through our three months training and, bromide or no bromide in the tea, we were always ready to show off in front of any holiday making girls. Unlike our bible basher, we did not lower our pants to our ankles. This would have inhibited our forward movement or make any other motion difficult as I would soon learn a few months later in steamy Singapore, much to Big Ray's entertainment.

We approached our bayonet practice in the more conventional fashion. We charged bravely, clutching our rifles with wicked looking bayonets fixed, aiming at bags of straw swinging from wooden posts. Yelling and screaming in what we imagined was a very impressive and manly fashion as we attacked the swinging straw bag enemies dangling on the posts.

What would we know then? We were eighteen years old, and a wee bit on the green side. This would all change in a couple of months when we were due to insert real rounds into these rifles and sharpen our bayonets in earnest before taking on the Communist Terrorists in Malaya. But that was the future and we would have to find out for real. No worries right now, mate.

We marched back to barracks after our showing off session, glowing and sweating then dismissed to check our rifles back into safe keeping at the armoury before cleaning ourselves and heading for the mess hall.

I was one of the last to check in my rifle at the end of the afternoon's practice but something made me turn round just as I was entering our barrack block. I was in time to witness our religious nut case who seemed to have finally gone raving mad. Perhaps the strain of our basic training had proved to be too much for our Holy Roller - he was yelling and screaming cuss words while brandishing his rifle at one of our passing Regimental Police, not a good idea. The rifle was unloaded, but the bayonet was still firmly attached to his rifle when he made a mad charge at our cop.

None of us had particularly kindly feelings towards our home grown representative of authority but attacking the poor bugger with a bayonet was not to be recommended. The R.P. deftly sidestepped and quickly stopped our hero's mad charge with a powerful clout to the side of the head, knocking the nutter unconscious to the ground. Two bystanders were detailed to fall in, pick him up then haul him off to (I imagine) the guard house with the R.P. marching quickly behind them shouting, "left, right, left, right", as they rapidly hauled him out of sight, his boots scuffing behind him.

That was the last any of us ever saw or heard of our religious zealot. By the time we returned from the mess hall, all his gear had been mysteriously packed and removed. I can only imagine he must have been discharged on medical grounds as he was clearly 'mad as a hatter'. I sometimes wondered what happened to guys like him.

In my fairly short service so far, I had seen the mad *bible basher* disappear after attacking a Regimental Policeman with a bayonet, never to be seen again. The brave, muscular inoculation expert Nesbit also disappeared. Aptly followed mysteriously at some point by *The Great McBain*, hypnotist and magician, who was conjured away after our passing out group photo. None of us saw McBain again, probably disappeared in a magic puff of smoke.

12   THEN THERE WAS DREW

Drew was posted to the same room as me and was as normal as a guy from the South Side of Glasgow could be. We were in the ablutions early one morning at the start of basic training. Drew was using the sink right next to me. I was trying to be cautiously polite. After all, he was from a rough part of Glasgow so you never knew how these guys would react to even a very normal enquiry, observation or perhaps just a pleasant, *Good morning*.

The Glasgow population was made up from a mixture of both Lowland and an infusion of Highland Scots with a very generous measure of Irish immigrants fired by the huge exodus from Ireland during the Famine. This volatile mixture sometimes only needed a faint spark to set tempers ablaze but also produced some with a fantastic, quick sense of humour, unlike any other.

I seem to be equipped with good peripheral vision and could not help noticing Drew and the tooth brush appeared to be strangers to each other. Not too surprising. I have read that, during the early days of World War II, when kids from London were being evacuated to the country to escape the Nazi *Blitzkrieg,* that many of the working class evacuee kids did not to possess tooth brushes at all and were seemingly strangers to soap and water.

I was standing next to Drew, cleaning my teeth like a good Protestant boy, but quietly observing him as he just seemed to be standing there gazing at the toothbrush but making no move to start the cleaning process. Suddenly, his whole body gave a tremendous jerk, the toothbrush went flying as he took a few jerky but involuntary steps backwards till he made contact with the wall behind us and quietly slid to the floor with a puzzled look on his face.

One or two of us rushed to help him asking daft questions like,

"Are you O.K.?" What a stupid question this is but I believe it is the usual question asked even when some poor bugger has just been hit by a half ton motor car and is obviously preparing to meet his maker.

Somebody alerted one of our corporal trainers who got Drew to his unsteady feet and helped him back into our nearby room. He placed him on the bed where he just sat staring at something that none of the rest of could see. Drew just sat, staring.

However, the army routine allowed no halt to the military timetable. The rest of us just had to leave our friend and his teeth from Glasgow with the Corporal in attendance as we hurried to the canteen for mugs of morning tea (exactly the same as dinner tea, if you want to know) with slices of bread spread with breakfast marmalade. An army marches on its stomach, ye ken.

We rushed back from the canteen in what seemed like only a few minutes. Actually, it really was just a few minutes as our trainers seemed to make us run all the time from reveille to lights out. We made a quick check back to our room before having to rush down to parade on the square but Drew had been removed.

Removed to where we knew not, could have been a black hole as far as we were aware but, like the others who had disappeared from our ranks, Drew's bed was now empty, all his kit gone. We never got an explanation about his sudden departure, although I suspect he had had some kind of fit which would render him unsuitable for army service. This place was beginning to feel like the setting for some cheap horror movie, who would be next for the disappearing act?

13   THE DREADED KIT LAYOUT INSPECTION

There was an announcement that a mammoth bullshit kit inspection would soon be held. This is not exactly how it was worded on our orders pinned to the notice board but it was how we received the unwelcome news, how did these rumours get started?

The inspection was due to take place in two days' time. This would in theory give us time but not very much, to receive instruction and then to practice exactly how the kit should be laid out on the bed. The bed was expected to be a work of art all by itself; we were told to scrounge used cardboard boxes from the NAAFI. The boxes were to be cut into long pieces exactly six inches deep which were to be inserted inside an army blanket after being placed on your bed. Of course, none of us possessed a pair of scissors with which to cut the bloody cardboard, we had to adopt, adapt and improvise. Probably one of our guys had *adopted* a pair of scissors from somewhere.

This *adopting* theory had an interesting sequel: some years later in the early sixties when my rock 'n roll band was playing at Dumfries in the Borders - this will be a later story. However, this part is pertinent now. I had slipped out at a short break from our dance activities for a wee refreshment with the dance hall manager.

We were just about to enter the pub *The Hole in the Wall* for a wee drink - this pub became famous when *Robert Burns* the famous Scottish poet used to frequent the establishment a long time ago. When I ran into a great character I had first encountered during our basic army training back in 1955 at Berwick on Tweed.

Charlie was from the Scottish Borders and was, I think, the scissors liberator. The scissors were needed to cut and shape the cardboard for bullshit reasons during our kit layout inspection during our initial training at Berwick. Of course, none of us carried any scissors for this task. I guess somebody *liberated* the scissors from elsewhere.

It seemed Charlie was the only guy sent back to our original barracks for his release on our eventual return from the Far East. He was to serve his final couple of weeks at the depot in Berwick before his release. The rest of us were split up to be sent to various army depots around Scotland where we would be closer to our various home towns when our service was completed.

Charlie seems to have been left alone to while away his last couple of weeks at the Berwick depot. This was a thoughtless decision by the local army authorities. They should have kept him busy with some official duties. Instead, Charlie had kept himself busy and earned some extra income for beer money by lifting various articles from the newly appointed rest and recreation room.

This 'quiet room' was a recent advance in military thinking which had been started when we were abroad. It had been designed, I believe, as a calm and quiet place where military types could take a break from military routine to relax in a quiet and comfortable area. This room had several rather uncomfortable easy chairs, a TV set, a radio and also little tables where homesick, new soldiers could sit and write letters home.

Charlie greeted this new room with enthusiasm. While the rest of the military were busy elsewhere doing what military guys do to occupy their time during their busy army day, Charlie *lifted* anything that was not actually bolted to the floor. To be fair, he was only carrying out the old Scottish Borderer tradition of saddling up to ride out over the Border to 'lift' or rustle English cattle, then to herd them back home North of the border and into Scottish land before the local sheriff found out.

Where else did you think the wild American West tradition of cattle rustlers and sheriffs came from? It all originated in the wild border lands between England and Scotland, I am not sure how they take care of modern style cattle rustling now, but we certainly still have sheriffs in Scotland to this day.

Charlie established contact with a local second hand furniture dealer where he disposed of the TV set and anything else he could lay his hands on. It seems Charlie had passed himself off to the furniture dealer as a rich house owner living somewhere in the Borders. He claimed he had just returned from a holiday in Spain where he had fallen in love with that country and had now decided to sell his house in Scotland to buy another in Spain. His fake identity story was intended to back up his story that he was now selling his furniture before moving to Spain and starting his new life.

Charlie had cultivated a deep mahogany sun tan during his six week military sea cruise home and tended to stand out among the local very white Scottish natives on a cold April morning. He really looked as if he could have just returned from Spain as he claimed. Nobody at the army depot could understand how Charlie had managed to steal, move, deliver and sell the piano. Its disappearance was not discovered till the following Saturday night. It was sorely missed by the usual gathering of sentimental and homesick new, young soldiers who, confined to barracks during initial training, habitually gathered together in the recreation room on Saturday evenings to sing dreary sentimental Scottish songs mostly involving **a wee hoose in the highlands** *and* **a wee wifie far away**. A situation none of these eighteen year old young soldiers had ever actually encountered.

This sentimental and tear jerking twaddle was accompanied by the, usually out of tune, piano, now reported *missing* thanks to Charlie's clandestine activities. It was, however, too late to question Charlie. He had been released from military service on the previous Thursday and managed to disappear, *Scot Free*, from any provable blame.

Anyway, back to the kit inspection and basic shaping of the sacred beds. The result was like a precisely shaped woollen oblong display base, even before we started to get our kit ready for inspection.

I see from a recent kit inspection photo that our standards of fine crafting seem to have drifted downwards from the later drafts of young soldiers who followed us. The photo which surfaced to me later in my National Service was supplied by one of the young soldiers conscripted with a later draft into the regiment. It merely shows a sample kit lay out but is nothing like the bullshit work of art we were expected to produce during basic training. It's way below our standards in 1955.

I think it was around this point that I realised we had a problem. There was no way we could possibly use the beds for sleeping on the night prior to the great kit inspection. Time needed for bullshit bed layout did not allow very much time for sleeping. I could see a problem looming ahead.

We would have to make a quick visit to ablutions followed by an even quicker scramble to the mess hall. The kit inspection was scheduled to start at eight o'clock. We would have to dress in our gleaming uniforms by then, as we were also to be inspected along with the kit layout which took ages to construct properly. How in the name of the wee man could we get all this done in the time allowed?

It would be a good idea to make the kit display on the bed during the previous evening. It was a great idea with only one drawback, where was I to lay my pretty head to grab a few hours sleep after I had assembled the bull shit kit layout on my bed?

14   MR 'LETS GET ORGANISED' HAS ANOTHER BRIGHT IDEA

This was an army barracks, not a hotel with spare rooms. It looked like an uncomfortable night spent on a hard wooden floor was looming ahead, not a comforting prospect. Then, BINGO! I remembered the old army ambulance I had noticed when I first arrived at the bus depot in Berwick, now parked behind one of the buildings nearby. Situated in a quiet location, to my knowledge it had never been used since our arrival. It would make an ideal overnight hideout prior to the kit inspection.

A quick check proved I was correct in assuming the vehicle was not locked. It was on secure army property after all and it even had two stretchers installed. I conspired with wee Robbie to complete our kit layout display on the evening prior to the inspection. We could then saunter off quietly to occupy the ambulance where we would spend a comfortable night using our heavy army issue great coats as bed covers. We could leap into action the moment the bugle sounded in the morning and be well ahead of the game. Clever us.

That evening, our gleaming kit layout was on the immaculate beds, Robbie and I strolled away from our room with great coats slung casually over our shoulders secretly heading for the stationary ambulance nearby for a well-earned restful night prior to the parade looming early next morning.

The unlocked ambulance door posed no problem and we were soon inside the vehicle, unseen. The only teenie problem I had overlooked was that it was pitch dark inside. With the door securely shut, we had to rely on memory for moving around in the unfamiliar van. Not a problem, really, as all we had to do was claim a stretcher each and bed down for the night.

Robbie's voice came out of the darkness to admit he had, in his excitement, overlooked making a visit to the lavatory. He needed to pee before getting to sleep. I grunted at him to hurry up, go outside quietly, pee behind the ambulance and remain unseen in the dark. I heard him blundering about trying to find the unfamiliar catch which secured the door, muttering he couldn't see a bloody thing and you would think there must have a light switch somewhere. He started to feel about on the side of the vehicle where he imagined such a switch would be. At last he gave a satisfied Glasgow grunt and switched on with new found confidence.

There was no light. Instead, after a few seconds delay, a strange and alarming noise began to issue like a banshee wail from somewhere in the dark. This frightened the shit out of us and generated even more fright when the banshee wail developed into a full blooded alarm siren which was installed somewhere in the ambulance and drawing its energy from the vehicle's battery. We scrabbled about in the dark trying to relocate the bloody switch to turn off the screaming racket before it woke the entire barracks.

The noise was deafening. We were trapped and panicking in the dark when I accidentally located the lock for the door which shot open. We burst out in a heap on the ground. I have no idea who left it there.

The moon which had come out from behind the clouds gave us some light. But Robbie had lost his cool and we could not locate the siren switch again. So we grabbed our great coats and fled into the night followed by the banshee wail which must have awakened all of Berwick on Tweed. Even our Regimental Policeman, never the brightest light in the shop at the best of times, would be wide awake by now and heading for the source of the blast. Heaven help us if we were caught now, *guilty as charged!*

We slipped quietly into our building where all the lights were switched back on and mingled with the others, now roused and wide awake. We also faked big surprised yawns asking each other what had happened, who did it? Somebody eventually located the trouble and switched the siren off.

Gradually things quietened down. Lights were switched off again. Robbie and I had to bed down on the bare wooden floor beside our immaculate beds adorned with a full, military kit display. We spent what was left of a very uncomfortable night on the floor before the bugle sounded the start of another day

Luckily, the whole matter of the mysterious siren blew over as nobody could offer any explanation for the alarm so our names were never mentioned as suspects, too late now if anybody reads this.

15 THE MYSTERIOUS ANCIENT POLE SCRAPING CEREMONY

The entire training squad fell in one morning as usual, performed our daily session of smart, drill marching, with me issuing sotto voce instructions in the middle of squad.

Then, with Sergeant Fleming in charge and Corporal Donnelly fussing around us, we were wheeled to the right and issued from the barrack gates into the public street. It was an unusual turn of events for us to be marching along a busy street, first thing in the morning. We must be heading for something special.

After a while we swung onto the Elizabethan city wall, still surrounding the old part of town and wide enough for us to march along. We came to a smart but unnoticed halt beside what looked to me like a pile of heavy looking, black, telephone poles.

Sergeant Fleming told us to fall out and gather round while he and Corporal Duckett lit up their fags. It was then we noticed Corporal Duckett was carrying a small canvas bag which he opened and started handing out a safety razor blade to each of us. We were ordered to form into groups of four men, each group to manhandle one heavy, black, pole from the heap, place it onto a level piece of ground and sit on it, all of us, legs straddled over the pole, and all facing the same way.

On closer inspection, we found the heavy poles were coated in a bitumen type of material, probably left over from World War II when it may have been necessary for them to be painted thus, for some reason which was no longer important. The black, bitumen coated poles must have lain there for years till some anonymous ideas guy in the local council decided something should be done with this valuable commodity. This is where we came in.

Each group of four sat, spaced a few feet from each other, and started to scrape the bitumen coating from the wood using only a safety razor blade. Hard to believe really, but the Army Daze could be a difficult thing to figure out at times.

We spent the morning scraping away at these bloody poles but making little impression. Obviously the twit who had suggested we use the safety razor method on the poles had never tried it himself before issuing instructions for us to serve Queen and Country in this daft fashion.

Perhaps there had been some confusion and the twit had meant Queen Elizabeth I? It might have worked in long ago Elizabethan times, when the town wall was originally being built. They had a bigger pool of available labour and a large group of peasants could have tackled the job, overlooking the obvious fact that the safety razor had not yet been invented at that time!

I could see Sergeant Fleming was not in favour of having his training squad wasting time on this futile task. He let us have plenty of smoke breaks during the morning. "Smoke, if you've got them", was the usual order, causing the smokers to search around for any of the guys seen patting their pockets and who might have cigarettes about their person.

Nonsmokers like me just sat and looked out to sea, chatting and enjoying the fresh air.

The Sergeant let us potter about, leaving enough time for us to get back for lunch. We stacked the poles back in their original heap, carefully disposed of the used safety razor blades, and then marched cheerfully back to our depot wondering at the mysterious workings of the military mind.

Many years later, I happened to be driving through Berwick on Tweed to a business meeting nearby. As I had a bit of spare time, I parked the car in Berwick, and took a healthy stroll down memory lane along the old Elizabethan wall where we had carried out military manoeuvres.

There, like spotting a group of old friends, I came upon the familiar stack of old, wooden telegraph poles we had shared the morning with so long ago. They now had long grass reaching up through them, awaiting for their chance to make an appearance and, just like the fabled King Arthur, they could once again come to the aid of their country in any future troubled times. Why should Britain tremble?

16 SCRUFFY SOLDIER

Alfie McGinlay was another of our conscripts from Glasgow. He was a perfect contender for scruffiest soldier in our outfit and probably would qualify for the scruffy title in regiments throughout the land. Alfie was not dirty or unclean in any way, he expended as much effort as the rest of us in cleaning or wearing his kit, he just always managed to look like some kind of Neanderthal man masquerading as a British soldier.

He could not help it. At one time I rather suspected he would make the move to the ever increasing list of those who made a sudden disappearance from our training squad, but apparently just being scruffy must not have qualified even him for the quick wheech! Something else we found out about Alfie was that he could not march in step with the rest of us. Being about the same height as Alfie, I was positioned immediately behind him during drill squad training, and I was the first to encounter Alfie's strange style of marching.

Now, dear reader (I am assuming there might be at least a couple of readers out there, I still have a few friends) I realise you may have someone with military experience among you and no doubt you will be anxious to let me know that you and everybody else who may have had exposure to the military world, has encountered the soldier who marches in completely the opposite step from his comrades. Well, you can sit back in your comfortable chair and relax now, for nobody and I really mean nobody, could possibly march exactly like Alfie.

On the command, *"QUICK MARCH!"* Our hero would start off just like the rest of us by stepping forward with the left foot. However, before his left foot actually completed the first movement, Alfie's brain seemed to rescind the first order and decide that perhaps the right foot would have been a better idea.

Unfortunately, it seemed that Alfie's mind could not make up its own mind! This confusion led to the mental instruction from Alfie's brain to his foot arriving in a jumbled fashion, seemingly leading to a new idea of experimenting with another marching style altogether. Unfortunately, this new idea arrived at his feet a bit too soon. The result was the left foot only took its first short step about half the length of the steps being taken by the rest of us. Alfie's brain had apparently decided to abandon the idea of using the left foot as a leader. Instead it issued instructions to launch the right foot on its merry way but this step was of normal size which meant he was exactly half a step adrift from the rest of the drill squad. Pardon the pun, but this was no mean feat. If you don't believe me just take a couple of minutes and try it sometime, it's fairly impossible for a normal person, but Alfie was not exactly normal.

I was still responsible for calling out the timing for the various drill movements but marching behind Alfie was starting to cause problems with my thought process. I tried calling, 'Left, right, Left, right' to keep the guys in step but I was having to concentrate really hard with Alfie's head bobbing up and down in front of me. His style of marching seemed to include taking a brief skipping movement halfway through his initial step which affected his marching style in a distinctive manner which I found fascinating. It influenced not only my own marching but also most of the guys behind me. Not a good idea. I could see disaster looming.

Although I say it myself, viewed from the sidelines of the barrack square our drill squad must have looked pretty good. I felt responsible, being in sole charge of the time chanting which gave me a sense of pride and even a feeling of power. I was part of a well-oiled machine. It felt good, probably meaning that army training was taking hold of this civilian guy as I was feeling more and more like I belonged with the regiment. At least I felt like that till I remembered our *Alfie* handicap.

We were nearing the completion of the training period, the highlight of which was a march past of our drill squad, dressed in full regimental uniform complete with lowland bonnet and blackcock feather, Leslie tartan trews, white spats and shiny black brogue shoes. We even had a bagpiper in full regalia to play the regimental march, 'ALL THE BLUE BONNETS ARE OVER THE BORDER'. Much tartan bullshit, of course, but it was popular with the English holiday-makers when visiting Berwick upon Tweed. This also added a wee touch of romance to our swaggering marching style for the passing out parade. Photographs would be taken, parents were invited, so everyone would be **lookin' good, baby.**

Then I remembered Alfie and tumbled to a mental crash: there was no way we could look good with him around. Here endeth Plan 'A'

17 PLAN' B' WILL SEE US THROUGH.

It was around this time that I came up with Plan 'B', which I hoped might get us through the passing out parade with honour rather than disgrace. It would only take a wee bit of organising coupled with some obtuse maneuvering. I have already mentioned our old fashioned army buildings which bordered directly onto the parade square, and it was this situation that gave me the idea for Plan 'B'. On the day of the passing out parade day, we would be dressed and ready inside our barracks. When the command to get on parade came, we all would stream out and quickly form our smart drill squad on the barrack square, immediately outside the building.

This is where the *'Army Daze'* school of thinking came in. On the special passing out day, we would all duly stream out, **EXCEPT** for **Alfie**. He would be instructed to slide further upstairs at this point and remain out of sight during the marching display. He was instructed to take up a hidden position behind one of the old, heavy, post war time blackout window curtains in a deserted upper room and watch the parade from above. Brilliant!

We could then complete the passing out parade minus Alfie, featuring a successful marching display and showing off a bit. Afterwards, our drill squad would march smartly back to the starting point, coming to a halt just outside the main door. We would fall out and mingle for a while outside the building, feeling well pleased with ourselves. At this stage Alfie could quietly reappear and blend in with the mingling. There would have been no roll call before the march past. We were all captive bodies within the barracks. Nobody would think to count us.

I had cause to compliment myself for the perfect plan and solution which, if handled properly, would go smoothly. The big day would come to respectable conclusion with tea and buns being served to assembled guests and relatives.

At this point in a work of fiction, the carefully thought out plan would come to an unexpected halt because of a terrorist explosion or possibly the arrival of space aliens. But nothing of the kind happened. This is more or less a true story. Some names have been changed in case we ever meet up again, you never know.

Plan B worked like clockwork: the parade went well, so well that we marched off the parade square to applause from an appreciative audience. Alfie even shared the later congratulations from the invited crowd. I had convinced him that his evasive action had been a 'good idea' and he had been instrumental in making sure the parade went off smoothly. Anyway, this was true. If Alfie had taken part in our display, we would have been an entertaining laughing stock.

(Photo. Thanks to D.M.Smith. Photo News Service, Berwick upon Tweed).

Passing Out Parade, August 1955. Our training Sergeant Fleming is seated in the middle, with Corporal Charlie Ducket and two lance corporals. I am seated second from left with Robbie on my left. I am the good looking one.

At the following tea and buns affair, Alfie only managed to blot his otherwise good conduct by spilling his tea all over a visiting Episcopalian Minister. This supposed *tea spilling* may not have been totally accidental. Alfie was of the Roman Catholic persuasion, he also hailed from the Gorbals district of Glasgow where these little religious differences were taken seriously. The visiting, but now tea-stained Vicar was Episcopalian, go figure.

Alfie's strangled cussing which accompanied the *tea spilling accident,* was masked by quick thinking and loud talking from a nearby colleague. His carelessly dropped bun was spotted by another keen eyed soldier who swiftly dislodged it from the chair and kicked it away, unseen, into the crowd, just before a bulky lady approached to take the weight off her feet.

Alfie was unaware that his iced bun had been removed from the chair and he started to fumble around the stout lady's rear end in an attempt to locate the bun while she tried to sit down. Alfie's bunless and stricken expression must have been misunderstood by the fat lady who was the wife of the rather damp Episcopalian Minister. She struggled her bulky figure round to face Alfie and gave him, ***the look***!

Alfie recoiled and disappeared, mumbling an explanation in his heavy Glasgow accent, his rambling was, luckily, quite incomprehensible to the fat English lady who may have supposed Alfie was some sort of barbarian from the North, conscripted into the British Army, a supposition which was not too far from the truth.

18　PISSED-UP PERFECT PASSING-OUT PERFORMANCE

It was decreed that we were to be allowed out for one night 'on the town' to celebrate the completion of our basic training on Saturday. Sunday was reserved for peace and quiet which would give us a day to recover from our anticipated excesses of the previous night. None of us had been out of the barracks during the training programme, except for the route march and once for a marathon run. I managed to complete only a part of the run by hiding behind a bush not too far from the start, rejoining behind our best runner as he returned and then coming in positioned just behind him looking like a plucky second. Our period of incarceration had stretched from 12th May and it was now late August. I can only guess it must be something like doing about four month's time in jail. Luckily, the weather had been beautiful for most of the time. If our training had taken place in mid-winter I would perhaps have had a different song to sing. The thought of 'square bashing' during a hard winter on the East Coast did not appeal to me. No thanks. I was destined for warmer climes.

The great day for our celebration finally arrived and we were dressed in our best walking out uniform, tartan trews, white spats and all. Exactly at six o'clock we stood in line outside the guard room where we had to pass inspection before being allowed out into the fleshpots of Berwick. No problem there, although we were each issued with a special evening pass number which we were supposed to remember when we returned because, for some daft reason, we would need this number to get back in again! Why would we even want to get back in again was my immediate thought.

Big Ray and I had teamed up to check out the town pubs together. We were looking forward to swilling more than a few beers. We had bonded, being the only jazz fans among the training company but we were pretty much opposite in other respects. There was little chance of either of us hearing any jazz in Berwick upon Tweed in those days. However, we headed optimistically for the nearest bar, ready to get the evening started.

Ray had recently discovered a great drink called 'Black Velvet'. He had adopted the role of 'Man about Town' for my benefit and explained his was the poor man's version where cider was substituted for champagne then mixed with draught Guinness and served in a pint glass. It seemed a bit exotic to me, but champagne was out of the question. None of the pubs where we were heading for would be able to offer that class of refreshment, anyway. So I joined Big Ray.

Over the next couple of hours we tried more than a few. Ray was possibly a couple of pints ahead of me which I put down to his greater height. However, he did not seem quite as wobbly and daft as me, but by that time I was feeling no pain. I was 'beside myself with the drink', as they say.

Eventually, well refreshed, (there's a contradiction if you like) we made our unsteady way to the local dance hall. After all, it was a Saturday night and this was our passing out celebration.

19 THE NATIVES ARE GETTING RESTLESS.

If we had a plan at all, which was doubtful, it was to make contact with the local girls at the dance. We had decided not to restrict ourselves to meeting only local girls but to also consider *any* girls from *anywhere*. We had no contact with any women at all during the entire training months except for the old dear who managed our NAAFI canteen. In our teenage opinion she was way too old and probably 'past it,' as she must have been around thirty. This, plus the fact that she was slightly cockeyed and had buck teeth, rather ruled her out for us young and choosy gods. We could never be quite sure which of us she was looking at when she called out, **"Next"**.

However, none of our lads had considered the possibility that the local population would not welcome the sudden invasion of their local dance hall by our tartan clad army. This event only took place on one Saturday night every four months when each intake of new recruits completed training and 'passed out'. The native lads resented our intrusion into what they regarded as their territory, this, plus the fact that we were team handed and more than slightly pissed, talking with Scottish accents and from over the English border must have seemed to be an uninvited foraging attack from the hairy barbarians. Our severe army haircuts were certainly barbaric, in my opinion. Looking back, I guess the natives were probably right and reacted accordingly. General fighting broke out over the dance floor almost as soon as Ray and I reached the place.

The problem for the local lads was, although we were all mostly almost legless from excessive alcohol, we had just completed a fairly rigorous nearly four months course of physical exercise and were fitter than we had ever been or ever would be again. Formidable! This is according to Merriam-Webster, the formidable effect spread through the dance hall, resulting in exciting fear, dread and awe among the locals. It is where I first saw how effective and useful a seemingly decorative army webbing belt could be when removed from the waist, wrapped around the hand, with the brass buckles sticking up proud over a clenched fist and applied energetically to the head area of an opponent. Absolute bloody mayhem. The local guys never stood a chance and started to retreat, heavily damaged from the combined onslaught. Unfortunately, the local girls fled as well. The band faltered to a wheezing halt. The manager announced loudly and firmly over the microphone that all members of the army in uniform were now 'officially barred'; they would have to exit the premises at once or else the police would be called. We were so used to obeying orders from anyone in authority that we meekly left the building. Here endeth our romantic adventures for the night, a 'no show' situation. Bastards never even re-funded our entrance money.

Originally, our boast was about the type of girl we would pick, but I have not been able to remember a damn thing about any success in that department. Can't even remember much of anything at all except for Ray half carrying me back to barracks later where I disgraced myself by forgetting the stupid, special number I had been issued with before leaving that evening. For this misdemeanor I was severely bollocked by the thick, uncaring Regimental Policeman.

I remember arguing with the uncaring bloody Regimental Policeman in the guardroom when asked to recall the damn number. Apparently, I explained to the cop what a stupid idea the whole number thing was. It seems that I started to giggle in the middle of the explanation, but I managed to interrupt my lecture by throwing up on the guardroom floor. Not a good idea. I was saved by Ray who volunteered to haul me off to bed, promising to return immediately to clean up the mess. What a true mate. I would be able to return the favour to Ray on the occasion of one future, ill spent evening, in steamy Singapore city a few months later.

I was unable to remove my trews when we were eventually allowed to stagger into barracks. Two of my mates had to lay me down onto the bed, take off my shoes and nice white spats, each then took a leg of my pants to haul the garment from me. I was unable to help, having at last reached the passing out part of the evening. I was quite unconscious, feeling no pain. Tomorrow would be another story altogether.

Luckily, our last day was Sunday. Basic training was finished so I had the entire day to recover from our disastrous Saturday night out before smartening up to board the train for home on Monday. Back to Mummy to enjoy some embarkation leave.

20 EMBARKATION LEAVE- PENICUIK, SCOTLAND.

So I made the return journey home. This time I hoodwinked the *Army Daze* and travelled by train to Edinburgh, accompanied by my mates rather than wandering alone by bus across the Scottish borderland. I enjoyed the three week's leave. We had been awarded one week's leave at the conclusion of training, plus the regiment had been given two weeks leave prior to embarking for the Far East. No marching, running or being bossed about at every turn.

It was late August, lovely weather (it used to happen occasionally, even in Scotland). I happily dressed in my old jeans and shirt and generally 'hung out' although I don't think that expression was in vogue with teenagers at that time, but we certainly knew how to do it. I dressed up in full uniform one day for my mother to take a couple of photographs. My friend Dan Stephenson happened to call round that morning so I pressed him and his wee dog into service for a photo.

Dan, his wee dog and me.

Embarkation leave. Penicuik, Scotland. 1955.

Apart from posing for the photo, my army uniform hung in the wardrobe in my bedroom for the entire leave period. Shirt and jeans took the place of uniform, a feeling of wellbeing filled the vacuum instead of our continuous striving to obey military orders and attempt to be in every place at once and at all times.

I soon reverted to my pre army status of 'only child'. I often took-off for solitary hikes up into the Pentland Hills, the *'hills of home'* where Robert Louis Stevenson also used to roam as a young man. Thoughts of army route marches accompanied by lots of sweaty soldiers were pushed to the back of my mind. The hills were just a short walk from my house where I could relax, watch and listen to the curlews and lapwings. As I started to mount the slopes I would disturb the occasional red grouse from the purple heather. The grouse would explode from their hiding places before landing a bit farther away from my interference, giving their familiar call of, 'Go back, go back', before settling down as they went into hiding again. Yes - I was more than happy being on my own up in my hills of home.

I still remember one special evening which was not spent being alone. I went to a local dance, must have been a celebration for some event, the details of which I can't recall. Dances for whatever celebration it was were being held in two halls, on the same evening, and the purchase of one ticket allowed entrance to both dances. The halls were situated close to each other, but different styles of bands played, and it was possible to wander between halls to sample the different types of music.

I ran into an old friend from my schooldays, great girl, great dancer, and great company. Her name was Maureen - this is not her real name but it does contain the same amount of letters. I guess she will probably never read this sort of military book but, if she does, I am sure she will know who I am writing about. Even then, I realised she was a wee bit special but my thoughts on writing to her when I would be heading to foreign parts did not fit with my positive ideas on that subject. I knew that being apart for two years was just asking for trouble, arranging to keep in contact by writing was too much to ask any teenage girl. We hung out quite happily for the whole evening. This is not the prelude to a hot, steamy, teenage love story. It's written because I still have a very strong, happy feeling about that particular warm late summer evening which has remained with me ever since. We were very happy just being with each other.

When the dancing finished, we went strolling along, arms linked together with no particular place to go. I remember we actually wound up sitting on the kerb beside the road in the dark. Feet in the dusty gutter, just talking and enjoying being together under the moon well into the wee, small hours. Tomorrow did not exist for us that night. It was a balmy night, even in Scotland, beautiful big moon above. It was what we call, a **Gloaming** night. Summer nights in Scotland, situated in the North, never get completely dark. This light effect is called 'the gloaming'. Both of us talked and laughed for pretty much the whole magical night till we eventually realised the concrete we had been sitting on for hours was really uncomfortable. I happily walked her home before giving her a farewell kiss and walking out of her life.

I never did break my resolution not to write to any girl after I left for the Far East with the army. She was the only one I would have wanted to be with but my pig headed attitude did not allow for any of this mushy romantic writing stuff. It would be two long years before I would see her again.

21 WE HEAD BACK TO BERWICK ON TWEED

I was surprised that we all made it back to Berwick in time for the big move to Ballykinler army camp in County Down, Northern Ireland where our battalion was stationed.

One or two of the guys had been making daft claims of 'heading for the hills' rather than heading for active service in faraway Malaya. These claims had mostly been wishful boasting, although I did notice most of our young soldiers had managed to consume fairly heavy quantities of alcohol before reporting back to the depot. There was much visiting with each other in our billets, stories of drunken leave experiences, meetings with young women were claimed, the details mainly fictitious. Also much speculation as to what may lie ahead of us on the great Far East adventure.

We only spent one night there before we *entrained* (love that word) at Berwick upon Tweed railway station first thing the following day. We were destined for Glasgow.

22 THE BROOMIELAW QUAY, GLASGOW.

We arrived at 'The Broomilaw' in the Glasgow dockland which was the traditional staging post for Scottish Regiments to board ships bound for foreign parts over the many past years, way back to the busy old British Empire days. We only had to board the Irish Ferry from Glasgow to Belfast on our journey to join our regiment of The Kings Own Scottish Borderers stationed at Ballykinler army barracks in County Down on the coast of Northern Ireland. We would have a couple of weeks to settle in and be reassigned to our future positions within the regiment before we were due to sail for the Far East.

There are lots of Scottish marching songs attached to the Broomielaw. One of the favourite doggerel songs used to be sung by the departing *'JOCKS'*, as all Scottish soldiers were known. This was the song, **Wha saw the tattie howkers?** The tune was 'Scotland the Brave'.

This version also mentioned the 42nd regiment, The Black Watch, marching doon the Broomielaw. **"Some o' them wi' kiltie cauld bums",** referring to the kilted Scottish Highland Regiments' custom of *dressing regimental,* meaning nothing was worn under the kilt. Which gave rise (if you will excuse me) to the question and answer routine, *"Is anything worn under the kilt?"* The correct answer is, *"Naw, it's all in perfect working order".*

Last time I saw this custom was on St, Patrick's Day celebrations in Sheabeens Irish Pub when I lived in Colorado, USA, many years later. A bunch of guys came into the pub – Yes, the one on Chambers Road, Aurora, Colorado. They were all dressed in the kilt and led by a mad Irish guy, Mark Braden, who had obviously been influenced by the movie '**Braveheart**'. He paraded the whole kilted bunch onstage where, on the command, **"Go regimental"**. They turned their backs to the audience, bent over, lifted up their kilts and cried **"Freedom"** showing their bare asses to the audience. This kind of display used to be meant as a great insult to the enemy, but on this occasion it was greeted with wild applause from the friendly American audience who were quite unaware of the real meaning. As, of course, were the half pissed kilt lifting gang. I guess they had been performing this same show at several other bars on that *'St. Pat's Day'* before arriving, well primed at Sheabeens Irish Bar.

23 I VENTURE INTO INDIAN COUNTRY- SCOTTISH STYLE.

We had the prospect of waiting for a few hours in Glasgow before boarding the Irish ferry. My friend Robbie from Florence Street in the nearby Gorbals area, a sort of 'Indian country' to strangers, suggested I accompany him on a short visit to his place. We could have a cup of tea and something to eat, which would be a perfect break in a fairly tedious day.

Robbie's house was in a big, old tenement building where we climbed the stairs to find the door was unlocked. We were able to walk right in to find his old grannie sitting comfortably by the open fire.

"Ahh, it's Bertie," she said in a very pleased and welcoming fashion, "come away in, son, and have a cup of tea."

Robbie whirled round to face me, grabbing the lapels of my battle dress jacket, pushing his face right up to mine, "If I ever hear you using that name to me, I'll smash your face in", he hissed. He let go immediately, turned round to his grannie with a big smile on his face," Hello there, grannie, how's it gaun auld yin?"

'Bertie' would not be a name commonly used in the Glasgow Gorbals district. It sounded too English and soft, a clear invitation to a bashing. He gave no sign that he had just threatened to smash my face in, in fact he became the perfect host, pulling his mother in from the wee kitchen in the gleaming and spotless house to be introduced.

He never referred to the incident again, he never needed to - I had only seen Robbie looking like that once before. The occasion was during our early basic training when a much bigger guy than Robbie had started to take the piss about some now forgotten training incident. The other guy obviously thought he had nothing to fear from the smaller Robbie. In an unguarded moment he managed to pin Robbie to the floor, and was pushing down on his shoulders, laughing right above Robbie's upturned face. I saw that look on Robbie's face for the first time. No hesitation. Robbie spat upwards into the guy's face above him. The guy recoiled backwards giving Robbie just the time he needed to escape from the heavy weight.

'That's all she wrote', as they say. It took three of us to haul him away from the bigger guy who was already receiving a ferocious battering and probably making a huge mental note never, ever to upset wee Robbie. My friend Robbie was, what would now be called, street wise, growing up in the Gorbals area of Glasgow is a hard school, you tangle with these guys at your own risk.

Robbie's mum gave us cups of tea and scones. She was really pleased to see him at such short notice for they must have already said their goodbyes before he left for Berwick the day before. At that time, showing emotion was not really much encouraged in Scotland, I think it was regarded as a kind of display of weakness, best to be kept out of the way.

It was then I noticed his grannie had an Irish accent but was not really surprised for Glasgow had been a huge melting pot for various nationalities. Highland Scots had arrived here looking for work and lots of Irish people came for the same reason. They all joined in with the local Lowland Scots. The resulting mix of these peoples in Glasgow gave birth to, in my opinion, a very interesting race of humorous, intelligent and fiery people with their very own accent, sense of humour and Glasgow slang, a language which was rarely understood elsewhere, even in most other parts of Scotland!

Robbie said his brief goodbyes all over again. It was then I thought about my own goodbye to my mother. I had slipped quietly out of the house in uniform, kit bag over my shoulder and was halfway down the street before she realised what was happening. She came running out of our front gate, calling my name. My only reaction was an embarrassed wave of my disappearing arm as I turned the corner on my way off to far away Malaya with a good chance that I might not ever be coming back. I, callous wee bastard, never even turned round. Oh dear, *je regret*.

Our way back to the Broomielaw lay through the brooding Gorbals area, I was just like a bloody tourist. Everything in this area was new and different. I knew I would not like to live there but could not help checking things out as we walked through Robbie's home district.

Without realizing, I had been selected as a strange chicken, ripe for the plucking. Some guy suddenly appeared beside me to babble away at me in very fast Glasgow patter.

Robbie had carried on by himself for a few yards before he noticed I was no longer beside him. He wheeled around, made straight for the stranger, grabbed him by the lapels, stuck a 'Glesga Kiss' directly on his startled face, then spun him around to deliver a hefty kick on the arse.

"Get tae fuck, ya bas", was all he needed to say. The strange guy whose nose was now streaming blood, was off like a shot and, I guess, the chicken had been saved from an attempted plucking although I had no idea what all the fuss was about. Robbie stared at me, shook his head as if delivering an admonishment. "In the name of the wee man, ye shouldnie be allowed out by yourself .How you even manage to cross the street by yourself beats me", was all he said before turning around to lead the way out of this big strange city of Glasgow.

Nobody had noticed our absence and we arrived back to the Broomielaw in time to mingle with the other soldiers and board the Irish ferry bound for Belfast, Northern Ireland, on the sideways step westwards for the next stage of our long journey to the mystical Far East.

24 BALLYKINLER ARMY CAMP, NORTHERN IRELAND

My recollection of our arrival on the ferry to Belfast was a bit restricted, I had my unfamiliar new seagoing kit bag loaded on top of my back pack and resting on my neck. This extra weighty bulk caused my head to face downwards which gave me a clear view of my nice boots but looking forward was out of the question. This made the task of negotiating the slippery, upward sloping wooden gang plank very difficult.

My first impression of Northern Ireland was of seeing another pair of shiny black boots. But this time the boots were firmly anchored on the Belfast quayside just above my head level. As I made my way up the gangplank (why did a vision of peg leg pirates come to mind)? I was labouring underneath my full service marching order kit with my head pushed downwards. As I clambered slowly up the slippery gang plank my eyes connected to blue serge trousers above the shiny boots. Then. **'Shit!'**, a huge pistol was strapped to the leg of the blue serge pants.

I was now able to see the whole uniform, my first view of a Northern Irish Policeman. Coming from mainland U.K. where the cops are unarmed, this small part of the Island, separated from the Irish Republic by an imaginary line, is still technically in Great Britain. This always puzzles strangers

Army trucks were laid on to take us to Ballykinler army camp where we disembarked in fairly good order except we seemed to be without

Alfie, our scruffy soldier. One of the guys had seen him wandering away from our ranks to talk to somebody at Belfast docks. Alfie had a habit of breaking into conversation with strangers although he could also break a few heads if the conversation got difficult. A phone call was made which established that our vagrant was being held at the dock on suspicion of trying to go absent without leave or, A.W.O.L., as the charge goes.

A small truck was dispatched to pick up our untidy soldier, unfortunately for Alfie, none of our former training N.C.O's had accompanied us to join the regiment, there was nobody of any rank with us on our journey to explain Alfie's eccentricities. He was in for a severe bollocking when he eventually reached the Regiment. He looked aggrieved at being accused of some crime he had not even considered committing. The look of injured innocence on his face was a picture. He was minus his belt again, his shirt had come adrift, tie now untied and askew, I had to turn away to have a wee laugh.

25 SETTLING IN

We settled in to our new life and were paraded into a large room for an examination to see if any of us would be suitable or intelligent enough to join the regiment's signal platoon. We were each issued with a printed sheet of questions with a blank area for answers.

Question #1. When the phone rings, you pick it up and what do you say? (space for answer). I actually thought it must be a trick question so I hesitated for a bit until I saw everyone else scribbling away, so I confidently wrote, *Hello*.

You are probably wondering why I think this information is worth writing about. We did not have a phone at home back in the fifties. This was not at all odd because there were no phones at any of my friend's homes. Our local GP, Doctor Badger (he really was called Dr Badger) had a telephone. He lived in the next street and ran his office from home, so there was a phone at his address, but I was unaware of the existence of any other domestic phones in my area. This was not unusual during the early fifties. Luckily, I had worked in the sales office of our local paper mill and was already familiar with telephones.

Now confident, I moved on to question #2. What is the name of the Prime Minister? I managed to answer this correctly, also dealt successfully with the 3rd and last question although I now can't remember the question, never mind the answer.

The papers were collected, checked and, after a brief exchange between two Sergeants, about a dozen of us had our names announced. Apparently we were the bright ones and were informed we would report in the morning to start a signals cadre which would keep us busy for the following two weeks before sailing for the Far East.

The others must have appeared to be pretty dumb, probably cannon fodder I thought, as they were allocated to various rifle companies in the regiment.

The new arrangement meant a change to our accommodation, but Robbie and I were still roommates and we had a new batch of conscripts transferred to us from The Cameronians, another Scottish Infantry Regiment. This transfer would help to bring our regiment up to strength before we left for active service in Malaya. Once again, these new guys were mainly recruited from Glasgow and the Lanarkshire area where my Grannie lived so I was quite comfortable with them.

I was unaware that not a single army soul in the military had any concern whether I was comfortable with our new additions or not. I was still what is called 'a young soldier' and had not yet realised I was just 23139714 Private Wishart.A. Not eligible to be an individual or have any opinion at all.

We were soon issued our much discussed jungle green Malaya outfits although we were not to wear them yet. The command to change from our thick, heavy khaki battledress uniforms to the new, lightweight, jungle green gear would be given at some unspecified date during the troopship voyage.

No prize for guessing the order would be given when it was already too bloody hot for comfort, causing sweating inside our normal British uniforms. In any case our heavy boots would not be worn (no pun) on board the ship as the sailor boys did not allow it. Wearing our issue rubber soled canvas P.T. shoes on board would be obligatory. We would not look at all military while wearing normal U.K. army gear with canvas plimsolls.

The rubber and canvas green jungle boots looked cool and were very popular but the green lightweight pants and blouse did not appear at first to look very classy. It would take a few weeks in Singapore before we saw how cool they could look after frequent laundering and with the addition of exotic shoulder flashes plus some dexterous attention with a hot iron.

This would, of course, be the style affected by the *office wallas* stationed at cushy positions on Singapore Island. The real jungle soldiers operating up North in Malaya, were engaged on sweaty fighting duties against the Communist Terrorists or C.T.s as they were known. Unlike some of the 'cushy' postings in Singapore, there was no time or opportunity for *style* in the Malayan jungle. We would soon be receiving our new shoulder flashes which would elevate us right above any others. These shoulder flashes embroidered with their crossed khukuris (the traditional curved steel knifes from Nepal) would show we served alongside the very famous Gurkha Regiment but we would have to wait till we moved into Malaya before we were issued with these prize shoulder flashes. I still have mine.

I guess all the guys had, like me, been looking forward to the issuing of the new jungle hat. In those early fifties years we had all been brought up on Hollywood movies which, in the pre TV world in Scotland, had an enormous influence on our thinking which spanned every aspect from human relationships, love, marriage and just about everything else. I recall causing a bit of confusion when visiting a small restaurant in the small border town of Peebles by asking for the check after having been served with what was probably my first meal away from home in a restaurant. The waitress looked a bit puzzled at first then directed me to the rest room.

I don't think I had ever eaten outside our house up to that point. As far as I knew, the American guys in all the movies I had ever seen always asked for the check before leaving the bar for some regular adventures. I had a lot to unlearn from my background at that age, all that was about to change and I could not blame my Hollywood training for much longer.

The jungle green hat was a great disappointment to those of us who had been raised on Johnny Weissmuller exploits in Tarzan movies for that was where we had seen the Great White Hunter types, always scanning into the distance with far away eyes, their strong, tanned faces shaded from the merciless African sun by wearing a large hat.

None of us would admit it, but I know we had all rather fancied being able to pose in a dramatic stance while wearing a big hat and staring into the distance. Shit, we even had rifles now. What great photos we could send back home. We had still to learn that staring romantically into the distance would not apply to us in any way shape or form. The Malayan jungle would restrict viewing to a few feet owing to the impenetrable dense thick green foliage. Another Hollywood movie fantasy bites the dust. Jungle soldiers were never sun tanned either, the hot sun from above cannot reach them through the thick tree top growth competing for sunlight. The only suntanned soldiers were, perhaps, the cooks back at base camp.

Our jungle hats looked like nothing a great white hunter would be seen dead in anyway, especially if he was trying to die heroically. Our military version of a great white hunter's hat was a scruffy looking scrap of green material, mass produced somewhere that preferred to be anonymous. The hat looked more like a substantial handkerchief that could be crumpled into one hand. Wearing that bloody hat and doing even a lot of staring just would not cut it. What a disappointment.

On the plus side, it was a wonderful unmilitary piece of our new uniform as no two hats seemed to be the same style or shape.

We now had a chance to express our individuality, which we did with great style and fashion ideas. The only thing the hats had in common was when they were removed from us temporarily, then returned with our cloth Leslie tartan regimental shoulder flashes sewn on to the front, every piece of tartan in exactly the same place as all the other hats. Apart from that we were free to wear our jungle hats in any shape we cared to adopt.

We *young soldiers* were allowed for the first time, to wander outside the army area in Northern Ireland, but we were not allowed to wear civilian clothes. This privilege would come later when we had served in the army for six months. Very few of us took the opportunity to visit the nearest town which I think was Newcastle, County Down. We would have to wear all our regular army gear to do this and would stick out like extremely sore thumbs in our still new army uniforms and embarrassingly short army haircuts.

Just like the army jungle hat, most of us preferred anonymity. In our free time we would wander off in the opposite direction from the town and head towards the sea as there did not seem to be any formal barrier between the army camp and the sea. The beautiful deserted beach was only a short stroll away and we could see the Mountains of Mourne sweeping down to the sea, close by. The afternoons and evenings were still pleasantly warm. The sea swell had enormously smooth waves rolling in towards the sandy shore. We indulged in this free surfing activity and the couple of weeks we had to wait for our departure from Belfast passed pleasantly enough.

26 WE SHIP FOR THE FAR EAST
(Ahoy there)

The great departure day finally came and we were all loaded onto open trucks (This was the signal for a general outbreak of 'baaing' and freestyle mooing). We were being transported to Belfast Docks where lay the good ship 'Devonshire' waiting to transport us safely to the Far East.

Before leaving Ballykinler Army Camp we were decked out in full army moving gear or, as it is referred to officially, F.S.M.O. (Full service marching order). Every piece of kit I possessed was fastened somehow to my body, even an extra, smaller, kit bag for use aboard ship. My full kit was strapped, clipped or slung onto my body, one kit bag carried underneath my arm, the other one balanced behind my neck across my back pack, resulting in my head being forced downwards, face looking at the ground. Result, I could see bugger all.

The entire regiment was now filing in a single line onto the ship. Each man dressed in F.S.M.O. with all heads pushed forwards and facing downwards which prompted an immediate response to this new *Army Daze* affair when an enormous baaing chorus broke out from the increasing amount of young men crowding onto the vessel. We could only follow behind the guy in front. As each new line of men entered the ship, the guy in front was directed down a metal corridor where he could only plod forward unable to see where he was supposed to be heading, followed by all the other guys pushing along behind him, nobody appeared to have a clue where they were going.

It seemed to us that soldiers were being directed on board, and were then left to their own devices, that was the end of available direction to destinations. For all we knew, all over the huge, strange, ship, lines of khaki clad soldiers were plodding aimlessly up one corridor then down another. The line in which I was embedded was encouraged to descend even farther into the bowels of the ship down steep metal stairs.

We were confused, sweaty, tired of carrying the heavy and cumbersome gear so we did what soldiers have always done when in distress, we started to baa like lost sheep. God knows what we would have done if a fire broke out. As the baaing sheep noises increased in volume, they became mixed with giggles as the daftness of the situation dawned on us conscripts. The big advantage of employing sheep noises as a form of derision was that nobody could pin point the source of the baaing. When authority approached, the sheep noise would die down till the danger had passed then start up again when the authority moved on, still looking for any culprits.

There must have been some military method involved somewhere. I eventually reached the bunk, below the waterline, which was to be my home for the next month. The bunks on the ship were intended for us 'other ranks'. They were arranged in groups of three and attached to the three bunks on the other side. I had been allocated top bunk so threw my kit bag up there to confirm my ownership. I climbed up to follow my kit bag and was surprised to find another guy already occupying the top bunk next to mine. He seemed to have made himself comfortable and I guessed he must have had *the smarts* to somehow reach the ship without being involved with our sheep noise makers. He was ignoring me, lying on his side, facing away and already settled down reading a book.

I noticed a full two Corporals' stripes on his arm. I was still a *young soldier* as far as this guy would be concerned and I did not relish spending a whole month in such close proximity. Without turning round he surprised me by addressing me by name, "'Yer late, Wishart, and what was all that sheep shagger noise you fuckers were making?" It was only then he rolled over to reveal a wide grin on a friendly face.

He was Derek 'Basher' Gillies, an old Boy Scout mate from my hometown. *Basher* was a real Penicuik keep fit character, the first guy to set up a professional trampoline on the lawn behind his house. I went to see him in action after hearing about the new trampoline. He was not around when I arrived, so I wandered round behind the house to view the new toy. Still no sign of Basher. Then I heard a loud cry of, "Geronimo", from above. Looking up, I was just in time to see him leaping from the window ledge of an upstairs bedroom, right down onto the trampoline!

I had heard he was in the battalion but he was a regular soldier and Physical Training Instructor, away on a refresher course somewhere. He had come back just in time to head directly for the troop ship, and managed to bypass the great military move from the army camp to the docks.

Somehow, all our gear was stowed away in the dark bowels of the ship, probably keeping the rats company for the entire journey. Neither our kit not the rats were seen again till we arrived in Singapore in about a month's time. We were left with just our romantic sounding sea going kit bags containing such essentials as military issue drawers – cellular – green - pairs one. Other ranks for the use of.

Eventually correct bunks were found. We learned where the heads were located and the great journey was about to begin. My 18th birthday had taken place only a few months before. I was excited as a wee schoolboy when the huge ship started to vibrate and we were off to see the world.

Unfortunately, on my deck, the portholes in the heavily laden troop ship were just below water level and I could see bugger all of the big wide world! You will note from the ship's picture the lower row of portholes actually dip below the water line of our heavily laden ship. Guess where my bunk was situated?

The good ship Devonshire which transported us away to Singapore.

27   I SAIL FOR THE FAR EAST.

The great adventure was under way. See how quickly I can adopt nautical talk. I seemed to be very adaptable in these days, my only previous sailing experience had been an exciting but brief trip on an actual National Lifeboat on the storm tossed East Coast of Scotland during Lifeboat Day when I was about eleven. I also had a few hours experience fishing for mackerel, on a proper fishing boat sailing round Ailsa Craig off the West Coast of Scotland. Luckily, even these two short trips, made me realise I seemed to be impervious to sea sickness. I was able to loll on my bunk listening to the land lubbers around me complaining the motion of the ship was making them feel ill. As far as I was concerned, all I could feel was the throbbing of the huge engines buried somewhere in the bowels of the ship which filled me with forward looking excitement at the prospect of heading towards foreign parts.

We were blissfully unaware of the terrors ahead when we would reach the notoriously stormy Bay of Biscay off the Portuguese coast, located just a couple of sailing days away.

The Pipes & Drums, 1.K.O.S.B. play the Regiment out from Belfast under the direction of Drum Major 'Pony' Moore. 1955.

Army routine was quickly re-asserted, reveille was, as bloody usual, at six o'clock. In barracks, reveille was always played by a drummer/bugler after which a piper played *'Hey, Johnnie Cope are you wakin' yet '?* This is the normal reveille morning ceremony in all Scottish regiments, followed at intervals during the day by the bugle calls for other activities like Cookhouse, Defaulters, Mail Call, Parade Call, etc., and ending in the evening with the evocative bugle call, Last Post, followed by the piper playing Lights Out, a slow lament which could bring tears to a glass eye. However, if you happened to be close enough, the piper could be seen marching quickly away in the darkness while playing a slow march, pretty clever actually, but he was probably just heading for bed.

The naval troopship was not suitable for our army type traditions with bugle calls or bagpipe players. The pre-recorded Reveille blasted out at great volume daily from the P.A. system speakers on each deck. The volume was adjusted to maximum level just in case any sleeping beauties missed the musical treat. To make things even more alien, the recorded bugle call was different from the one we had been getting used to after joining the Regiment. This rasping, soulless dream chaser made what I imagined was a very British Army call. If it was set to words it would sound like, *"GET OUT OF BED, YOU LAZY BASTARD"*. Not a very encouraging sound on our first morning at the start of an adventuring sea voyage to the romantic Far East. It seemed that all my illusions were being dragged out from my head, one by one, before being quickly dispatched.

I was brought up reading tales of the old British Empire from Africa to Hong Kong, Singapore and India. My grandfather, Corporal Munnoch had served with the Seaforth Highlanders in India, and I was keen to follow in his footsteps to see what this roving kind of life involved. So far I was not experiencing any of the romantic shit.

We were each allocated tasks and activities to keep us busy in the mornings. I was lucky to land the daily task of cleaning the Sick Bay which actually turned out to be a plum job. Sick Bay was located in the Out of Bounds (for us Other Ranks!) area of the ship, and it appeared to be unoccupied for the entire voyage.

I reported to the deserted Sick Bay each morning, to have a quiet and private shower before selecting a comfortable chair and continued reading my book for a couple of hours of peace and quiet. This was o.k. by me, I was an only child and never quite got used to having crowds of people around. The Sick Bay was permanently empty so nothing needed cleaning. For a couple of hours after breakfast I could pretend I was a man of leisure taking life easy on a sea cruise. I would often take regular peeks out of the porthole which, unlike the one on my deck, was above the water line.

P.T. on the open deck of the ship was scheduled immediately following our regular morning duties. Must keep the chaps fit, you know.

Our Physical Trainer in charge of these activities was my bunk neighbour Corporal Derek *'Basher'* Gillies. He marched up and down the deck, barking orders in a very Nazi fashion, keeping his evil eye out for any slackers. None of the guys were aware that Basher and I knew each other. I was in the 1st Penicuik scout troop while Basher was in the newly formed 2nd troop, and there was a great deal of friendly rivalry between the two. This, plus his two stripes of army authority, gave him an excellent opportunity to indulge his wicked sense of humour whenever I appeared on the scene.

We were moving steadily further south into warmer weather causing us to start sweating and Basher would continue marching up and down among the long lines of us snaking along the deck, barking out orders till he arrived at my space. He would immediately come to a halt beside me, pretend to take an interest in my poor performance before deciding to make an example of someone he would describe as 'an idle soldier'.

He was a real *ham*, playing to his captive audience by making loud comments about my apparently feeble physical performance. He would order the others to stand/sit at ease to concentrate on me as a slacker, all the while there was a wicked twinkle in his eyes, hidden behind his fairly thick glasses. I guess his eyes were the only weak part of his body as the rest of him was built like a brick shithouse. "Right you," he would say, "let's see you do some press-ups, then."

I would have to assume the position, and start performing in front of the whole assembly who were more than happy to sit watching me sweat while they took their ease, wondering what I could have possibly have done to upset the nasty Corporal. After about 20 pushups Basher would add his own contribution to the entertainment by placing his foot on the small of my back, calling, "Come on lad, push!"

This particular part of the act brought much amusement to our audience. Basher even managed to introduce a fresh slant to the daily show by adding new pieces of business to add to my embarrassment. However, I eventually managed to invent an excuse myself to extend my time to the fictitious cleaning of the Sick Bay and completely avoid the bloody daily P.T. show for the rest of the voyage. I confided the news to Basher later that day when we were in our bunks just before Lights Out. His only response was an enigmatic but wicked grin behind his comic book. Daft bugger.

28 TERROR ON THE HIGH SEAS!

Question - PIRATES.?? Answer – NO, Navy Porridge !

When we could just about see the distant Spanish coast, the weather began to warm up. Even better, permission was granted for us from below decks to sleep on the open, top deck at night. All we had to do was take a blanket and pillow when darkness fell, and head upwards until we cleared the fetid atmosphere existing below the water line where each deck was occupied by several hundred sweaty soldiers.

I was surprised that not many of the guys took advantage of a chance to exchange our airless bunks for the opportunity to sleep in the fresh air under the stars. The only entertainment after lights out below deck was listening to old jokes. These stories were interrupted from time to time by the fascinating and various types of sound from great, horrendous farts. Our below deck soldiers managed to display a wide and entertaining range of farts, often accomplished by contorting their young bodies into interesting shapes. We seemed to have had more than our fair share of beans with our seagoing fare and our stomachs were adapting to the change.

Why stay below when we could escape to the fresh air and romantic nautical atmosphere by bedding down above board? Every evening I headed for the open deck above, armed with my pillow and blanket. Not many guys followed my healthy example of sleeping underneath the stars on a hard, wooden bench on a ship at sea, how strange.

There were a number of benches bolted securely to the deck at various intervals. After nightfall I had no problem in securing one all to myself by merely spreading my blanket and pillow on top. I was then master of all I surveyed which was bugger all really because of the darkness, the only farts rending the night were all my own and not to be sniffed at!

Two nights passed in this peaceful fashion, each night I soon fell asleep and slept very soundly, dreaming of the mysterious orient ahead until awakened by the usual blasting recording of a bugle call on the loud speaker system at 6a.m. in the bloody morning.

Technically, we entered the normally stormy Bay of Biscay off the coast of Portugal late on the afternoon of the following day. I had noticed no great difference in the weather during the day time. Come evening, I gathered my bedding and headed for the deck and fresh air. I selected my favourite bench and settled down pretending I was a salty old seadog. This was just like those damn movies which usually had me believing in the stupidest of things till they were proved to be a load of old Hollywood crap. And so I drifted peacefully into oblivion.

I went to sleep on a solid Clyde built, safe and trusty British ship. This reliable vessel seemed capable of sailing confidently over any of the fabled Seven Seas, strong as the Rock of Gibraltar.

My premature awakening was due to an urgent shaking on my shoulder. My eyes opened to the alarming sight of huge banks of sinister black waves with frightening white crests towering way above me, apparently about to thunder down and sweep me away. The safe and trusty ship seemed different now, bit more on the vulnerable side than when I had gone to sleep. The frantic shaking on my shoulder was from a scared Military Policeman, hanging on like a human limpet to the metal support on my bench. The waves were rolling headlong across the open deck, washing right up to his thighs and I had been sleeping through all this?

Apparently, he had made a previous sweep of the deck, but must have splashed right past me in the dark. He had been sent back above board for a second time to have a final look and to make sure none of the stupid young soldiers had been overlooked after an unexpected storm broke.

I had been in the blissfully deep sleep of the just, and had objected to his frantic shaking but woke to find white stuff crashing over both of us. The scene was something like I had only seen when I went to see a Noah's Ark movie. Actually, I am lying about this part, I could not be dragged, kicking and\or screaming to see a Noah's Ark movie, except possibly to have a good laugh!

Even in the dark I could see huge, white crested waves towering over the ship which was rolling and wallowing through deep troughs in the suddenly storm racked ocean. The Bay of Biscay's reputation was certainly justified that night. The Military Policeman had been violently pushed sideways by a wall of water. He had grabbed onto my deck bench to keep his balance and avoid being washed overboard and that was when he had noticed me fast asleep on my bench and still fairly dry in my elevated position, slightly above deck level. The bench was securely bolted to the deck but I was not!

He woke me, bundled me below deck, pulled the heavy metal door shut and followed quickly behind me, the poor bugger was actually scared shitless. I guess I was still half asleep or I should have been joining the scared shitless club as well. Being sound asleep, I must have escaped the flooded deck as I was a couple of feet above it. That was when then I realised I had been rescued just in time, before the next crashing wave could sweep me away to Davy Jones's locker with just my wee military pillow and blanket for company, wheeeech!!

My sense of relief changed immediately when I descended to our deck which was situated as far down as you could go. I was about to take my last step from the rung to the deck floor when I recoiled just in time, managing to step back quickly upwards to avoid a brown wave of vomit sweeping across the floor.

That was the only time when I felt nauseous at sea. I must have been the only guy on that lower deck who had not upchucked. The dim night lights revealed the small but disgusting brown wave as it slopped about to the motion of the fiercely rolling ship, I guessed most of the sea sick guys had tried unsuccessfully to reach the heads before being sick on the deck. Others had only been able to get their own heads clear of their bunks just in time to add to the brown wave.

It was a nightmare scene. Luckily, my bunk space was fairly close to the entrance so, with a quick hop, skip and jump, I made it to my bunk at the top, well clear of the disgusting mobile mess below. And so to bed dear reader, away from a sickening experience I hope never to repeat.

29 PORRIDGE

The morning bugle recording aroused me to a view of the brown vomit wave still splashing around beneath me. However, by employing my perfect timing, once again, I evaded the brown slush and made it safely to the top deck albeit rather scruffily dressed and unwashed. Reaching the head to wash was out of the question.

I had considered slinking off to the hospital room where I usually spent my early mornings 'cleaning' the place. I always took my private shower there but I realised the Sick Bay might actually be full of sick people at this time and quickly changed my mind.

I headed in the opposite direction and made it safely to the Mess Deck (different type of mess - naval talk, you know) where I always ate well. Apart from the inevitable porridge, this was the place to find kippers, bacon and eggs. Kippers for me! The Merchant Navy looks after their sailor boys properly, unlike the Army of that time. I found the army food to be bloody awful. Our four weeks afloat with the Navy gave us a welcome break from the Army Catering Corpse as I called them. It also gave me, at least, a healthy appetite from exposure to the fresh air. I remember our favourite cat call concerning Army cooking. "Who called the cook a bastard?" Reply was, "Who called the bastard a cook?"

That morning, instead of having to stand in line for my meal, it seemed I was the only guy who had any appetite. The Mess Deck was deserted apart from only one other brown job (army guy) .He was seated alone in the huge empty Mess, tucking in to breakfast. I didn't know him but he seemed to be observing me closely while he ate.

I collected my usual breakfast of kippers, porridge, bacon, eggs, toast and tea, the whole schmere loaded onto the naval aluminium meal tray which had several shallow embedded impressions to take the various courses. This made meal times a pleasure and avoided sloppy mixing of different courses with each other if the ship was rolling due to bad weather. The ship was not the only thing heaving vigorously on that choppy morning.

As I made my way towards a convenient table I had to paddle and move sharply to the side on one corner of the deck to avoid a strange grey mess on the unusually sticky floor. When I joined the other guy, he told me he had been watching to see if I coped successfully with the messy floor or would I fall victim to the slippery obstacle by losing my feet and depositing my porridge over the floor where it would contribute to the mess. The last three guys had gone arse over tit at that point and he congratulated me on a safe journey.

The two of us sat together in the empty mess, betting each other on the outcome of the new diners progressing with their porridge. However, even this amusement started to pale after a while as there were very few diners that morning. The vessel was still pitching and heaving although not quite as fiercely as before or perhaps we were just acquiring a sailor's roll, adjusting to unaccustomed motion.

Not many of the others had been able to copy our new rolling and walking system and were probably still lying and dying in their bunks for all normal discipline seemed to have been abandoned. The recording of the stirring bugle reveille call had tootled out at six a.m., as bloody usual, but that was about the only thing that stirred on board ship that morning.

I did not fancy descending below to my lower, puke covered deck area again, so I took advantage of the lowering of normal army rules, picked a convenient, if still pitching, bench on deck and passed the time watching the heavy Atlantic seas. The only other people I saw were occasional sailors going about their business. There were no army types, and I stayed happily on my undisturbed bench, watching the world go by or more accurately, going up and down as the ship pitched wildly from looking down into wild grey seas then up into heavy rain filled grey skies the next. I gazed ahead searching for the first glimpse of The Rock of Gibraltar which was scheduled to appear later that day.

Gibraltar was sighted as we entered calmer waters of the wonderfully blue Mediterranean Sea. We squeezed past the huge slab of rock that was the Rock of Gibraltar. Obviously, I had never seen it before but I recognised it immediately. It was so bloody big and could not be missed..

It was an unmistakable chunk of the British Empire right before my eyes, this was the life of adventure as far as I was concerned so I clung to the rail to drink it all in. I had been brought up with tales of travel, derring do and the old British Empire, also large helpings of fictitious Hollywood nonsense and I was more than ready for this sort of stuff. Bring it on!.

30 THE MEDITERANIAN

We entered the Med, big difference here. It seemed small compared to the Atlantic. We could even see the distant coast occasionally and no more Bay of Biscay capers.

Next morning I was back to my duties in the sick bay which was empty as usual, I guess most sick people had been feeling too sick to go to the sick bay!

I looked out of the port hole and there was an Arab dhow right before my eyes. I knew what it was but thought that kind of ship belonged to the history book. This was an actual working boat, amazing.

This was the same area where ancient boats from my own country had, thousands of years ago, plied their trade shipping tin mined in Cornwall, England. These pre-historic, small boats headed for ports where tin was a much valued material. Tin was essential to mix with copper to produce the recently discovered bronze, resulting in strong sword blades thousands of years ago. I could not help wondering if they had sailed their primitive boats right across the Bay of Biscay, as we had on that stormy night, or perhaps they had clung close to the shore of the land that would eventually be called Portugal. My bet was they must have clung to the shoreline, their boats loaded with precious cargo of tin. They must have been very brave voyagers. They were Celtic men from what would eventually be named Cornwall, the south west tip of England and the last refuge of the

Celts in that area. I guess the ancient Celtic sailors must have been daft as well as brave.

The traffic around us had increased too. As soon as my time in the deserted Sick Bay was up plus a wee bit extra time to evade the wicked Basher Gillies and his P.T. sessions, I was up on deck, leaning over the ship's rail up at the sharp end taking it all in: foreign shipping, porpoises, even flying fish as we sailed into warmer waters. This was, indeed, another world.

Some of the best shots in the regiment were allowed access to the blunt end where they spent their time shooting at bobbing targets thrown from the ship before the floating bottles and cans disappearing behind us. They seemed to be having fun but I was more than happy up front at the sharp end, just savouring this new experience.

31   SUEZ CANAL

The Med ended too soon for me. Our first stop was Port Said in Egypt where we joined the queue of ships gathering to sail through the Suez Canal. Traffic was one way and ships went through in convoy style to make sure traffic flowed smoothly. We were only in Port Said for a few hours, so there was no time for shore leave. No big deal, I thought, viewing the area from my vantage point at the ships rail, the place seemed to consist mainly of dust and flies.

Entertainment was freely provided by *bumboat* proprietors, these guys had what looked rather like large row boats crammed with cheap tourist goods which they were more than willing to sell to the troops.

The sale transaction was achieved by verbal bartering from the troops crowded on deck with the bum boat owners bobbing in their boats below us. If a, usually disputed, price was eventually agreed by bargaining, the chosen article was placed in a little basket securely tied to a cord which was then hauled up to the ship's deck by the potential customer for inspection. If the goods passed, the customer removed the purchase. The agreed money was placed in the basket which was then lowered back to the waiting bumboat man.

The bargaining pantomime gave us great entertainment, welcomed by the Jocks hanging over the ship's rail on deck. Even the new experience of sailing the high seas was paling after about a week of being held captive on the ship. We were all beginning to walk with a bit of a roll, as they say, so bargaining with the natives provided a welcome break.

There was no language problem. It seemed to us the bum boat souvenir sellers appeared to speak good English judging by the barrage of comments floating up to us at the rail. Of course, the Second World War had only ended a few years previously, and lots of military activity had taken place in Egypt. These guys even seemed to be speaking with Scottish accents. *"Hey McGreegor",* they shouted," *The Black Watch, that's the sheep shaggers, that's right"?*

They had guessed correctly we were a Scottish regiment, although not the one referred to, but that was all the same to them. The crack exchanges between us and the vendors below provide a lot of fun until, somewhat regretfully, our ship was added to the required number of boats in the queue and we set off for the Suez Canal to resume our journey.

I had been looking forward to seeing the Suez Canal which, after the expanse of the sea, looked a bit on the narrow side.

I saw the occasional clump of palm trees here and there to relieve the monotony for a bit and was thinking of going below to write a short letter to my mother. My conscience was bothering me because she would be wondering about me, as mothers do. I had sent a note when we arrived in Northern Ireland but she had heard nothing since then. My mail could be collected from the ship at our next port of call which would satisfy my conscience for a while.

Unfortunately, my guilt feeling had to be taken care of at a later date. Suddenly I heard the magic sound of bagpipes playing in the distance. I strained over the ship's rail to locate where it was coming from and, Lo! There stood a lone piper from the Royal Scots Regiment, stationed somewhere in Egypt at that time. He had been transported with his bagpipes to play us through the Suez Canal. He was not the only soldier to be transported that day. This was a pure piece of history for me. To add to my delight I recognized the piper: he was John Brown a friend of mine from my hometown, his mother and mine were good friends, some coincidence.

We emerged into the Gulf of Aden and the Red Sea later that day. Bloody hot, unbearably hot. Surely the authorities would leave us alone to sweat it out in peace. Unfortunately it was not to be. Those of us in the Signal Platoon were still undergoing training when a new announcement was made. The good old *Army Daze* had surfaced again. We were ordered to forget our initial training and adopt the all new military signaling procedure halfway through our course. This new procedure complicated things quite a bit for us. We were only getting used to saying Able, Baker, Charlie, Dog, etc. when everything we had learned was changed to Alpha, Bravo, Charlie, Delta and so on, all the way through the alphabet.

No big deal, I hear you cry. However you did not have to try to take in new information at two in the afternoon in the bloody awful heat of a roasting metal ship with no air conditioning when sailing through the bloody awful hot Red Sea. So there!

32   ADEN

The dull routine was soon broken when we reached the old coaling station at Aden. The ship stopped for a few hours and we were allowed to go ashore, albeit walking with a bit of a roll, as they say.

Aden was a big disappointment. If this was the Mystic East, you could keep it. My main impression was of dust, heat, dirt, poverty and veiled women who looked not at all mysterious even to our sex starved young soldiers. This was not the mysterious orient I thought I knew through Hollywood eyes. No lovely oriental women, no intriguing bars, no bars at all, of course. There was not even a single, solitary bottle of Coca Cola to be seen or obtained anywhere.

Ray Reid and I hung out for a few hot and rather boring hours, resisting offers from a series of scruffy locals promising to take us to see a donkey shagging a woman if we would give them a reasonable sum of money. The money was for the scruffy guys, not the donkey or the fictitious woman. We were growing up fast, although Ray was still way ahead of me. We were sure the situation would change once the money had changed hands, probably they would take us to see a mosque or some other boring Middle Eastern building, conveniently forgetting the first attraction which probably did not exist anyway.

I can only guess the soldiers, who were present in this area during the war, must have started this particular donkey rumour. British soldiers have a strange sense of humour.

Aden seemed to consist of a dusty lane which allowed us to wander along on the East side of the street, all the way to where the street tailed off onto a dusty track. We crossed over to the West side of the same street to return back again to where we had begun with nothing of interest in between. The nonexistent attractions soon wore down any slight interest we might have started out with in that dump, we were only too happy to queue at the dockside for the next liberty boat back to the ship No wonder there is a Scottish Army pipe tune named, *The Barren Rocks of Aden.*

The Barren Rocks of Aden.(the fabled donkey is resting in the foreground).

33 CEYLON

Sacred elephant at the Temple of the Tooth, Ceylon. Poor thing, it only had one tusk. I felt very sorry for the animal. It spent most of it's time restricted to the temple with only the occasional trip outside to take part in religious parades dressed up in the silly trappings.

This part of the journey was fairly uneventful. We stopped for a day at Colombo in Ceylon or Sri Lanka, as it is now known. This was a welcome change from Aden, a bunch of us managed to do a bit of sightseeing, although there really was not a lot of time to do anything properly. We did not even look for somewhere to have a meal.

In the years since that visit, I have seen lots of TV programs by a host of seemingly endless so called Master Chefs all willing to show us the food delights of Sri Lanka with loads of great spicy dishes we might have tried when we were there. But what would we know? We were just a bunch of eighteen year old Jocks let off the leash for a few hours, probably as dumb as a bag of spanners about life in general and exotic foreign parts in particular.

In any case, we had been sternly warned by our officers about of the dangers of eating strange foreign foods which would certainly result in a case of '*Gippy Tummy*'. The same tactic was also advised regarding any contact with, '*foreign wimmin*', which would probably result in a, '*case of the pox*'.

These grim warnings were confirmed when we would be compulsorily marched into makeshift cinemas from time to time to see short but frighteningly graphic films. These short but shocking films illustrating the resulting dangers of contact with foreign women, although the women portrayed in these film looked disturbingly British. I guess the film making was, at that time, dictated by the dire post war economy in the UK and it was a case of one size fits all as far as the cost of providing different actresses went.

If we were to judge from the English accents and white complexions as portrayed on the VD films, most of us young eighteen year old soldiers went through our army service believing all women prostitutes were white girls from London.

The original warning of not consorting with girls like that was easily complied with as far as we were concerned, for none of us ever saw girls like that in the Far East. We happily allowed our jumping hormones to leap about when confronted by dusky or tinted Eastern ladies. We quite happily parted with some money to these young ladies and, hopefully, the rest was history as the romantic saying goes. Of course, part of the monotony of our almost monastic military existence was being devoid of any female company at all. There were no girls in our army of the 1950's. This new-fangled approach to military life by introducing women into the service did not start till the early '60s, too late for us. I often wonder what it would have been like to have some girls around. My old fashioned, traditionally bound mind boggles at the prospect.

Unfortunately, we accepted the warnings about eating nasty, foreign foods. As far as I know, nobody would even touch the stuff. We, therefore, missed the delights of tasting curries in Colombo and stir fried noodles in Singapore. My discovery of faint imitations of these treasures was slowly acquired much later back in the UK, when both Indian and Chinese foods began to be accepted back home.

We actually did have a rather daring eating adventure later during our military service in Malaya. This was when our adventurous cooks from The Army Catering Corps or *Corpse* as we called it, would throw something they referred to as curry powder into a grey, meat stew concoction which immediately turned the mess to a pale green colour. They offered this mess for an occasional treat or as an alternative choice when they had beef stew on the menu. Actually there never was a menu. You got a ladle full in your mess tin of whatever was the disgusting offering meal of the day. The green *curry* was an alternative treat which, I think, was a passing salute to any of our regiment who had perhaps served in India during the old Empire days.

I had never seen or met any of our older soldiers who claimed to have served in India. Certainly none of our cooks from *The Catering Corpse*, (as we called them) had been in India, so I guess the green curry day was another fable generated through re-telling for years rather like the donkey and the woman in Aden. Incidentally, the green curry treat was bloody awful.

I was so disgusted by the regular offerings prepared by our Catering Corpse that I once led an adventurous and hungry band of food explorers on an expedition to the nearest small town of Batu Pahat in Malaya's, Johore State where I had heard there was a Chinese eating house.

The Chinese owner was delighted to welcome us into his rather primitive establishment. The welcoming consisted of a broad grin and much gesturing because of the language difficulty. We attempted to request chicken soup which we illustrated by hunkering down, hopping for a bit and clucking like a hen. This acting part was probably influenced by the memories of 'The Great McBain', the hypnotist we met during our basic training days. The owner watched our antics closely for a minute then grinned, nodded and made for the kitchen from where loud clanging noises emerged. He eventually put delicious bowls of Chinese chicken soup with noodles on the table before us to be rewarded by blank stares from us ignorant peasants. We had actually expected white coloured Campbell's chicken soup, like the tinned soup we had back home. Eventually one of us tried the watery looking stuff with bits of things floating in it and grudgingly admitted it was eatable but nothing like the real thing by which he meant good old Campbell's tinned soup back home.

The next course was to be our big treat. We had tried to order steak and chips. There was a bit more of a delay with this request, I guess our loud mooing impressions did not really cut it. I later discovered our new Chinese restaurant owner friend had scurried out the back way to a butcher and returned eventually with bits of some kind of meat (probably pork) which he tried to cook to our liking by slicing it into thin strips, throwing them into a hot wok before sliding them into a large dish garnished with fried onion and other tasty vegetables which he placed on the middle of the table.

After we had prodded and sniffed at the food for a while. One of our guys actually tasted a little bit, chewed and rolled it around his mouth before swallowing it while nodding approvingly. We were hungry and had also committed to buying a meal from this guy who then re-appeared with a huge bowl of steamed rice and set it down before us. He must have thought we were a right bunch of dummies when we just looked uncomprehendingly at the rice. Our only previous experience with rice was when it came in a can which contained rice pudding, what the hell were we supposed do with all this rice? A couple of the guys started muttering with each other, a bad sign with this lot. Luckily, the restaurant owner piled some rice on a plate, added some of the cooked pork and veg.and handed the plate to me for my opinion. It was delicious, I immediately shoveled more food onto my plate to indicate it was o.k. and the other guys dived in enthusiastically. So far so good but we had only been using the big serving spoon to dish out the food, how could we actually manage to eat the stuff?

Chop sticks were lying on the table but there were no knives or forks. We had seen Chinese people in Singapore City eating from small bowls by using chopsticks. They always lifted the small bowl up close to their mouths then somehow shoveled in the food. By now I was so hungry and game for anything. I grabbed a couple of the strange wee chop sticks, lowered my head down to the bowl and clumsily started to raise bits of food towards my mouth. Not much success to report there. I then tried lifting the bowl up to my mouth trying not to think about my mother's horrified expression if she could see my bad manners. No worries. My mother was thousands of miles away and I shoveled the tasty food into my mouth with the chopsticks. Great stuff.

You have to understand, I was eighteen years old. The farthest I had been till now was London when I was sixteen, not a lot of my contemporaries back home in Scotland had even been that far. This was the life as far as I was concerned, it was costing me nothing and I was even being paid, I was absorbing it all greedily. The days of foreign travel, jet setting and more affluent lifestyles was unheard of and still far away, near impossible for a working class guy in the 1950s.

The only guy I had known who had ever been in the Far East was an unlucky prisoner of the Japanese during the war. Poor bugger, he was lucky to even just survive what must have been a horrific experience.

What could happen to me in these foreign parts? Possibly be shot? End of foreign adventure story, but that sort of stuff never entered my soon to be endangered head.

34 ARRIVAL in SINGAPORE

Sadly, I remember the first sights and smell of Singapore docks with no great affection. We were disembarking from the Troop Ship and I remember the smell quite clearly. A high percentage of raw sewage was featured which marked it out for me to make a mental note and avoid this area whenever possible.

I was surprised to see what I assumed was a group of coolies engaged in loading a nearby ship manually. I have a memory of the coolies conveying the shipment into the vessel with the cargo in bags loaded onto their heads! This particular scene was right out of Conrad or else I witnessed a time warp of some kind. This was, after all 1955. Perhaps the local government had overlooked this particular activity or maybe a movie was being made, although I saw no sign of any movie cameras.

The British Raj had taken over once again after the war. They were keen to show the natives how good and kind they were to a grateful people now liberated from one type of slavery and back to another.

However, the Second World War had ended ten years ago. Perhaps the coolie activity would teach the natives that the Brits were back to stay, that, of course, was why our fresh boatload of soldiers had arrived. Even with our regular addition of fresh blood to the governing system, the old regime was already doomed with the sounds of 'Verdeka', meaning 'Freedom', already being shouted with more and more fervour by the natives in the streets of Singapore island.

I must have somehow missed part of my geography lessons at school - the cause of my missed knowledge was probably due to the eccentric lady geography teacher. For some reason this batty lady formed an intense dislike for pupils from my home town who had qualified and had been transferred to her nearby Senior Secondary school at Lasswade. She used to refer to us as *'the water rats'* from Penicuik. She completely ignored us, refused to address us and gave her Geography lesson to the local kids only.

The bad attitude of this teacher probably contributed to my rather sketchy knowledge of geography for I thought Singapore and Malaya were one and the same. I now realised that Singapore City was built on the large island of Singapore. Malaya was another country altogether, it was situated over a causeway to the north. Malaya was where all the fighting took place. We were to be billeted at an army barracks on Singapore Island for a few weeks of re-organising and re-grouping, before heading north for active service over the causeway, the short stay in Singapore was another welcome distraction for me.

We were loaded onto a fleet of army trucks to be driven to Selerang barracks on the east side of the island and close to Changi village which was on the coast beside the South China Sea. This was more like it. I hoped things would be more Oriental soon.

I noticed all the trucks were without canvas covers which would have been installed on all similar trucks in the UK. This was partly because the heat generated in canvas covered trucks would have been unbearable for the passengers as we were only a few degrees from the equator. I soon found out this rule actually applied to all trucks operating in Malaya. The main purpose for removing the canvas covers did not allow for the comfort of the troops but was to allow a clear line of returning fire from the truck for instant retaliation when ambushed by terrorists. It also provided quick access to the ground for personnel to make a swift exit over the sides from the targeted truck to take up defensive positions and get on with the urgent business of returning fire towards the ambushers.

35 CHINATOWN IN SINGAPORE ISLAND IN THE 1950'S

Business addresses all on ground floor. Lots of shouting, bargaining and industry taking place down there. Accommodation was above, washing hanging out to dry. Movie theatre located at far end of street.

I worked my way through the rest of the guys in the truck to gain access to the rear of the cab where I could stand for a clear view as we were driven through Singapore. This was the Orient I had heard and read about and I was now actually part of it.

We drew away from the heavy, stinky smell of the dock area, into a whole new scene where the smell and sounds were very different with lots of loud hammering and shouting in Chinese from some unseen source of either industry or construction taking place.

Most of the Singapore citizens seemed to be Chinese rather than the native Malays. There were lots of street vendors selling food by the roadside. Their various spicy offerings contributed to the heady and hot atmosphere of the city, so different, so strange, bit scruffy but not at all like scruffy Aden. This was what I wanted to experience.

We left the city to travel the few miles to the army barracks, palm trees all over the place, till we were driving through a fairly clear area where a large, forbidding, square type of building came into view on our right. It was so different from what we had already seen and some of the guys were wondering what it was. I, alone in this crowded truck, could tell them. It was the notorious Changi jail. I had read about it in a book written by an Australian soldier who, with hundreds of others, had been incarcerated in there after the British Army had surrendered Singapore to the victorious and vicious Japanese Army in 1942.

The treatment of the imprisoned soldiers was scandalous with ill treatment, severe beatings, very little food, overcrowding. They even threw in the occasional indiscriminate murder, possibly for 'light relief'. The Japanese Guards were pure bastards with very few exceptions. There was no medical equipment apart from an improvised system implemented by the prisoners' own Allied medical people who had no medicines or hospital facilities at all.

Russell Braddon, the Aussie writer of *'The Naked Island',* managed to survive, even after being force marched up through Malaya in unimaginable conditions to take part in the construction of the notorious Japanese death railway. He laboured and suffered there until his final and welcome release to freedom when the Japs gave in at last after our Americans allies managed to finish the war by dropping the atomic bomb on Japan.

I was aware there had been a high proportion of Scots imprisoned at Changi Jail. The Argyle and Sutherland Highlanders had been the last of the British Army to cross the causeway to Singapore when retreating from Malaya. Their sappers then blew up the causeway link to Singapore with the Japanese troops hard on their heels.

The Argyles had made their withdrawal over the causeway with pipes playing defiantly before taking up their new defensive positions on Singapore Island. They must have been completely puzzled when, a few days later, the decision was made for the entire British Army to completely surrender and they had the surprising order to stand down.

I tried to explain this to the rest of the guys in a condensed version but most of it was lost in the general road noise and babble. Anyway, the mood lifted as we approached Selerang Barracks with its modern looking, big, white buildings with spacious accommodation and, crowning it all, more bloody palm trees!

Charwallahs, Selarang Barracks, Singapore 1955
"Anybody wanna tea, mucker"?

I awoke next morning before reveille sounded, wondering where I was. The familiar sound of huge ship's engines throbbing was replaced by a strange voice intoning, with no urgency, "Anybody wanna tea, mucker"? I opened one eye above the sheets which had been issued on our arrival at Selarang barracks the day before, no other bedding seemed to be needed as the temperature was already high, even before six a.m. We were only a few degrees from the equator and the humid heat, at first, was overpowering.

It was then I saw my first Char Wallah. He was an Indian guy, squatting just inside the entrance beside a large, copper urn which was heated by charcoal kept alight in a special area at the bottom of the unit, giving off an intriguing scent, unfamiliar to me. I suppose you would call him a tea vendor. He carried a large ruled book with him, it slowly dawned on us that tea was available to help us to gather ourselves together before heading for the ablutions prior to wandering over to the mess hall in the early morning sunshine for breakfast.

This was more my style, and in complete contrast to the usual treatment expected by us young soldiers so recently subjected to what we had considered to be harsh early morning military treatment. It had always seemed to be accompanied by much shouting and yelling with lots of running about on our part.

Even the bugle call, when it came a few minutes later, seemed to be different from the scratchy recording of a bugle broadcast over the loud speaker system on board the troopship which had been our home for the past month.

Our own duty buglers and pipers had already taken over at Selerang. The bugle call for reveille was the more familiar 'Charlie, Charlie', call. It was followed by the piper playing 'Hey Johnnie Cope are ye wakin yet'? This is the pipe tune played at reveille in all Scottish Regiments. It commemorates the lightening surprise dawn attack and quick defeat of General John Cope, commanding the British government forces crushed at the battle of Prestonpans by the mainly Highland Jacobite army in 1745.

The Char Wallah had no interest in Scottish history. His attention was focused on obtaining new customers for his daily tea vending service. This first mug of tea was complimentary. Very clever. It would not cost much to enjoy this wonderful early morning service and nearly all the guys gladly accepted the first free mug.

When we were well and truly hooked, Bushti, the charwallah, then produced a much thumbed ruled book to record your name against which he would enter future small charges for tea and any other costs incurred during the rest of the day for other purchases of cool orange drinks, sandwiches, etc. For some reason a fried egg on a bread roll was called an 'Egg Banjo'! These and other goodies could be obtained at their big tent erected conveniently just behind our building.

Charges for each service were reckoned up on a weekly basis to coincide with our pay parades held every Thursday. We would line up for our weekly pay in the open air, the ceremony administered by a Pay Corps officer. The Char Wallah would squat discreetly a little distance behind the pay officers' table, clutching his ledger. As soon as we received our pay, we saluted the Pay Officer, made a smart turn to the right and fell out before marching at a much slower pace round the table to be accosted by the char wallah. We would then pay him for the services provided over the previous week. The account book system seemed to work out pretty well. We also received an overseas pay allowance which eased the pain slightly. To be fair, the Charwallah service was never exactly a luxury service.

I turned over in bed to reach for my mug on the bedside locker and was surprised to see another Indian guy squatting on his hunkers there with his hand in one of my boots which was being buffed to a high shine by the shoe brush held firmly in the other hand.

He greeted me with a friendly good morning smile as if he had been cleaning my boots all his life. He was the Boot Wallah engaged on a complimentary early morning boot polishing service which, according to Indian service tradition, would now qualify him to clean my boots each day for a small fee during my time of service. I was experiencing the tail end of the old British Raj. Once it was the prevailing system in India, written about by Rudyard Kipling, which I thought was over. But here I was on Singapore Island in the 1950's actually experiencing the death throes of an extinct system once totally accepted in the old British Empire.

It seemed Indian contractors were only doing what they had always done in India which was to contract and supply each British Army regiment with a different, now much smaller, army of Indian servants who would provide an early morning tea service and boot cleaning services. We would see the great contracting man only infrequently when he paid a visit to his workers at the char wallah tent pitched conveniently near our barrack block. It was easy to pick him out, he was tall but he really stood out in the head department because his hair was bright orange due to frequent application of henna dye, a bit weird at first sight.

When the remaining troops moved from Singapore to complete the transfer to Malaya in a few weeks' time, the char wallahs moved with us. I spotted what seemed to be an extra truck attached to the end of our convoy, full of smiling Indians, complete with all their gear, quite amazing. When my time came for the move 'up country' I had said a premature goodbye to Liba, our boot wallah. He was remaining at the garrison in Selarang, I imagine his services would not be needed among the guys on active service in Malaya where jungle boots were more the norm than leather army boots. He would be attached to the next regiment coming to occupy this area on Singapore Island. This was before I realized I would be remaining in Singapore to complete our much interrupted signal training course before being sent to join the rest of the regiment in Malay. We would be customers for our boot wallah for a few more weeks.

There was also a complete laundry service to save us scruffy young soldiers from more exertion.

The laundry workers were known as Dhobi Wallahs and I imagine this also was a service once provided for the British in India. It was, of course, a very slick operation. Our bundles of washing would be collected in the morning and returned next day, clean shirts and uniforms starched and pressed for, of course, a small fee. Most of the Dhobi Wallahs seemed to be Tamils, very black guys, probably imported from Ceylon.

There were also a few local Malays employed around the barracks. They were a friendly happy go lucky bunch, but mainly it was Chinese people who operated and owned most of the businesses on Singapore Island.

I recall mentioning on more than one occasion in the middle 1950s, that the Chinese would, within our time, rise to play an important part in the business community of the new world, then being formed. They seemed to be in control of most of the business interest on Singapore Island; they also owned lots of the rubber plantations and tin mining operations in Malaya. I reckoned it would not be long before they were calling the shots over the rest of the world. Of course, my forecasting in the 1950's is now coming to pass. However, nobody paid any attention to the ramblings of a wee, obscure guy from Scotland. I guess I was just a wee, thick, bugger from Penicuik. What would I know?

We also had the services of a wee Chinese woman. Even I could see she was no terrorist, she was tiny and carried a small bag and a little wooden stool which she set up just inside the entrance to our barrack room, ready for some sort of business. Her bag contained an array of needles, threads and wool. She was the, *Sew sew woman,* she had no English and sat patiently and silently until we understood what it was all about. She would then gladly receive our shirts to have buttons sewn on and woolen socks darned. This service was almost better than being at home where I had been taught to darn my own bloody socks.

Wee Sew, sew woman at Selerang Barracks, Singapore. She would sew our buttons back on and even darn our woollen army socks.

36 WEE SPOT OF EGYPTIAN P.T. (BRITISH ARMY STYLE).

Wednesday afternoons were set aside for sports activity. Being daft and Scottish or even just being Scottish and daft, most of the guys trooped off somewhere to play football in the horrendous heat of a Singapore afternoon.

I was also Scottish but not daft, and more inclined to the 'Mad Dogs and Englishmen' attitude where, according to Noel Coward the natives seemingly, *'banged a gong and ran'* from the heat of the mid-day sun to take cover in the shade, leaving mad dogs, Englishmen and the likes to suffer from the heat.

McGinlay, our 'scruffy soldier' was still with us, serving as a rifleman in Dog Company which I thought was rather appropriate. Being Wednesday afternoon and Alfie being from Glasgow where football was a religion, he would join the other sun lovers heading for the nearest football pitch. Being around Alfie was enough to inspire me to good ideas. I liked him and looked forward to his weekly pre-football visit to our billet. He came to our building with shoe laces dragging along behind carelessly tied boots. He was seeking other kindred football loving spirits to join the regular weekly exodus to the football field. This gave me a simple but artistic idea.

I noticed when the other guys just wandered off in the heat towards the football pitch in a casual bunch, there was no marching or head count involved. I carried out my simple plan where I would disappear into the ablutions, wait there for a while until any stragglers had cleared out from the barrack room. I would then reappear beside my bed like magic, clad in only a towel, ready for some Egyptian P.T. This was the army description for lying on the bed in a horizontal position, either reading a book or perhaps just dozing quietly in the afternoon heat, but with the big louvered doors wide open and securely hooked back to allow any passing breeze to enter and waft through this now restful place.

37   JUNGLE FEET

I was practicing my Egyptian PT while clutching my well-thumbed copy of *The Pickwick Papers* on a quiet Wednesday afternoon when the peace was disturbed by a strange voice floating up the stairs calling, "Jungle Feet, jungle feet?" in a questioning sort of way.

The strange voice was followed by the entrance of an equally strange and broadly smiling Indian man. He was dressed in old fashioned cream coloured trousers and open neck white shirt. His brown feet peeped out from his wide bottomed trousers revealing his natty leather flip flops. He carried an old leather bag of the type once referred to as a Gladstone bag, sometimes also described as a doctor's bag. He spotted me which was quite easy as I was the only guy there and approached with a beaming smile as I lay with my bare feet sticking out at the end of the bed.

"Got any jungle feet, John? I fix". He beamed as he reached out quickly to pinch my toe between his thumb and forefinger. I squealed at him in surprise. He was still smiling but his keen eye had spotted a corn on my left little toe. I was p.o'd as I can't stand anyone touching my feet and he was gripping my one and only corn rather painfully.

The corn was a legacy from a recent hard winter in Scotland. Early one Saturday morning while on my way to join the grouse beaters, I had been unwise enough to allow my old leather boots to get soaking wet. We were temporarily employed each Saturday for a day of 'beating up' the grouse for the sport of the shooters - it made a bit of beer money for me to spend in the pub on Sat. night. I found it hard to resist showing off by splashing through a stream rather than walking the few extra yards to cross by a little bridge. I had to wear the wet boots for a whole day trekking across the local moors and earned a seemingly permanent corn on my small toe on that particularly cold and wet day.

Still beaming, Jungle Feet let go of my toe and, with a great flourish, opened the doctor bag.

"I fix jungle feet", he repeated confidently, showing me a tin of some unidentified sticky paste which he quickly smeared on my affected toe. I started to object but he dismissed my muttered complaint with a quick professional motion of his hand while his other hand delved again into the magic bag, producing a roll of cotton wool from which he tore a small piece and stuck the cotton to the sticky stuff on my toe.

Somehow The Great McBain and his conjuring tricks came to mind as I stared at the decorations on my foot.

"What happens now?" I said, "I suppose you set fire to it?"

I was so busy looking at my foot that I failed to notice he was still in action over the bag. Quick as a flash he produced a box of matches. He lit a match and rapidly applied it to the cotton wool on my toe where a huge sheet of flame shot towards the ceiling. I also shot up from the bed, cursing at Jungle Feet who was standing back, still beaming, the spent match still in his fingers, looking well pleased.

It is difficult to look aggressive and threatening from the horizontal position, with a smoking foot, when clad only in a green army towel. To be perfectly honest, I was not feeling any pain either. Only my cool had been disturbed. Jungle Feet was standing at the foot of my bed, still beaming, confidently expecting some reward for his professional services. To be fair, when I inspected my toe there was no trace of the hard, little round corn which had been there a few minutes ago. To tell the truth I never saw it again.

Just like The Great McBain, Jungle Feet also appeared to be a great magician and as usual I could not explain how it was done. This was the mysterious East, so I could only conclude it must be magic. I fumbled in my pants pocket draped over my locker, and gave him the two Straits dollars he requested. Still beaming he wandered out of my life and away down the stairs to become another strange, but memorable, little episode in *My Army Daze* memories.

38   GUARD MOUNTING

I did my first and only guard mounting in Selerang barracks.

The routine was for thirteen selected private soldiers to be marched onto the square before six p.m. for guard inspection by the duty officer of the day. Twelve was the required number of soldiers for the night guard duty but Thirteen soldiers were paraded and the smartest soldier was excused from night guard duty altogether.

After completing inspection the duty officer would nominate the man he considered to be the smartest soldier. This man had earned the title, *stick man*, excused from guard duty for that night. The officer would notify the duty sergeant who would bring the squad from the *at ease* position to *attention*, identify the particular soldier then instruct only that soldier to take a smart turn to the right and dismiss.

The lucky guy would march off the parade ground and disappear back to barracks where he would usually get rid of his rifle, get changed and join his mates for a game of cards, bottle of beer or whatever. He was chosen as *stick man* and was excused duty for the night, leaving the losers to continue with the guard mounting and march off to the guard house to start their boring duties for the night.

The only task ahead of the stick man was to report to the HQ office the following morning where he was actually issued with a cane, hence his title *stick man*. He would then find a shady spot to the rear of the office, select a newspaper from the office with which to while away the morning and pass the time away.

The only chance of any action would be if the Regimental Sergeant Major had run out of fags then the stick man was dispatched to the N.A.A.F.I. building for a packet of cigarettes, remembering to take his little cane with which to march, now wearing his daytime shirt sleeve order with well starched shorts and short sleeved shirt, like the smart soldier he was.

This would be the only effort he would be obliged to make all morning till the sun got really hot around noon when he could then be briefly glimpsed marching off again in a soldierly fashion, cane tucked under his arm, looking very purposeful. One would assume he was going about some more important business.

Not so, although it was certainly important to him, this time he was again marching smartly as before, but now heading for his own barrack block. Mindful of the sound advice, *'Bullshit baffles brains'* he could indulge in perhaps some Egyptian PT and snooze the afternoon away till tea time.

I recall being told about one enterprising soldier who had investigated the *Army Daze* state of military mind and adapted it to suit his needs. This soldier seemed always too busy to be on normal chores and duties usually reserved for the other, ordinary soldiers. In reality, he was putting *Army Daze* to good use. He carried a folded piece of white bond paper in his hand, and if an officer was spotted on the horizon, he would pick up the pace to a good marching clip and disappear round the nearest corner into oblivion.

Onlookers presumed his folded paper carried a message being transported from one army office to another, and nobody ever questioned him. In reality, it was always the same, neatly folded piece of blank paper he kept clean in his back pocket. He was probably heading for a quiet, shady corner where he could have a smoke from one of his free fag issue cigarettes in peace. It would not have been correct for the stick man to be seen smoking on duty, not good for discipline and all that old crap, don't ye' know.

Our bond paper carrying warrior soon became a man of legend. He expanded his paper carrying scam to other days and could often be seen marching smartly to nowhere, minus his smart stick but clutching his official looking piece of paper. According to the most recent shit house rumours, he is still serving his country somewhere, still drawing his pay and doing bugger all.

The reason for thirteen soldiers to be paraded for guard mounting was simple. The idea was they would all vie with each other to be smartest soldier, the winner to be excused duty while the rest of the twelve comparatively scruffy soldiers would march off to the guard room to commence a boring twelve hours of guard duty of two hours *on*, followed by four hours *off* when you were allowed to sit but not lie on a bare wire sprung bed frame. Boots could not be removed and sleeping was a punishable offence. Must keep the lads awake and alert in case of emergency.

I must have been comparatively scruffy that evening when it came my turn for guard duty. I was unprepared and not at my best for selection as the smartest soldier. This smart soldier tradition was new to me; perhaps I had been day dreaming when it was announced. At any rate, I was dispatched to guard the Motor Transport compound for my first, and only, two hours *on,* etc.

Fortunately, there is bugger all twilight in that part of the Far East. It gets dark quite suddenly just after six p.m., so I closed the wire gates of the M.T. compound behind me, locked them for security, clambered into the cabin of a big army truck, got comfortable and snoozed my way through both of my two hour slots of night guard duty.

However, I was disturbed during my second stage of duty that night. It was about 12.30.a.m. I was back into the cab of what I was now calling my truck when I was awakened by a loud, insistent rattling at the wire security gate. I had taken the precaution of slipping the padlock shut then pocketing the key, can't be too careful, you know, I was technically on guard and liable, I believed, to be shot if found to be asleep on duty.

The cause of the bloody racket was a young, green, Second Lieutenant just about my own age and only just posted to the Regiment. He was, like me, carrying out his first night as Duty Officer and, unlike me, he was probably looking for promotion and prepared to make a good impression to let everyone know he was for sure on the ball tonight.

My first impulse was *bollocks to him,* but decided against following that impulse when I saw he was he was accompanied in the gloom by the familiar figure of the Duty Sergeant obviously a wee bit pissed off at being dragged away from his mug of tea in the guard room.

The young Officer started a blustering verbal attack at me through the wire security fence, demanding to know why the gates were locked and why was I not standing beside the gate when he decided to check the place.

Two can play this game was my second thought. Full of bullshit, I came to attention, started ranting about security procedures about which I was sure neither of us knew anything about. I was throwing in statements like, "Can't be too careful these days, **Sir**, lots of strange characters about, **Sir**", just making it all up as I went along.

Anyhoo, you would think my brain had a mind of its own for it had wandered off all by itself to consider the advice Sergeant Fleming has instilled in me during my basic training, *"Remember, Wishart"* he had said, *"Bullshit baffles brains"*. Baffle brains it did that night, the green Lieutenant had no comeback whatsoever, merely mumbled something about, *"Well done, good man"* etc. which was his best and only line of defense before marching off back into the darkness followed by the Duty Sergeant who paused to give me a thoughtful look under the light beside the locked gate before turning away to follow the new young Officer.

I could only guess the Sergeant was also thinking along the bullshit lines as well when I marched smartly back to my comfortable but, out of sight, cab to continue my interrupted snooze.

I mentioned this guard duty was my first and last duty for the entire duration of our stay at Selerang barracks. If it had not been for a touch of the Daze affecting my brain, it would have been possible for me to avoid guard duty right from the start. Qualifying for smartest soldier was no problem for me as I rather enjoyed putting on a smart uniform, taking care that all the correct bits were gleaming, hair cut horribly short, boots shining. All I was required to do was turn up for parade, my previously mentioned talent for smartening up did the rest and I would be ordered to take a smart turn to the right and fall out. The other guys were marched off in the opposite direction to serve their twelve hours of boring night duty.

There was a slight problem with the uniform which prevented me becoming an instant *smart soldier*. During the voyage to Singapore, we had been issued with our jungle green uniforms. These outfits were intended for jungle warfare. They were a bit floppy and obviously very new, not at all suitable for British Army bullshit parades. We also had strict instructions to have jacket sleeves rolled down and long pants to be worn after six p.m. in the evening. We felt like real prats when dressed like this for an evening out in Steamy Singapore, not at all cool.

The reason for this order was supposed to be as a guard against mosquito bites which caused malaria, although it was a known fact the Singapore area was virtually mosquito free owing to fairly strict insect control.

Added to this we had to take anti malaria pills, I think they were called either Paludrin or perhaps

Mecaprine which were dished out to us first thing on muster parade each morning, taken under supervision by the Duty Officer. Seemed to us to be a load of army bullshit but, to be fair, this daily parade went on during all of our Far Eastern service. As far as I know, nobody contracted malaria.

The uniform problem could be helped by frequent laundering whether needed or not which removed the sheen of obviously newly issued clothing material. The green colour soon faded to achieve an 'old soldier' effect, a look which was much affected by the young soldiers at that time.

We already had a sunburnt appearance from our month long sea voyage to Singapore. This tanned look plus the frequently laundered and starched jungle greens enabled us to do lots of posing when any new replacement units arrived from the recently introduced air flights from the UK to Singapore. This allowed us to shout witty, old soldier, cat calls at the new, painfully white, obviously new young soldiers. Oh how we laughed as we called, *"Get yer knees brown"* or, *"Get some time in",* plus other witty sayings which, we thought, marked us out as very urbane, quick witted types. What the new guys, ashamed at their pallid looks, thought has not been recorded.

Frequent laundering with heavy starching would soon take care of my uniform and would lead to my being a consistently smart soldier, spending the whole guard duty night in my own bed and fetching fags next day for the Regimental Sergeant Major, then practicing Egyptian P.T. with cool, old soldier flair.

My cool, old soldier flair attitude to suburban guard duty ceremonies in Singapore Island would come to an abrupt halt as soon as we were transferred over the causeway into Malaya, an extra stick man was surplus to requirements up there.

The practice of gunfire, tiffin and especially the quiet time caper, quickly faded away when we received orders to stop with the fucking about on Singapore Island and get ourselves up into Malaya to tackle some real soldiering. Pity really.

39   WRITING LETTERS BACK HOME.

My Singapore sleep habit was similar to my outdoor sleeping habits on board ship. I used to drag my iron bed across the cement floor, through the big, louvered doors onto the veranda where I would spend my night in the cool, fresh air. Back inside the billet room there was a strong wire line installed the full length of the room on each side, above the lines of beds. Our mosquito nets were strung on a metal ring from these wires, one green netting cocoon above each bed. We used them for the first few nights. However, there was no real need for them and the few mosquitoes that ventured into our huge, airy rooms were soon gobbled up by the many geckos who shared our accommodation.

Like the nets, the geckos were a novelty at first as they wandered about above us. They seemingly anchored themselves vertically or completely upside down on our walls or ceilings. The only time I used the mosquito net was to give me a bit of privacy in the evening if I was either reading or not wishing to be disturbed when writing the very occasional letter home.

I only wrote to my mother. Writing to any girl friends was, in my opinion, a waste of time. We were away for so long that it would be a sure way to court disaster to the friendship if the girl got fed up waiting and decided to send a 'Dear John' type of letter instead of a 'Happy Birthday' card. No girl had asked me to write to her anyway! One girl wrote to me - once. Unfortunately, she broke the news that a friend of mine, Pete Ketchen, serving in Cypress with the Royal Scots, had been killed when a terrorist chucked a hand grenade into his passing army truck.

The girl was very upset about Pete, so was I. However, she finished the short letter by saying she would not know what she would do if I got myself killed. That was enough emotion for me. I can't remember sending an answer back to her, a thoughtless, selfish act on my part, one I have regretted ever since.

Sunday morning. Me with the Sunday Singapore issue of the Straits Times. Dig the army haircut.

Harri, our Char Wallah at mid day. It is Ramadan and Harri is Muslem, he must fast during the day. We are located very near the equator and the heat knocks him about a bit, he takes advantage of a quiet hour to conserve energy.

40 SPIKE.

Big Ray and I were sitting on my bed chatting one evening. It was around closing time for the wet canteen, Ray strolled out onto the veranda then turned round and silently but urgently beckoned me to join him.

"It's Spike", he whispered quietly as he motioned for me to hurry over to duck down behind the small wall on the veranda. We were above and out of sight from the small, very drunk old soldier who had obviously just left the wet bar in the N.A.A.F.I. building. He was 'beside himself with drink' and now making his unsteady way across the hallowed barrack square which was strictly off limits and reserved for military drill functions only.

It was forbidden to walk across the barrack square. Even if you wanted to go from a building on one side of the square and cross to another building on the opposite side, it was necessary to walk all the way around to get to the other side. (Did somebody mention chickens?) Here was one of our very own 'old soldiers' weaving his drunken way home, right across the sacred square to his billet, brightly illuminated by the huge, full moon above.

I never knew his proper name but Spike had soldiered with the regiment for many years, all over the British Empire, often during very active service, with more than his share of battle scars. The most recent disfiguring wound had been inflicted in a pitched battle in Korea. He had been hit in the face by shrapnel and now affected a large, bushy moustache to cover a bit of the damage.

Right now Spike was feeling no pain. He was probably soldiering in his befuddled brain somewhere in India when Ray's voice made him stop as if he had marched into a brick wall.

"Spike", Ray said into the dark and steamy night, in a loud, quavery, stage whisper voice. "Spike", we're comin' to get you, we're comin', Spike". The very drunk old soldier was struggling to stay upright, he could hear but not see the speaking ghost but he was ready to fight it whatever it was. That bloody ghost was going to be made to suffer if Spike could just get hold of it. He twisted from side to side, arms reaching out, trying to pin down the elusive, malevolent spirit.

"A'll get ye, ya bastard, a'll get ye", he threatened, weaving this way and that in an effort to locate the source of the spooky voice. We, of course, were out of sight on the balcony above him, doubled up with silent laughter. It seemed to Spike the voice was coming from the night sky, "A'll get ye, ya thievin' bastard, I know you're somewhere in the Empire", he yelled as he raised his arms, grasping impotently into the night sky. His final effort spun him backwards where he fell on his arse, unable to get up and was reduced to incoherent mumbling still waving his arms about.

I started to feel sorry for the old guy, lying on his back, arms feebly waving like an overturned beetle. Spike was probably in his late thirties by now and would soon be reaching his time to be released from the army service, not very well equipped to face future civilian life.

Luckily, some of his mates approached, having come the long way round the square in the more conventional way. They could see Spike, illuminated in the bright moonlight, flat out and raving to himself. It seemed as if he was unable to get to his feet. His buddies could see no sign of authority, and quickly ran across the sacred square, heaved him to his feet, dragging him off to sleep in safety. We withdrew discreetly from the veranda, giggling and choking with laughter, like the insensitive clods we were.

41 STRANGE HAPPENING.

A strange thing happened to me around that time we teased Spike. One night after lights out, in my bed which I had dragged out onto the veranda, I woke suddenly to see a dark figure standing at the end of the bed, the figure was totally silent, without any movement. It seemed to be observing me but it was impossible to see anything of the face owing to the very bright moon behind the figure. It was really just roughly like a human shape and I thought it might be Spike wandering about still drunk from his usual evening activities at the wet canteen. But this figure was silent and immovable. Our old soldier Spike would probably have been swaying and muttering a wee bit.

I thought the strange figure might be something from the supernatural but that was just too much to comprehend, my only way of dealing with this situation owed a lot to my imaginative childhood protection. I had a theory that no ghosties or bogles could harm me when I was fast asleep. I made a kind of sleepy, grunting noise, rolled onto my side, pulling the sheet over my head and feigned sleep.

I could not think of anything else to do at the time except make deep breathing noises. Still hearing no movement from the dark figure, I had a sly peek from under the sheet, nothing there at all. Oh, I forgot to mention the other reason for my not seeing any eyes, the *thing* had no head!

It was a fact the place was haunted. Ghost stories abounded in this tormented area since its terrible experiences with the Japanese guards during the last war. This was the main reason that the solitary sentry position at the isolated old motor transport compound was one of the least attractive positions for night guard duty.

I have already stated that I preferred to sleep most nights out on the veranda wearing only a sheet for cover. The veranda at the opposite side from my official bed space area provided what I considered to be the perfect position to experience a new dawn on a Far Eastern morning.

It faced away from the barrack square towards the distant city of Singapore with exotic views of very foreign trees I had never seen before. I could also see the South China Sea from our veranda. The sounds from the char wallah provided the eastern affect as he prepared our morning tea during the discreet early morning tea making ritual noises. Our char wallah Bushti tended to mutter to himself in Hindi while making the tea just inside the entrance to our floor. His early morning muttering gave a magic effect to my Far Eastern experience as a young soldier.

This low muttering between char wallahs while preparing the early morning tea was a sound which had been heard for many years by serving soldiers in India. My grandfather must have heard it when serving long ago in India with the Seaforth Highlanders.

Now it was no longer heard except for locations like ours which still had its char wallahs, boot wallahs, dhobie wallahs, jungle feet 'doctors' and old 'sew, sew' women. All this nostalgia would soon be no more as the old British Empire shrank smaller and smaller to finally disappear.

I usually awoke some time before the official rousing time of six a.m. I preferred to be ahead of the mass of unwashed bodies soon to erupt into the ablutions. Our showers had no method for heating the water. There was never any need for this soft, pansy, method for shaving and showering. The water was always tepid in Singapore. Each hairy male body contributed to the morning outbreak of coughing, encouraged by smoking our free weekly fag issue of cigarettes, also lots of hawking, spitting, farting and all the other manly sounds of Her Majesties' army soldiering in the Far East preparing for another day.

These sounds were hardly an appropriate welcome to the fresh Far Eastern dawn and the sensibilities of romantic imaginings by a young Scottish soldier.

The view towards the South China Sea from my balcony in the morning.

Influenced by my 'only child' background, I could wake myself to order by thinking of a suitable time to rise before I went to sleep, if you know what I mean. By rising early from bed I managed to shave and shower before the daily human eruption started. I was then to be found, leaning on the balcony, gazing upwards into the, fresh, early morning cloudless sky at the regular early sprinkling of beautiful parachutes, gently drifting earthwards.

I watched this wonderful parachute show every morning but only mentioned it casually to Robbie one day as we went to the canteen for what some guy with a sense of humour called breakfast which always consisted of overcooked pieces of fried bacon actually floating in a huge puddle of melted fat in a big metal tray. I went mainly for a mug of tea and piece of burnt toast. Anyhoo, Robbie told me the morning display was put on by members of the Special Air Service when they performed their early morning parachute training exercises.

I realised they must be the same guys I had often seen around nine a.m., probably returning from their early morning parachute training. They seemed to pay no attention to our rules and bullshit regulations, making their merry and irreverent way right across the sacred parade square wearing bits and pieces of military type uniform. They were obviously from some sort of army unit, wearing quite unidentifiable dress as far as I could see, with absolutely no regard for the sort of rules we were subject to.

It had occurred to me there seemed to be no effort on the part of our officers to discipline these tearaways as they horse-played their merry way across the square. In fact, I sometimes had the impression they must be invisible to anyone but me.

Being a National Service conscript, I was averse to any kind of military bullshit. I was certainly subject to it for my two years army service and had to conform to it, or else! What made things so different for these 'special' guys? John Scott, one of our signal platoon bunch of young soldiers was sitting beside us in the canteen and clued me in. John had been over at the dhobie laundry on the edge of camp, trying to trace a missing item of uniform which had failed to be returned to him. On his way back he had run into a Training Sergeant from this mystery unit.

The Sergeant shot a stray dog with his pistol just as John came on the scene. The dog was tethered to a post when it was killed. John was so taken aback at this seemingly cruel act that he aggressively asked the sergeant what he was playing at. John Scott was a dog lover, he was raised in Glasgow and could handle himself so his approach was hard. However, the Sergeant looked as though he could take care of himself. Having second thoughts, John approached the situation with caution as the other guy was still holding the loaded pistol.

The pistol-packing Sergeant explained that stray dogs could be a big problem at the barracks because they formed packs of hunting scavengers when their numbers grew. These roaming packs could turn dangerous; there were feral and there was also a high likelihood they could be rabies carriers. It was the practice in these parts to round them up and shoot them on a regular basis. As the Sergeant explained bout the stray dog problem, John noticed he had a Glasgow accent. By the time the shooting situation had cooled down, John and the Sergeant were chatting like old friends.

John learned the hard looking Sergeant was also a member of the Special Air Service. He was responsible for the training the young S.A.S. guys, all Maoris from New Zealand, on their daily parachute jumping exercise. They were a law unto themselves. As members of a unit of Special Air Service, they certainly did not answer to any of our Senior Officers, nor did they take orders from anybody else but their own training Sergeant who seemed to be in sole charge. The Scottish Sergeant put them through their para jumps, followed by strenuous daily PT exercises which took place undisturbed on a corner of the hallowed parade ground.

They were a work hard and play hard bunch of guys who obviously rose from their beds earlier than us to take advantage of the comparatively still, early morning conditions on Singapore Island for their parachute jumps before returning to our barracks for their physical exercise.

What they did for the rest of the day was a mystery, probably shot stray dogs, cats or stray people, for all we knew. I do remember they all seemed to return by taxi from a mysterious 'somewhere' during the night, well after our evening lights out routine. Their taxis were often driven off the access road and right across our taboo parade ground towards their billets, accompanied with lots of shouting and laughing. It seemed to me that strong drink might have been taken. They were a bit of a mystery and, strangely enough, none of our officers appeared to see them or remonstrate against their noisy antics.

It seemed John had been complaining to the S.A.S. Sergeant about the length of time we were spending on the training cadre for the regimental signal platoon. Most of our battalion had moved 'up country' into Malaya. Their jungle training was completed and they were on active service, spread out in their individual rifle companies to form a huge perimeter across Johore state. Our little happy band of brothers was still held in Singapore to complete our signal training cadre which had been delayed by various interruptions from our departure in Belfast with all the distractions till arrival in Selerang barracks to settle in, reform and commence our training yet again. We were awaiting orders as radio operators to be allocated to our various rifle companies already in place at their Malay positions.

The S.A.S. Sergeant had listened to Johnny bitching for a while, then interrupted with a suggestion. Why not sign on with the S.A.S.? Apparently, there was no buggering about or time wasting with this unit. They were even involved in some very covert activities which none of us ever heard about. Unlike us, discipline in their mob was barely discernable, based on establishing a strong bond with comrades who could be counted on in a tight spot.

42   I DECIDE TO VOLUNTEER FOR THE S.A.S.

It all seemed rather exciting and romantic to us. The unit had originally been conceived by an adventurous Scottish guy, David Stirling, during the Second World War. The S.A.S. had gained quite a reputation as a rather special, hard hitting force with more than a little mystic surrounding them. The unit had been disbanded after the war as it was thought they would of no further use. However, Britain still had lots of trouble spots all over the world and the S.A.S.Regiment had been reformed. This all sounded very attractive to John and me. We decide to join up and have some adventure - you must bear in mind we were eighteen years old and daft.

We would have to sign on for the three year minimum term of regular Army service, of course. We had just started our two years compulsory conscript National Service, and one extra year would be no problem for us. We were in the same age group as the Kiwis who were being put through their training and the only sounds we heard from them was their exuberant laughing and joking as they carelessly strolled or drove in taxis over our seemingly holy square; they were even paid more than us. It started to sound better and better. John and I gave no more thought to any further doubts or details, this sounded like the life for us.

What to do? It was agreed we should approach Sergeant John the Bastard for advice. After all, he was what we considered to be an old soldier and was, in any case, our signal platoon Sergeant. He was not a very popular guy with us young conscripts as he seemed to be more concerned with discipline rather than dispensing information about signaling techniques. However, we would be free of too much discipline when we joined the S.A.S. but in the meantime we needed guidance on the correct method to follow and achieve this move.

I honestly cannot recall the Sergeant's real name. He was always John the Bastard or just *JTB* to us. The one thing I do remember about him was the day he carried out a quick pre inspection of our billet before the orderly officer was due to have a look at us. He came marching out of our ablutions, all red faced and blustery, grabbed the nearest guy, instructed him to get a scrubbing brush to erase a scribble he had found on the wall. Some daft bugger had, in a fit of spite, scribbled on the wall, *Beware of John the Bastard*. JTB followed the designated scrubber into the ablutions because he was curious to find out who 'John the Bastard' actually was. He re-emerged with what looked like a satisfied grin on his face. He had found out that the terrible JTB was, in fact, himself. He still had to act his part of John the Bastard while secretly bursting with pride. Fame at last.

John Scott and I should have paid attention to the message scribbled on the shit house wall, 'Beware of John the Bastard'. However, we were young and foolish and decided to seek advice from JTB on how to apply for a transfer to the S.A.S. He had no clue, but told us he would check it out and get back to us. We did not have long to wait.

43 GUILTY AS CHARGED.

About half an hour later JTB burst into our room looking all official and dangerous and frightened the shit out of us, *"Scott and Wishart"!* He shouted. *"On your feet, come to attention, NOW! Quick March to the Company Commanders office, Left, Right, Left, Right,"* he bellowed, chasing the two of us downstairs at a hell of a pace and wheeling us straight to the Company Commanders' office. It certainly did not reassure us when he muttered to us as we entered the office, *"You are for it now. You are on a charge"*.

Without ceremony he pushed the office door fully open. Then, with much stamping of boots, he placed us at attention before our Company Officer, a fairly elderly (to us) man of about forty. *"Hats off!"* commanded JTB. Apparently you have to remove your bonnet when being charged. I had no idea why and no reason was given. All I remember was a large dose of *Army Daze* enveloping me. I was quaking in my size 8 army boots, the nice and comfortable former brown ones, wondering just what sort of crime I had unwittingly committed.

The elderly officer sitting at the desk before which we stood to attention, hatless, seemed to have a wee touch of *Army Daze* himself, not quite sure of how to proceed. It was then I realised this was probably all JTB's doing, neither he nor the Company Officer had a clue about how to handle our situation. JTB had probably advised strict discipline as a solution. *"Just give them a bollocking, sir"* he must have recommended, *"frighten the shit out of them. That should do the trick sir,"* he must have said.

The company officer waffled on for a few minutes about how we young soldiers were important to the Regiment. He told us our battalion was waiting impatiently in the steamy Johore jungle for us to complete our signal training when we could join them to them help kill Communist Terrorists for the honour of the regiment.

We had stupidly overlooked our obligation to the Regiment and should by now have been looking forward to getting sweaty and stinking in the Malayan jungle. Instead, we could look forward to heaving out dated and heavy radio equipment through the mud for Queen and country. Naughty, inconsiderate us. There would be no more delays in our case as our signal course had now been completed at last (not our fault!). Soon we would be totally involved in the soldiering business. There would be no more visits to the seaside at Changi beach or chasing 'loose wimmin' in steamy Singapore city. He tried to paint an attractive picture of us happily heading into the Malayan jungle to face dirt, discomfort, snakes, possible sickness or even a more than possible sudden and messy death.

John and I failed to focus on the happy picture he was trying to paint for us. We were more inclined to think of the Happy World and our regular trips to steamy Singapore when finances allowed. In that direction lay the dens of iniquity where taxi dancer girls were available and would partner us on the wicked dance floor provided we purchased enough tickets to pay for the tatty dancing service.

I was aware of the naughty dangers just waiting to pounce down on us in Singapore, but I also knew of the dangers lurking in the other direction of the Malayan war zone over the causeway which led away from Singapore. My old, romantic ideas about the old British Empire were fast vapourising. As far as I was concerned there was no contest.

However, on a cautionary note, I recall one night when I had perhaps taken strong drink in steamy Singapore. It all seems a bit on the vague side now but it was possibly late December and I may have been celebrating Christmas. I seem to remember a female was involved. My attention was drawn to a Christmas card on a shelf in her tatty wee apartment room. It had caught my attention because it was an officially printed regimental military Christmas greeting card. It was tastefully inscribed, *'Merry Christmas and A Happy New Year from the 1st Battalion, The Argyle and Sutherland Highlander's.* Not really very reassuring situation when you consider a battalion at full strength consists of around one thousand men!

Never say but, always say however, as an old friend of mine used to advise. It seemed that our transfer had ground to a halt right there in the Company Commander's office. The Officer finished by giving us a fatherly talking to. He also considered our previous good behavior. He offered to let us off this time and he would forget our immature attitude. Our supposed 'case' was dismissed and we were ordered by JTB to replace bonnets, take a smart turn to the right and bugger off rapidly back to our billet where nothing more was heard of, or ever again mentioned, about our little scheme.

With the benefit of hindsight, I imagine we could have pursued our transfer to the S.A.S. by other means. After all, we were volunteering to sign on rather than being just National Service conscripts.

However, I have since heard reports of the actual rigorous training with the S.A.S. The reject list was reported to be pretty high, this was information we had not considered. Qualifying as rejects had never entered our impetuous heads, what would we do if we only achieved the 'reject' list? If rejected, we would be returned to our own Regiment as regular soldiers with still three years of service to complete in any one of the rifle companies in the sweaty jungle, not a very attractive idea.

Big Ray threatening to bash my head in unless I had a plan to lose my virginity.

44 IS YOU IS, OR IS YOU AINT ?

My mate, Big Ray from Jedburgh, regularly enquired about two things. One question was had I had managed to find out where we could go to hear live jazz in Singapore? We had tried jumping into a taxi, ordering the driver to take us to hear some jazz only to be puzzled when we were deposited at some whore house instead. It was only when we realised the taxi drivers had very little English and girls always seemed to be involved with army personnel taxi rides. The taxi drivers just assumed it was, 'business as usual' and they always took soldiers to a whore house. The drivers were awarded a small commission for every successful delivery of keen, young and horny, military customers. We fitted this description quite well. However, our sights were firmly centred on being able to sample some jazz music and any girlie project was shelved for the time being, but not for long.

Ray's second enquiry was usually about my virginity. Was I still or was I not? This was an inevitable question whenever we met.

It took us a few weeks to find good jazz. Surprisingly, it was situated at the nearby Changi Royal Air Force Base located a fairly short stroll away from us. I think it is now the site of Singapore International Airport.

The Royal Air Force Base was located fairly close to ours. However, the location was as close as we would get. There the similarity between the two branches of British military service ended. For starters, the RAF had a jazz club which was held on base once a week. Modern jazz music was provided by very talented Air Force personnel playing good music to an audience of sun tanned young men casually dressed in shorts and Hawaiian style casual shirts. Theirs was a very different world to ours.

Ray and I were as suntanned as any of the young Air Force men but there the parallel ended. We had not yet completed our initial six month period of service and we still had to wear military uniform when 'walking out'. Six p.m.was the official time when the military had decided we should also guard against mosquito attacks. We were compelled to wear long pants instead of shorts, with jacket sleeves rolled right down as well. We must have looked like a right pair of eejits in the RAF *holiday camp* surroundings. The entire Regiment was indoctrinated into believing we were at risk of contracting malaria unless we followed *Army Daze* regulations. The rest of the population of Singapore must have been immune and, of course, members of the Royal Air Force (also known as The Brylcreem Boys) did not catch malaria!

Surprisingly, we were quietly accepted by the casually attired group of young, mainly English, modern jazz fans in spite of our military attire and heavy Scottish accents. Jazz fans, particularly modern jazz fans are an eclectic lot with a strong leaning to what would soon be known as the cool generation which was even then beginning to raise its unflappable head in the mid-fifties. We bought a couple of soft drinks and settled down to enjoy a few hours of surprisingly very good jazz.

Being more than slightly inclined towards the cool approach to life, Ray and I immediately joined the club of modern jazz aficionados which soon happily almost coincided with the end of our young soldiers six month compulsory order forbidding the wearing of civilian clothing. We were then able to mix on a fairly even keel with the young, sun tanned, Hawaiian shirted gods at the RAF jazz club.

While we had managed to acquire a pretty good sun tan on our outward bound sea voyage, we had drawn the line at Hawaiian shirts, choosing instead smart plain white shirts laundered and full of starch. These smart shirts would pass inspection when we had to exit our army camp via the guard room, where the sight of a pansy *American style* shirt would probably cause an outbreak of something akin to apoplexy. The very least we could expect for risking any departure from our daft army dress code would be a severe bollocking accompanied by bulging eyes and veins as the bollocker (just invented that word) vented his outrage at the two young soldiers. Of course, trying to flout the imaginary dress code would mean a trip back into our billets to get changed into a more suitable attire to gain the approval of some clod of an ex turnip harvester or Cheuchter which was our way of describing any country people, but particularly any members of our small, gallant band of Regimental Police.

It never seemed to enter these regular army brains that the government spent huge sums of money on advertising the sunny prospects of joining the army as a career. Running simultaneously with this recruiting campaign were the *Army Daze* clods daily dispensing the daft army daze rules and regulations in complete contrast to the recruiting advertising campaign. Many thousands of young, some very bright, civilian National Service conscripted soldiers who, after exposure to this kind of old fashioned army crap discipline would never, ever, consider joining the British Army as a career in those days.

The decision that John Scott and I had made about joining the S.A.S. was inspired by a desire to serve with other, like minded young professionals for a life of action and adventure which, I imagine, had no room for the hidebound regular army discipline which was currently part of our old fashioned army training.

This traditional training method had previously managed to send young men marching into battle in nice, orderly straight lines, preferably wearing nice, white belts crossed over their chests to provide an easy X shaped target for enemy sharp shooters. This old fashioned type of approach was indeed *Army Daze* style of thinking which, surprisingly, was still fairly evident in parts of the 1950's army.

We always looked smart when making our exit through our army guard room. However, the blazing sun quickly reduced our shirts to floppy, soaking wet pieces of material caused by our excessive sweating. Luckily, the blazing sun also made a fairly quick exit at that time and we could always look forward to a comparatively short stroll in the relative cool of the early evening on our weekly visit to the RAF jazz club.

The jazz club also had a few girls, probably nurses from a nearby military hospital, hanging out there, dressed in casual, light, civilian clothing. They even wore shorts. Oh- the legs, the legs! This was 1955 in the British Army. We were not used to this kind of thing. To us, this place seemed more like a holiday camp than a military establishment.

There was a really neat swimming pool near to the RAF base which, I think, we had access to. I never actually checked to find out if rough, army personnel like us were allowed to visit the pool. However, it seemed nobody was prepared to challenge our decision to use it. So that, as they say, was that.

On Wednesday afternoons, I would sometimes gather a few Egyptian PT enthusiasts together. Bearing in mind that Wednesday afternoons were devoted to athletic diversions, I decided to put another one of my Alfie inspired ideas to work and head away from our army barracks for some swimming exercise at the pool. Any kind of 'heading away' from our army base during the day was not really allowed except for official military exercises. I decided to put this to the test and invent an 'army exercise' of my own.

A few of us would dress according to our newly granted permission to wear civilian shorts and short sleeved white shirts.(daytime hours only – after six p.m. long trousers must be worn, mosquitos ye know). We rolled the swimming pants into our jungle green army issue towels, stuck the smart green bundles under our left arms, and, keeping in mind Sergeant Fleming's information that bullshit always baffles brains, and also being unsure whether we were officially allowed out of barracks at this time of the afternoon, I promoted myself to *pretend* corporal. I then marched *my men* in an orderly fashion right past the guard room where you were normally required to 'sign out' for any activity outside army barracks. I was really testing the bullshit baffles brains school of thought and we ignored any thoughts of actually entering the bloody guard room, cap in hand so to speak. We made a smart turn to the left at the barrack exit still marching in military fashion to disappear away from the puzzled but not well informed gaze of the Regimental Policeman on duty outside to guard room. We would continue to march in good order till we were out of sight behind another bunch of bloody palm trees.

My accent is what I believe is referred to as, 'Educated Scottish', whatever that means. However, I sometimes adopted my, officer class, silly twit, voice for the benefit of the guys as we passed the Regimental Policeman standing on duty at the guardhouse entrance. We were all dressed in shorts and short sleeved white shirts and our issue P.T. canvas shoes. An Officer marching his men for some physical activity could be wearing much the same type of clothes as *the men.* At least this is how things would appear as far as our not too bright Regimental Policeman was aware.

I frequently pretended to be a young lieutenant type as I marched along at the head of my men. I was never quite sure whether or not the guard on duty would attempt to challenge my authority. I guess I was really seeking to be the centre of attention at that age and would throw discretion to the winds. *"Smarten up a bit, you chaps,"* I would order loudly as I mentally promoted myself from Corporal to

Lieutenant. I would get carried away with my new identity, even turning completely around, full of bullshit and now marching smartly backwards to face our guys who were marching along enjoying their part in the show. *"C'mon, McNeill,"* I would say in my, *silly twit* voice, *"Get these shoulders* beck*, you look more like a facking wet hen than a smart soldier. Mustn't let the regiment down, must we?"* I would then turn nimbly around to resume facing the front, still keeping perfect step, marching with *my chaps* like a keen, popular, young lieutenant taking his men out for a healthy swim on the exercise afternoon, dropping the occasional silly twit type of cuss word, just like the rest of, *my chaps*, as we passed by the regimental policeman, till disappearing from his sight round the corner.

We could then dissolve into our daft, laughing routine like any other bunch of normal, rule breaking teenagers. Behaving like the non-military civilians we were as we headed for the swimming pool where there was no army discipline and where we could spend a carefree couple of hours in the sun, safe from exposure to *Army Daze*. Almost, but not quite, like normal, almost adult, people.

I managed to wander through my entire but short military service employing this method. Daft as a brush, as the saying goes.

I was pleased to find out two years later that someone had suspected me of something but could never put his finger on exactly what I was doing. On my discharge pay book I discovered a handwritten comment *'Wishart has a highly developed sense of humour, NOT NCO material'*. This observation was hand written, obviously added after the usual typewritten remarks in the character description section.

It slowly dawned on me that the comment, being handwritten, must have been done by someone in our orderly office just before my discharge and was quite unofficial. The handwritten entry must have been by someone who thought in the same way as me. I then realised it was more of a compliment than anything, gotcha! It had to be Sergeant McIntosh who was in charge of the orderly room.

It was then that I remembered one night before our weekly pay day not long after our arrival in Singapore Island. Time must have been dragging a wee bit that evening. We were all broke and unable to partake of the city's fleshpot delights. I invented a caper which called for some noisy and energetic audience participation. There was no military law breaking involved and our activities could probably come under the heading of *daft!*

I was, and still am, an admirer of the musical offerings of Spike Jones and his City Slickers, particularly the recording of *At the Races*. This is where Spike and his daft band portray in audio an actual day at the racecourse complete with radio compère giving a running commentary describing the horse racing, the whole band making horsey noises, etc.

I had arranged for two of our guys to sit at the ends of opposite beds, holding a broom handle stretched between them to provide a makeshift horse race course jump. The rest of them lined up in two's, taking turns to race down the room then, prancing like horses, each one attempting to jump the hurdle. The two guys holding the broom handle hurdle raised the hurdle bit by bit in reverse limbo style after the participants had completed one pass. The whole thing was accompanied by my shouted comments as I tried to remember all the Spike Jones vocal gems. This included such renderings as I could remember when I imitated the radio commentator shouting, *"And it's banana, banana, banana, banana pulling away from the bunch"* and other gems. The session was accompanied by horse neighing noises and fanfare sounds. And yes, we did have a bugle handy. I blew merry tootles, I was awful clever, you know.

The other guys involved in our, simple, homespun race might have been at a slight disadvantage. Unlike them, I could hear the Spike Jones record, broadcasting clearly inside my head. I have been told I must have ears like a shithoose rat, never actually having seen a shithoose rat I will just have to take the remark as a compliment.

This scene might not appeal to my more sophisticated readers. However, you must bear in mind this was 1955. Probably none of us could even spell 'sophisticated'. We had nothing but our inventive minds and very few opportunities with which to amuse ourselves. No TV, no cell phones and only one small, battered radio with uncertain reception. This radio only seemed able to provide weird Chinese music and even that came in small, irregular, surges from time to time rather like a frightened, uncertain, virgin in our midst.

I happened to look up in the middle of a loud, horse neighing impression on the bugle and noticed

Sergeant McIntosh who was duty sergeant that night. He must have been attracted by the daft noises coming from our barrack room and was standing in the shadow just outside one of the veranda doors. Our eyes met, he gave a short conspiratorial grin, shook his head in a resigned kind of way before leaving us to our daft evening.

When I look back on these times and think of the hand written remark in my army pay book, it is perfectly clear. Sergeant McIntosh, a wee, perceptive Highland man with a sense of humour was in charge of the orderly room. He must have been the author of that short but succinct hand written comment. The above happening was just after we had completed our signal training and before we were moved from the Island of Singapore to rejoin our regiment in Malaya which brought an end to excursions to the big city.

Big Ray and me. We are dressed for a 'big night out' at the Royal Air Force jazz club. You may notice that waists were higher in the mid fifties. Also please note our Billy Eckstein shirt collars. This was my idea and I had the wee Sew, sew woman stitch the collars back into something close to the popular fashion style. Unfortunately, the severe army haircuts rather spoiled the effect.

45   A FLATULENT WHORE IN SINGAPORE.

However, it came to pass that Big Ray was determined to resolve the question of my still intact eighteen year old virginity while we still able to visit the wicked city of Singapore.

It happened on a Saturday night when the two of us usually took the opportunity and also the passenger bus which picked us up at the bus stop near the entrance to the barracks and transported us to the steamy City of Singapore Island. Saturday night was our favourite time to head for Singapore. The army held its weekly pay day on Thursdays and we would probably still have some Straits dollars left intact in our pockets by Saturday.

Our usual heady delight was a visit to the Cathay cinema where we could enjoy the air conditioning experience. Once we saw a movie featuring the great American singing group, The Platters. Magic! The movie featuring The Platters that afternoon was actually a bit of a bonus for Ray and me. The novelty of the air conditioning system was the main feature in the movie theatre that day. Located as we were, close to the equator, it was sheer luxury to revel in the delights of the cool cinema for a couple of hours, away from the hot and steamy humidity outside on the streets.

Leaving the cinema building was like receiving a wet punch in the face. It was now after the witching hour of six p.m. We had not yet gathered enough service time to entitle us to wear civilian clothing and were still dressed in jungle green uniforms. We were already pretty close to being laid out ourselves after we left the air conditioned cinema. Our shirts turned dark green when the sweat started to pour down our backs again.

46　GOODBYE VIRGINITY.

Ray was determined to get me closer to the actual losing of my virginity. After leaving the movie theatre, we meandered into a less well known district of the city where we were openly accosted by small groups of working girls, mostly Chinese. I had never been attracted to an Eastern female, I can only think it must have been the shape of their eyes. I may have been influenced by Hollywood movies portraying Japanese with slanting eyes. They were the bad guys in lots of war films.

Ray soon took care of the eye problem, it was now dark and it was difficult to see the girl's eyes anyway. He impressed on me that this affair should not take very long, we could hurry up and get it over with as quickly as possible. This would leave us plenty time to get to the Union Jack club and drink a few beers before catching the last bus back to barracks. It was at this point that he started using *we* instead of *you,* how strange.

He added the tempting attraction that, for my sake, he actually repeated, 'for my sake', he would be prepared to get involved and pick up a girl for himself, provided I paid for her services. This would enable us to at least be in the same building, if not actually together, when I had completed the session. He was doing all this just for my sake. What a great guy he was.

I usually had a few bucks in my pocket in these days. I was a nonsmoker and virtually a nondrinker at that time and was one of the few who might still have some cash on nights before and, sometimes, for a few days after, the weekly pay day. Ray must have had the impression that I had a money tree hidden away somewhere. Cash seemed to be no problem that particular night.

The setting sun solved the eye shape problem and we were soon in a gloomy lane with an open and fragrant monsoon drain running along just beside us. How romantic. The street lighting was practically nonexistent in this area and I could not see the eyes of the small Chinese woman Ray had picked for me. I was more interested in avoiding falling into the open drain.

Ray chose a slightly taller girl for himself. He also did the talking, such as it was. He even arranged the price which was agreed upon after a few pidgin English words with the Chinese girls. He told me how much I should pay for the two of us before we were led to a very basic dwelling house nearby where Ray and his girl disappeared into a room. My girl led me through another door where the only furniture was a raised wooden platform which I soon gathered was some kind of sleeping bunk but with only a few cushions for comfort.

'Sod the comfort', I thought with the full amount of my hormones flooding through my eighteen year old, fit and willing body.

'Sod it again', was my next thought. Here I was in my full olive green army uniform, including long pants which were lovingly wrapped firmly in the old Indian Army style puttees round my ankles just above my huge puddle jumping army boots. This outfit had taken me quite a long time to assemble as the puttees had to be wound several times around the bottom of my pants, making sure the pants were held in place before securing the puttees firmly with the attached tape, carefully wound evenly several times around my ankles, giving a very smart uniform appearance.

This performance would take several minutes to complete each leg. It was not something you would want to undo except for undressing before hitting your army sleeping cot last thing at night.

The current arrangement with the lady of the night made no allowance for sleeping. You could, if you wished, extend the time of the performance but there would be an extra charge for that. This was not in our plan. I could almost hear Ray saying, *"Not another bloody problem"*.

He would probably be finished with his girl now. Here I was, standing in the middle of the floor with my pants tied round my ankles, plus socks and boots still securely on my feet, not yet even near to starting on the great quest. However, you will be pleased to know that romance is not dead, especially not for a wee eighteen year old Protestant guy from Scotland.

I dropped my pants and drawers, green, cellular, down to my ankles where they were firmly anchored by my puttees and boots, then taking little, short steps I waddled awkwardly but gallantly across the floor, firmly hobbled in my temporary cloth manacles and army boots. I scrabbled clumsily and noisily onto the bare wooden sleeping platform, very uncomfortable on bare knees more used to contacting at least some kind of mattress. I then more or less fell on top of the waiting Chinese girl who had removed most of her clothing and was probably wondering why I was wasting time, after all, time is money in this game.

Thankfully, she was obviously more used to this activity than I was. You must appreciate I had never actually done this kind of thing before. There was no way I could rely on any of my previous experiences for guidance.

My prior experience of similar (but not quite) situations mainly included tedious wet faced kissing with my chosen, warmly dressed, girl. Shit! The only way she could be warmly dressed in wintertime Scotland was to put on layer after layer of warm, if unromantic, wool clothes which provided an obstacle course to any ideas of foreplay, hanky panky was definitely out of the question. The two of us looked like a couple of waddling teddy bears. She all wrapped like a comforting, woolly gift and me in huge but warm duffle coat with heavy sweater underneath. We clutched each other, leaning on a sturdy fence to her front garden in the middle of a freezing cold Scottish winter before I saw her safely into her house while I hobbled back home in the dark, doubled up with sexual frustration.

Sometimes I was lucky enough to take a girl to the warm picture house as we called the movie theatre back then. When the movie was over we would once again face the cold winter night when I walked her back home. One girl's mother had a house quite close to a telephone box which was located in a fairly remote street. This particular box was not patronized very much, particularly on late and cold winter night in Scotland. We could squeeze into the old, red phone box (remember them?) and I would reach up to unscrew the light bulb, plunging us in almost darkness. There was a street light nearby which illuminated our frozen breath as it formed into clouds. How romantic.

You must remember that all this took place during the early 1950's. Average age was about 17 nobody had their own flat or apartment in those days. It would be another decade before the great sexual revolution would start to happen in the swinging '60's, perhaps the weather had improved due to global warming by then as well.

I now tackled this new, strange and humid, Far Eastern sexual freedom in great, if clumsy, style. My polished and gleaming boots drummed on the bare wooden boards, beating out a great rhythm but I was a bit concerned about damaging the shiny surface on the toes of my boots as I bounced inexpertly but with great enthusiasm on top of the girl.

My bouncing was so energetic that a huge and very loud fart was suddenly expelled from her! It was so sudden and quite unexpected and it actually rattled on the bare bed boards giving it quite a resonant booming quality. I dissolved into laughter which was so infectious that she started to laugh as well which seemed to encourage more farting noises. We were laughing so hard and I guess my virginity came and went almost unnoticed at about the same time.

The loud laughter attracted the attention of Big Ray and his consort on the other side of the thin wooden partition wall. He rushed naked into the room to see the cause of the disturbance, his wee Chinese friend more modestly hesitated at the open door. Ray exploded with laughter when he saw my romantic, virginity-losing costume, tangled around my ankles. My boots still held firmly in place with the damaged polish on the toe caps played peek a boo through the folds of my long jungle green pants.

I considered how lucky I was having Big Ray as my friend. He even offered to help me to get rid of the leg encumbrance around my ankles then we could all have another go, in peace and quiet this time, provided I had enough cash for a repeat performance for both of us.

I reminded him severely that I was Scottish and the very thought of spending extra cash in this wanton fashion did not appeal to me. After all, I had inadvertently provided light relief to all within earshot rather than personal satisfaction for a job well done. I would prefer to forget the embarrassing episode in what I thought should have been an important milestone in my life. I had achieved losing the virgin state he had always requested, could we go now and have a cold beer? I would buy.

That night I headed for bed and a dreamless sleep. So much for the great adventure, it seemed to me this sex thing might not be all it's cracked up to be. I could only hope things would improve with practice, as the soldier said to the girl.

47 I HIT THE NEWSPAPER HEADLINES, AT LAST!

Before completing our signal training and prior to moving up country to rejoin our regiment, a few of us were chosen to form an honour guard. We would have our picture taken and be featured in the Edinburgh Evening News back home.

Apparently we had a professional football player assigned to our Regiment to serve his National Service. He played for one of the Edinburgh teams and a sports writer back home wanted to write a piece about our hero. He would be described as fighting on active service with the Kings Own Scottish Borderers in Malaya.

It then occurred to someone that this was Singapore not Malaya which was a bit further north where the real bullets were flying. It was decided to borrow a Hollywood idea and use one of our issue machetes to cut down a few bushes from behind the cook house building to make a bit of a fake jungle. Our celebrity football star, suitably attired in jungle green uniform, could be placed in front of the bushes, looking real fierce with some black grease paint smeared over his face and waving a rifle about. I could only hope the rifle was not loaded.

It must have also seemed a good idea to have some of the smarter soldiers to do a bit of posing in tandem with this sporting pantomime taking place nearby. We could probably use the services of the same photographer to include our little charade honour guard photo in the *Evening News* publication.

A good photo in the local newspaper back home could possibly attract some new business to the local Army Recruiting Shop in Edinburgh.

After all, we were the official Edinburgh Regiment portrayed by the castle image on our Regimental badge although it never really looked like Edinburgh Castle to me.

So there we were, parading on the hot barrack square at mid-day, close to the equator and hotter than hell. We were dressed in our best white parade jackets with hot and heavy tartan trews, rifles etc. Just like, Noel Coward's 'Mad dogs and Englishmen'.

Our fat Quartermaster from Northern Ireland had been put in charge of us because he just happened to be there at the time and 'everybody has to be somewhere'. Most of the Regiment was presently serving up country in Malaya. The Quartermaster was still in Singapore and was discovered being quietly busy closing down the storage operation in the relatively cool darkness of the Quartermasters Store. He was pressed hurriedly into service with the rest of us for this special guard.

Unfortunately for us, the Irish Quartermaster was alarmed by the sudden limelight falling, uninvited, on him. He panicked and paraded us onto the hot square, long before a photographer appeared. The man from the newspaper was probably still chatting with the celebrity football guy who was posing in front of the home-made jungle area constructed behind the cookhouse. After all, the photographer had been sent to take a picture of our football 'celebrity' and I am willing to bet nobody had thought to tell him about us standing in the midday heat on the parade square. He had been invited to have a wee refreshment at the Officers Mess when he had disposed of our 'celebrity' and had no idea we were wilting in the heat. We were about to find out that communication was sadly lacking between the interested parties on that long, hot morning on Singapore Island.

If the Quartermaster had any sense, which he obviously did not, he would have kept us in the shade of the nearest building until the photographer showed up and was ready to do his bit. Instead, he had us paraded to attention on the square. Now read on.

(Photograph. Thanks to The Scotsman Publications).

Here we are, actually standing stiffly in the 'present arms' position in the bloody heat. The fat Quartermaster was usually more involved with parading blankets, mess tins etc. in his Quartermaster's Store rather than parading people. The silly bugger should have known better than to have us standing to attention on the heat blasted square on Singapore Island almost on the equator at noon, the very hottest part of day.

The official photographer eventually arrived behind us. We were still standing to attention but wilting fast as he dawdled, chatting to an officer. Probably realising it must be about lunchtime and the proper moment for some liquid refreshment, without warning, he appeared from behind us, clicked a button on his big camera and was gone. Job done.

Unfortunately, I was done as well, as heat stroke took over. I staggered forward before Paddy had time to dismiss us and crashed to the ground on top of my rifle, this was probably the only time I regretted being chosen as one of the smart soldiers. The photographer missed my performance, he had turned away to head for the free drinks at the Officers Mess. He did not see or hear my couple of staggering steps before the sudden transfer to the horizontal position. Even the loud sound my rifle made as it hit the tarmac followed by the dull thud made by my head, did not attract his fast receding attention.

He could have taken a good picture of me sprawled flat on the square. I could imagine the headlines in the *Edinburgh Evening News*, '*Spunky Scottish Soldier Succumbs, Silently in Sticky, Steamy,*

Singapore'. See details supplied be our foreign correspondent.

The *Edinburgh Evening News* eventually published the only picture the photographer took of us that day. While he missed my change from consciousness to oblivion, his camera almost caught it - I am in the process of fainting, eyes already half closed and body starting to pitch forward.

My mother cut the picture out of the newspaper weeks later. It shows us on parade. If you look closely (I am the second soldier on the right.) You can see my eyes are actually closed. These details would probably not be noticed when printed on newspaper quality paper of the time.

My recovery was aided, unnoticed, with a mug of tea made by the charwallah. If still in doubt and just to prove the authenticity of the picture, you can view the overweight Quartermaster on the left of the front row.

48 THE FIJI REGIMENT HAND OVER TO THE K.O.S.B.

The Kings Own Scottish Borderers took over the active service, front line territory of Johore State, Malaya from the Fiji Regiment at the end of 1955. Above picture shows some of the Fiji regiment posing with a recent 'bag' of Chinese terrorists.

Our Headquarter Company moved into the former camp of the Fijians at Batu Pahat in Johore while our other rifle companies set up for business in individual company camps straddled across the state which gave us quick access to any trouble spots as and when they cropped up. Our only contact was by wireless and each company started regular foot patrols in the surrounding heavy jungle, keeping in daily radio contact with our Gurkha friends who were in overall control of the area.

Our Pipes and Drums were at Singapore docks to play the Fiji Regiment away from port. This was a moving ceremony which, as far as I was aware, was unofficial. The Pipes played a slow lament as the Fiji troop ship pulled slowly out of the docks. Then the Fijians replied by chanting a traditional Fiji salute of brave men, hardly a dry eye in sight.

We grew close to the Fijians during the short time we were involved with them. This bond grew stronger one night in the Union Jack Club in Singapore when a fight broke out between a bunch of army soldiers and a small group of heavily outnumbered Scottish guys from our regiment. I have used the word 'small' advisedly for most of our lot were originally from the Glasgow area of Scotland where most of the guys were fairly short by nature, something to do with their poor diet during the late 1930s. It seemed their tempers were also fairly short and fights with 'the auld enemy' were a regular occurrence.

The Fijians present in the club bar were at first puzzled at the sight of the outnumbered, small white men battling it out with the larger group of also white, but taller men. The big, tall Fiji's immediately decided to intervene to help the outnumbered small men who talked 'funny'. They mistakenly assumed the smaller, outnumbered men would soon be in trouble but decided to even things up a bit anyway by joining in on our side.

I say, our side, because I was actually present at this little fracas accompanied by Big Ray. We had been to see the Frank Sinatra movie, *Love is a Tender Trap*, at the air conditioned Cathay cinema in town, and just had time to visit the medium sized but non air conditioned Union Jack club afterwards for a quick beer before catching the last bus back to our barracks.

I think I may have previously mentioned that Big Ray came from Jedburgh situated just a few miles from the Scottish Border. In the long forgotten bad old days of unrest between our English neighbours to the South of the Border and Big Ray's ancestors in the Scottish Borderland to the North, there were always a few scores to settle; all that was needed was something to fan the still burning embers, any old excuse would do.

Ray found an excuse the first minute we strolled into the bar just in time to see the beginning of the evening's entertainment. We saw an English military guy seemingly flying accompanied by an enchanted chair! Both objects were soaring through the air and over the beer bar together. The flying illusion was shattered when the airborne guy slithered along the bar and came to rest when his head connected with an ornate ceiling support post. The chair carried on all by itself until it smashed into the decorative mirror behind the bar, completely shattering the nice engraved large mirror.

This feat had been instigated by a huge Fijian, surrounded by a group of English military guys determined on revenge. The big Fiji was in his element, laughing like a drain while energetically cracking a few heads together. The scene was like one of the staged bar room brawls featured in Hollywood Wild West movies, except this involved real blood. Anybody knocked to the floor remained on the floor, nobody got back to their feet, shook their head Hollywood fashion, then started to fight again fresh as a daisy. That just does not happen. Ray contributed to the mayhem by grabbing one of the opposition by the scruff of the neck and smashing his face into the wall; he slithered down and sensibly stayed down.

The Military Police had just been summoned. Probably about the same time as we walked into the bar. Their arrival was dangerously imminent and none of the participants wanted to remain in situ when the military cops made an appearance. The punishment meted out for causing a scene like this would not be pleasant and the bar room cleared quickly. Big Ray and I gave up any thoughts of having a beer. We made a smart about turn to disappear into the humid Singapore night.

This little affair was outside of our regimental jurisdiction area. Even the very drunk Jocks realised that. They scampered away into the night as steadily as they were able, leaving the military police to puzzle over the wrecked bar. Our Fiji pals just carried on with their beer drinking; they were due to sail for home in a few days and did not give a fuck for anybody. Plus, each of them was over six feet tall, who in their right mind would want to tangle with them anyway?

WE MEET THE GURKHAS.

We had arranged to meet our opposite numbers, the signal platoon in the Gurkha Regiment. I am kneeling on left. Our Platoon Commander Lieutenant Henderson is seated second row. I notice Sergeant John the Bastard was with us that day, probably keeping a fatherly eye on us. These guys are so smart, we looked like a bunch of scruffs.

49 MARCHING ORDERS

Headquarter Company had established their base at Batu Pahat, the former Fiji base in Eastern Johore, Malaya. The few of us still remaining in Singapore were having our small numbers depleted daily on orders from the Regiment as they settled into their new location in Malaya. Whether we had been temporarily overlooked or perhaps mislaid, John Scott and I were beginning to feel a bit lonely, all our signaler mates had now been sent to their allocated rifle companies.

At last we received our marching orders one morning from an uninterested office wallah who must have been ordered to remain at the old Orderly Office in Selerang barracks to tidy up the odds and sods. I guess John and I qualified for that category.

Our orders were unlike the instructions issued to the other guys. They had been told to get their bodies on parade, then to board a truck and were dispatched to their various destinations in Malaya. John and I were told to roll up our bedding and move only as far as another building at the other side of the barrack square in Singapore (remembering, of course, to avoid walking directly across the sacred square). We then had to carry our bits and pieces the long way round to claim a bed space in an otherwise deserted and empty building and await further instructions. Another *Army Daze* situation was approaching. We could get no further information from the office wallah, mainly because he had no further instructions for us. There was nobody else around to ask either. We settled into the other, deserted and spooky building across the opposite side of the sacred square as directed.

We were used to having other guys around us. They could be annoying at times and often we would get pissed off, some of them were forever cadging, ranging from borrowing boot polish (how the hell can you borrow boot polish?). Perhaps you could take a spoonful of the stuff and return a replacement later. Some guys tried to obtain the loan of a favourite shirt for a night out carousing in Singapore. The borrowed shirt would probably never be returned. Occasional optimistic borrowers even invited a definite refusal to any attempt to cadge cash from you to pay for an evening out. One smooth talking bastard even managed to borrow a pair of casual shoes from me. I think he gave me a sob story about a fictitious function which he had to attend where wearing casual shoes (mine) was essential. I eventually had to ask him to return my shoes a couple of weeks later. They had obviously seen lots of action and were sadly in poor shape by then.

However, annoying as other guys certainly were, it is strange for only two guys to be situated alone in a large empty building, especially when it gets quite suddenly dark at around half past six in the evening.

We were used to hearing shouts from an Orderly Sergeant ordering us to 'Get these fuckin' lights out', at 11 p.m. after the bugle had sounded Last Post and the duty Piper had played his Flowers of the Forest lament.

Even our faithful charwallas had departed for Malaya, last seen as they packed themselves into an army truck and were driven off to rejoin the rest of our regiment. Now we would have loved somebody to turn some lights ON at half past six as the building was starting to get dark about that time. Even the usually irksome sound of a Glasgow voice cadging, "a wee tate o' yer polish", would be welcome. But no sound came, just the occasional bang as one of the unsecured doors to the veranda was caught by a sudden draft and slammed unexpectedly against the wall. This unscheduled forlorn banging noise gave us the willies. We rushed round the gloomy vastness of the huge empty room, switching on any light switches we could find, checking to make sure all the doors to the veranda were hooked firmly open. No more scary bangs in the night, as the soldier said to the girl.

Could it be that the big, bad, brave, potential SAS volunteers were starting to feel a wee bit nervous all by themselves? Bloody right we were! We had heard stories of hundreds of dead bodies, killed by the Japs and buried beneath the barrack square during the Second World War. Perhaps the location of the buried bodies was a myth but the killing, beatings, tortures and plain starvation stories were all true and all these bodies had to be buried somewhere around here.

I had already witnessed the mysterious and scary black figure standing at the bottom of my bed only a few weeks ago. Might just have been old drunken Spike, but I don't think so. When this place was full of daylight and Jocks, it could be quite cheery and comfortable. A deserted night spent here was quite another story. Changi Jail had its own horror stories and it was located just down the road. The whole area had a reputation for being haunted.

I was relieved when John suggested we take a walk over to see if the NAAFI beer bar was open. We intended to do the only sensible thing which was to get pissed before trying to spend a lonely night by ourselves in this bloody place.

The next morning dawned bright and sunny, as always in this area. Our heavy drinking of the night before had driven away any of the threatening potential ghosts and ghouls from our thoughts. We had even built up our courage and weaved our drunken way across the sacred square back from the bar to our temporary billet, knowing most of our superior officers had left to join the regiment. However, we were left with not only just bloody hangovers but also the worrying thoughts about our future and what was to happen to us. We were each a bit concerned in case the spectre of our attempt to obtain a transfer to the SAS might have been resurrected. Why had we alone been selected for isolation? Why were we not heading up into Malaya like the rest of the guys?

Luckily, there was a happy ending. A couple of hours later the office wallah guy finally made it to our new location in the isolated lonely leper colony to which we seemed to have been banished. It appeared he had received instructions for us late the previous afternoon but did not consider the news was of any urgency so had postponed walking over to tell us in the overpowering afternoon heat. He had also lingered over breakfast tea and enjoyed several mugs of British Army tea before wandering over to give us the news. Why should Britain tremble when there are guys of this calibre to defend the country?

50   PIPES AND DRUMS.

The direction of our next move was solved. John and I had been transferred to the Regimental Pipes and Drums. John played the pipes and I used to be a drummer with Penicuik Pipe Band.

This was great news for both of us. No more signal platoon duties for us, being obliged to hump the big, old fashioned World War II vintage army signal radios on our backs, plus carrying all the other gear required for patrolling in the jungle. However, we had to remain where we were for the time being as the Pipes and Drums were presently on board a Royal Navy destroyer heading north on the South China sea to take part in an official goodwill visit to Bangkok, Thailand. They would return to Singapore in few days to hook up with us. We would be driven North to the new location of HQ Company over the causeway in Batu Pahat, in Johore State, Malaya.

The Pipes and Drums are the crème de la crème of the regiment, never referred to as 'The Band'. There already was a regular instrument playing army military band with us, as in all British regiments. We called this military band rather disdainfully, 'The Girls'. The Pipes and Drums are different. Exclusive to Scottish Regiments, they are infantry trained men first and foremost, able to carry out the same duties as the man in the rifle companies. The best shot in the regiment was one of our pipers. An earlier soldier, Piper Dan Laidlaw, was awarded the Victoria Cross during the World War I for playing the Borderers into battle with the Regimental March, 'All the Blue Bonnets are over the Border'. Stirring stuff. Although unarmed and shot through both legs, he was downed, but continued playing the pipes as the Regiment charged and victoriously took the enemy position successfully.

Members of the Pipes and Drums were usually regular soldiers. Two year conscripted soldiers like us were seldom considered, this was indeed something special for John and me.

A few days later we joined the Pipes and Drums in Singapore. They were full of tall stories and far-fetched tales about Bangkok. We loaded our kit onto a couple of three ton trucks, drew our rifles from the armoury and we were off at last, heading for active service over the causeway connecting Singapore to the State of Johore, Malaya for the next adventure. On the way to the causeway leading to Malaya we were entertained by the guys from the Pipes and Drums with tales of their exotic doings in sexy Bankok. Having only recently carelessly lost my virginity, I was at last able to give the occasional knowing nod of approval to their imaginative stories. I was finally, 'one of the lads'.

51 SETTLING IN

We settled in quite happily at H.Q. Company now based at Bhatu Phahat in Johore State, Malaya. Instead of being billeted under canvas as I had expected, we were allocated a wooden hut with floor raised above the ground. I initially thought the raised floor was to keep us free from snakes, although it was more likely intended to keep the air circulating around the hut in this steamy country. Security was relaxed with armed guards only at the front gate. I imagined we were relatively secure from attack by Chinese Terrorists in this secure area although I had misgivings about the funny shaped and heavily wooded steep hill beyond the wire right behind our hut. However, I was fascinated by the whooping sounds made by the gibbons living on the strangely shaped conical hill behind us as they went about their daily business. At first hearing, they all sounded the same. However, after listening carefully to their whooping greeting to the sunrise every day I began to recognize the different sounds between mating couples as they serenaded each other. They even joined in with group choir singing, a fascinating sound. This soon pushed any security concerns to the back of my brain.

I was even offered a brightly coloured parrot for purchase, although I managed to decline the offer. I was worried about what would happen to the bird when I eventually moved on. That, combined with the added leg pulling involved for being a parrot owner, "Ahoy there, matey", type of thing with the bird perched on my shoulder rather put me off.

We were living in comparative luxury compared to the rest of the battalion in our rifle companies stationed in their individual, securely fenced in camps spaced out in a multi-mile perimeter around our allotted area where the real action was encountered.

Our happy wooden home in Batu Pahat, Johore State, Malaya.

Our Officers discouraged us from becoming pet owners, mainly for the reasons I have stated. Most of the guys respected this but one old soldier Willie who was nearing the end of his service could not resist adopting 'Junior' a mischievous little monkey, I mean the monkey, not Willie. The monkey and Willie shared the same bed at night. Sometimes, in the cold light of day, it was discovered that someone had pissed in the bed. Willie had been very drunk on these occasional bed wetting nights but he could never argue with conviction that the monkey was to blame.

52 AMBUSH !

We were no sooner settled in when were instructed to be prepared to leave the following morning for a few days duty as armed escorts to a convoy of trucks delivering ammunition to some units stationed in the middle of bandit country. The ammunition was to be picked up from a depot in Kuala Lumpur, the Malayan capital where we would stay overnight. We would then head north through the mountains to make the delivery.

By the time we reached K.L. it was late evening, we found our overnight destination and heaved our packs onto our designated beds. Jock Winton and I considered having a stroll out into the city but, having been warned the next day would be long and tiring. We decided to listen to sound advice and crashed into our beds instead.

First light next day saw us arrive at the munitions depot where we transferred from our two Bedford trucks to half a dozen trucks of the Malay Regiment which were already loaded, ready to go, each complete with a smiling Malay driver. We allocated ourselves in small groups of three or four to each truck with the canopies removed as was the custom. This gave us good all round vision to employ fire power plus the ability to vacate the truck and take better cover behind or even underneath it, should the occasion demand.

We were alert and watchful as the trucks left the city outskirts driving through mainly rubber plantations and scrub, starting the slow, steep, climb up into mountainous country west of the Main Range, the road winding sharply upwards through steep mountains thickly covered by primary jungle. We soon reverted to being tourists.

The road wound its way ever upwards following great swirling S-bends clinging to the sides of the slopes. It was so steep in places that our trucks were brought to a position level with the tree roots on one side but almost above the tree tops on the other roadside. We could almost reach out and touch our buddies in the other trucks driving round the bends below. We saw monkeys swinging about in the tree canopies, almost beneath us as we negotiated the steep hills. An evolutionary thought crossed my mind - we were on the same level as our ancient relatives, the monkeys. This situation made me think that would be about the right level for a bunch of army infantry guys and the monkeys. It did not bear thinking about. However, our open bed truck was an ideal platform for viewing the monkeys and the brightly coloured parakeets on top of the trees, we let our jaws drop and made oooing and aaahing noises, just like the bunch of big kids that we were.

It was also an ideal spot for a bloody ambush. Thank goodness the Chinese Terrorists must have been occupied causing mayhem at some other place. They passed up an excellent opportunity to chop us into little pieces as we crawled slowly up the steep hills.

Of course, our little expedition had not been publicised in any way, even the smiling wee Malay drivers had only been alerted early that morning to prevent any accidental information on destination, cargo, personnel strength, timing etc. from slipping out accidentally.

We finally reached the top of this first mountain only to find what seemed like another whole range of hills ahead.

My daft sense of humour had not deserted me, although my heart was quite often in my mouth on the slow, vulnerable journey upwards. I had observed on the earlier, gentler hills leading towards the mountain range that our truck tended to back fire noisily after cresting a hill as soon as our driver lifted his foot up from the accelerator pedal. The driver kept the back window of his cab open so we could have some kind of conversation going to while away the miles. His English was pretty basic, but he was a pleasant and happy wee Malay man. I thought he would be willing to be part of my stupid antics.

As we started to descend, I reached through the open window and gestured for him to remove the pedal from the metal as they say. He laughed and took his foot away sharply, I guess he intended to do that anyway as we were now about to descend rather sharply down the mountain, but even I was not ready for the loud bang that rang out amongst the echoing mountain tops.

The effect was instantaneous, with the exception my companions, all the guys in the other trucks hit the floor with rifles pointed frantically upwards and outwards ready to take on all comers. They were all sure an ambush was taking place. Luckily, the action to 'take on all comers' did not happen and none of our guys let fly with any live rounds, after all, there was nothing but the loud bang from our truck to respond to anyway. By now everybody was jumpy but they all held their fire although it took a few more bang alarms on our descent before they realised it was our truck which had caused the panic. By the time we had crested a few more mountain tops, our escorts had got used to the scary noises coming from our truck, and managed to relax and even laugh a wee bit.

However, I made the guys on my truck swear to keep silent about my having started the panic in the first place, although they were still laughing about it, and I only got their assurance when I threatened to say we were all involved if I was ever accused. That shut them up. After all, we were on active service in well-known bandit country, but I was convinced this daft leg pull could escalate into a court martial affair if the facts surfaced, so complete silence was needed and, thank goodness, agreed to.

But I could get no sense out of the wee, happy Malay driver who continued to create the bangs at every available opportunity. I thought he was a wee bit daft, anyway, and, as they say in Scotland, "a joke's a joke, but keep yer arse off the curtains".

So far, we had no contact with the Communist Terrorists. They could have been all around, us but they were able to stay hidden in the heavy jungle, choosing exactly where and when to appear, usually with disastrous results. It was right at this point that disaster struck.

We were slowly climbing towards the crest of the last mountain before descending into the next valley when a mortar bomb exploded just wide of the truck ahead of us. This was no truck backfiring. This was the real thing and was followed by erratic rifle fire from a position somewhere above us. We, in turn, rapidly vacated our former position of seated sightseers and re-appeared with rifles at the ready from a safer place underneath the trucks.

A second mortar bomb landed near the first explosion, but luckily it was about as far away from the truck as the first had been. The bandit who had fired it had not yet corrected the range. The frantic but erratic rifle fire was no better, but was heavy enough to keep us pinned down underneath our trucks. It would only be a matter of time before the bastards got our range and down would come cradle, baby and all!

Something had to be done and done bloody quickly. In my case the priority was to remove my body from the close contact I had accidentally made with an ant hill located in the verge at the roadside where I had thrown myself behind a wheel and in the lee of our truck. This wrecked ant hill housed a colony of large and vicious looking red fire ants, looking for revenge on the great home destroyer, i.e. ME!! I was temporarily out of sight from the C.T.'s somewhere above us as I cowered flat on my stomach. At least I was out of sight until the bastards corrected their range on the mortar and scored a direct hit which would probably add to my plight by setting fire to the available petrol in our tank.

This thought prompted a quick and not very dignified scuttle/crawl to put some distance between my delicate parts and the vengeful fire ants. I hurried to take shelter behind the wheel under the cab, the same limited space which the wee Malay driver occupied when he tumbled away from his seat in the cab above. Silly bugger was not laughing now. He had forgotten to grab his rifle in his panic to hit the ground and seemed to see me as some sort of savior, although we were both scrabbling in the dust, seeking ownership of the shrinking available space behind the wheel of our truck.

Geez. Is it just me or does anybody else experience having their mind taking a bit of a wander about during moments of extreme stress? I was concerned about the looming attack to my person from the fierce red fire ants, and was temporarily almost unaware of the peculiar whirring sound made by the live rounds as they sped through the air towards us before colliding with a loud thump as they hit our truck. Let's look on the plus side and call it 'multitasking' rather than day dreaming. At least the loud thumping noises were coming from the body of the truck rather than mine.

I glanced from my hiding place behind the protective wheel and spotted the last truck in our convoy. It had been experiencing some problem with the smooth running of its engine and had fallen quite a way behind the rest of us when we were climbing, the engine labouring a bit as it slowly maneuvered behind us up the steep twisting slope.

The truck below had stopped immediately when the driver heard the first mortar explosion, and the truck was hidden from the ambushers by the thick forest between us. As a result the convoy as seen from above looked as if ours was the last vehicle in the group. Luckily the soldier in charge of our small three man section in the slow truck halted below us was Corporal McFadyen, a veteran of the recent Korean War. He was an ideal leader and the very guy to have around when things took a nasty turn - he was not a bad piper either. McFadyen was leading the other two guys plus their driver from the Malay Regiment. They were well concealed in the bush below us but moving rapidly upwards and to our right. They drew level but remained out of sight from the C.T.'s. They were approaching a spot about fifty yards to our right where, I guessed, they intended to break cover for a quick sprint across the area of exposed road heading to a suitable spot slightly higher than our attackers. This would give McFadyen and his guys an advantage over the C.T's and hopefully the tables could be turned with a vengeance.

Our guys must have been spotted as they raced over the exposed road. A couple of rifle shots were fired in their direction but were wide of their mark. Then there was silence, briefly broken by a hurriedly fired mortar bomb which this time exploded even further away from its intended truck victim which indicated to us the attackers had spotted the rapidly approaching avengers led by McFadyen. Realizing they had bitten off more than they could chew, they had panicked and loosed off a final mortar shell before fleeing.

Our lot were not encumbered by women and kids but were ready and willing to retaliate. Led by the resourceful McFadyen, the guys from the truck with the faltering engine completed their flanking operation and arrived at the spot where they could have routed the ambushers. There was no sign of our attackers, only some flattened undergrowth and a few empty shell cases. Our, would be killers, had fled into the dense jungle. There was little point in trying to follow them as they were used to this area and could be far away by now. All we could do was to radio the attack position to the troops covering this mountainous area and perhaps give them a lead to be followed up.

The attacker's firing had been so erratic we guessed this had not been a prepared ambush, but probably an opportunist idea when our convoy had been spotted climbing slowly upwards on the mountain. The only blood shed was from McWhirter when he cut his knee by landing heavily on the road surface as he vacated the bed of his truck. We had a quick head count followed by a traditional 'Brew Up' of British Army tea made from some emergency rations, carried by one of our forward looking types before re-boarding our trucks to continue with our ammunition delivery.

Our truck convoy beginning to climb up into the mountain range with our load of ammunition. Apart from the backfiring antics by our wee Malay truck driver, it was all very hush, hush. Until the real, big bang came.

Some of our brave members of the Pipes and Drums ammunition convoy escort taking part in the old British Army ritual of tea drinking. They had sacrificed their drinking water to the tea making ceremony then refilled their water bottles with very important tea. Bloody awful bread sandwiches had been thoughtfully provided by the military authorities early that morning and consumed after our 'wee bit of bother' excitement.

Strange as it may seem, the leader of the C.T's, Chin Peng had been highly regarded by the Brits during World War II. He had even been awarded an Order of the British Empire decoration for his services against the Japanese. He was a good friend and ally to British hero, Freddy Spencer Chapman who survived as a much decorated fighter behind Japanese lines in Malaya for over three years.

But the tables had turned, Britain's former friend Chin Peng, OBE, was now Malay's most wanted man, being hunted in the impenetrable jungle. He was mainly responsible for my regiment's recent arrival in the Far East.

The Communists who had taken to the jungle to defy the old British rule had set up school classes in selected parts of the jungle where lectures on the Communist system were held secretly. Their young men and women referred to themselves as Freedom Fighters who fought against our young men fighting for the British Empire.

Most of our young men were conscripts on National Service serving the obligatory army term of two years, the majority of us unaware of any particular reason for being there. This was our necessary spell of army service. It was what was expected of us at that time. We did as we were told. I guess after two world wars, followed by armed enemy eruptions everywhere, British lads expected to be called to active service in the military to deal with trouble spots all over the world. That is how things were in those days.

I have a photo of a couple of C.T's who had been ambushed and killed by one of our patrols. They look about the same age group as my conscripted guys and me. They had probably been indoctrinated by studying Communist propaganda while we on the other hand were influenced by the

Capitalist system. What a bloody waste of young human lives, makes me wonder if we will ever learn.

We did not question why, although the old Empire façade was now beginning to crack a little. A blossoming new sense of humour was spreading over the old country; traditional systems were being held up to ridicule. The old regimes and ways of doing things led by chaps wearing silly bowler hats and other traditional habits were being laughed into history. My former Boy Scout outlook on life as it might have been in the British Empire days had now pretty much evaporated from me. It could not happen quickly enough as far as I was concerned. It's a funny old life.

53 SUBLIME TO RIDICULOUS

Including for your titillation a little bit of indecent exposure

Next day it was almost as if we had been sentenced to a spot of hard labour. Somehow I was reminded of our morning spent scraping telephone poles with razor blades during basic training which now seemed to have been a long time ago.

It appeared some local landowner had needed a small favour, probably a friend of the Sultan of Johore. He must have requested help with removing a heap of rubble at a tin mine plant. Guess which rubble removing bunch was selected? CORRECT! We swopped our pristine white drill jackets for jungle hats, P.T. pants and boots - this costume to be set off by us carrying both spades and rifles just in case the C.T's decided to pick on an easy target, ripe for the picking. Some wag suggested the spades might be intended for whacking any attacking C.T's. That would teach 'em.

We had been told at this stage of the game that progress had been made in gaining the upper hand during the conflict in certain areas. These 'certain areas' would now be considered to be safe areas. This was one of the 'safe' areas. We arrived at the unwelcome conclusion that the shovels were really intended for shoveling dirt rather than fending off attacking bandits

All I remember from that particular day at the tin mine is lots of laughing and joking, a wee bit of shoveling exercise and lots of dry dust which leads me to the excuse to show the picture you have all been waiting for, the INDECENT EXPOSURE one!!

That's me, second from left, not shoveling but trying to look busy. Move to next page for the indecent exposure photo.

THE INDECENT EXPOSURE PHOTOGRAPH

This is Drum Major Tom Black in very casual dress. The half obscured guy behind Tom is me, accidentally showing off my white arse. I had discovered a well and was innocently washing off the day's dust. You can see the primitive bucket, rope and well. Some perverted humourist spotted my camera which I had inserted into my empty boots outside the well area. That's all folks, good clean fun, bring the kiddies.

54 CHARACTERS AND HARD MEN IN THE REGIMENT

Big McGlin was one of our various Glasgow 'hard men' serving with the regiment. Thankfully, I did not come into contact with him very often. He had trained with our other training company during my time at the depot in Berwick -on- Tweed. I heard he had a bad reputation even then and should be avoided.

On joining the regiment, he did not qualify for the intake to our signal platoon and was allocated to one of our rifle companies now serving in Johore State in Malaya. He was big in stature, mouth and attitude, bit of a bully really, probably a mess of insecurity which might explain his behaviour to a psychiatrist. He was a pushy sort with a bad attitude, always ready to dish out a 'smacking' at the least provocation, a right prat. He did not fit in with the rest of the guys and was very unpopular as a result. Certainly he was not the type to be selected for a close knit platoon on jungle patrol.

His behaviour brought things to a head eventually. His Company was stationed in what we called the 'Ulu', somewhere in Johore. At one particular period his Company had two separate platoons absent on patrol at the same time in the jungle. This left the camp with only a few of its usual complement of active soldiers. Darkness falls early in that country, there was not a great deal of camp activity to occupy the guys at the best of times. They were isolated with nothing much to do and a bit frustrated at being permanently stuck there.

No little jaunts down into Singapore. No little jaunts to anywhere. There was no anywhere to jaunt to around there. This was active service in the thick, humid, bloody awful, Malayan jungle. Service in this part of the world usually involved long periods of seeming inactivity, interspersed with short bursts of frantic activity, usually an ambush either perpetrated by the C.T's or, more hopefully, by the British Army.

Unfortunately, the monotony was broken by McGlin's bad behavior. He struck a smaller guy during one of his frequent outbursts. Most of the other guys could be classed as smaller guys considering McGlin's stature. This time the smaller guys banded together and struck back with a vengeance: a group of them surrounded McGlin, armed with a variety of makeshift wooden clubs. They laid into him with a long suppressed vengeance.

He was severely beaten for the first time. Most of the other guys in the camp, hearing the noise joined in to take their long dormant revenge out on McGlin. Some of the new additions to the fray were armed with the parangs normally reserved for attacking jungle vegetation. The rising situation did not look good for the big bully McGlin. He certainly did not qualify for the title of flavour of the month in the camp and things were beginning to look very ugly. McGlin, badly beaten and bloody, ran back to the temporary safety of his tent. The illusion of safety provided by his tent was very temporary in his case. A group of the other soldiers surrounded the tent, bent on continuing McGlin's punishment.

McGlin's stature had qualified him as the Bren gunner when on patrol, the semi-automatic Bren machine gun was bigger and heavier than a normal rifle. McGlin had been cleaning his Bren before the altercation had broken out. The weapon was still sitting on the ground in the active position with legs extended at the entrance to the tent. He threw himself down behind the gun, slapped in a loaded magazine and in a panic induced frenzy, loosed off a few rounds towards his attackers. The attackers realized just in time that the silly bugger was about to fire and split away from the front of the tent. They narrowly escaped from McGlin's mad, but badly aimed, outburst of live Bren gun rounds which flew wildly upwards into the night sky.

Sudden stalemate! Everybody froze, including (thank God) the big, loony, McGlin. What was nearly about to happen was the unthinkable. What did the impetuous guys waving their parangs intend? Was their next step being to lop the odd leg from McGlin, perhaps even an arm and leg or just a wee ear to teach him a lesson? Was McGlin about to mow down a fairly large amount of his erstwhile comrades with a fatal burst of crazy fire from the loaded semi-automatic Bren gun?

Murder was still a hanging offence in the 1950s. For all McGlin knew, it was probably punishable by execution from a firing squad for military offences. He was now standing erect but still grasping the Bren gun, shaking violently in the entrance to his tent, raving incoherent threats at the shocked other guys.

Further moves at this point would certainly lead directly to the unthinkable.

Luckily, our Regimental Padre was visiting McGlin's company for a couple of days. He came running out of the darkness, closely followed by the alarmed Company Commander. Their approach introduced a touch of sanity to the situation. The Padre slowed down as he approached a possible headline grabber scene. A situation like this was to be avoided at all costs. How would this little story look if it was reported back to the press in the UK?

The Padre walked up to the, now deranged and extremely dangerous, heavily armed McGlin. Talking quietly but forcefully, he led him firmly from the Bren and made him sit down quietly on an army bed in the darkened interior of the tent. All the time he spoke in a low but authoritative voice, calming down the stressed McGlin.

Meanwhile, the Company Commander got a grip of the other erstwhile violent and almost mutinous soldiers. He also got a grip of the loaded Bren gun and removed it from the vicinity. He diffused the dangerous situation by issuing orders for someone to contact H.Q. company by radio, requesting a truck to be sent a.s.a.p. complete with armed escort to fetch whisk McGlin off for psychiatric examination.

Needless to say, McGlin was never seen again, he seemed to have joined the small group of soldiers in my intake who were transferred from the normal to the 'suddenly missing' brigade.

It was fortunate the Padre was in the camp that day to avert almost certain mayhem. I later found out the same Padre had also been with the regiment when they served in the Korean War a few years earlier in 1952. Almost over run in action against hordes of the Chinese army, some sections of the Regiment were so hard pressed by ammunition running low that they were forced to use shovels and even threw full beer cans to fight the heavily outnumbering enemy.

Private Bill Speakman 1st K.O.S.B. was awarded the Victoria Cross for his brave actions that day in Korea, Also in the front line that day was the same quick thinking, Regimental Padre, who gave council to the men who had come through an almost impossible situation in Korea without becoming totally frayed, thanks mainly to our Padre.

55 SPOT OF PIG SHOOTING

Just to illustrate the variety of life available to the young soldier while serving Her Majesty in foreign climes, we were detailed for a few days of 'stake out duties' somewhere in Johore State.

The task was for our Regiment to encircle a large and swampy area where a big body of C.T's was reported to be lurking. The army plan was to lob mortar bombs into the swamp in an irregular pattern, then pick off the bandits as they tried to escape through an encircling ring of keen eyed sharp shooters (us)! Our platoon was positioned at the edge of a rubber plantation which ended abruptly at the start of an area of secondary jungle which, it was understood, led to the swamp where the bad guys were reputed to be hiding.

Secondary jungle means jungle that has been cut back at some stage, but left to reassert itself which it does with a vengeance, resulting in very heavy growth. This can be even more impenetrable than the original jungle which is bad enough. We were fortunately placed amongst the plantation of widely spaced skinny rubber trees which provided no cover at all, but cover was not our problem. All we needed was a clear line of fire to mow down any escaping C.T's. That was the plan. I cannot take credit for this plan but I certainly approved it for the odds were stacked very much in our favour.

We got ourselves organised into the usual British Army routine of two hours on duty followed be four hours off. However, in this case all of us were more or less on call at all times, the possibility of having your head blown off certainly concentrates your attention on staying alert and alive.

We had drawn emergency rations including wee stoves for cooking the interesting KP rations. This allowed a few of us to relax while experimenting with the food stuffs, all water bottles were full, the rest of the patrol in guard positions so, all was right with the world. Apart from the bloody mosquitoes which were driving us nuts in spite of having face netting.

The face netting made us look a bit odd which was not unusual, although the poor bugger who had been a wee bit tardy with applying his net had been severely bitten, and his face had swollen in great style. The swelling left just two evil looking slits for eyes which gave him a really scary appearance, more like a sort of Hollywood Fu Manchu which would give any escaping Chinese Terrorist something to think about. There was even a proposal bandied about for a while suggesting he be left apart from the rest of us to crouch alone for the C.T's to encounter. We reckoned the sight of him would make the bandits turn and flee.

You can see we had all been brought up reading comics where the hero could always resort to amazing feats of valour in a tight spot. According to our action comics, quick thinking applied to possible danger could be enough to save the reputation of the British Empire and its soldiers. By trouncing a heavily armed enemy (usually a fierce Zulu type) with a really sporting, good, clean, manly punch to the chin, a dangerous situation could be avoided.

This idea for leaving McCausland with the swollen face all alone to scare the C.T's was shelved when somebody announced the gooey mess of bully beef heated over the tiny, smelly stove was ready for dinner.

We settled down to the dreary but reassuring rhythm which dragged on to the next day. We adjusted to the irregular exploding from the mortar bombs provided by our mortar platoon. They were gaining experience and at the same time enjoying the good feeling state of mind gained by lobbing their bombs into the huge swamp area in irregular patterns. But there was still no activity from any fleeing C.T's.

About this time on the second day we had lowered the water to the near empty level in our aluminium water bottles. I was bored out of my skull so volunteered to collect all the water bottles then wander off to find the stream we had crossed the previous day where I could replenish our water supply. We had the means to purify the stream water in our survival packs.

I was joined by Piper Charlie Jeffery who had surprisingly offered to help. He was a strange, dour, wee Border man who tended to keep himself to himself. I assumed he was as bored as me, only too glad for the chance to take a break. We festooned ourselves with all the aluminium water bottles we could find then picked up our rifles and clanked off along the track. The usual silent state of movement was not considered necessary, our mortar platoon had seen to the noise problem with their shelling, our total of around twenty rattling empty aluminium water bottles fastened to our persons ruled out any pretence of silent movements anyway.

We had no problem finding the little stream which, I guess, was a run off from the large swamp our mortars were shelling. The water had a rather muddy look about it but we trustingly added the prescribed number of little white decontamination pills as we filled each bottle.

We re-attached the now heavier bottles to our persons and waddled back to re-join our mates about half a mile away. We followed the track along its meandering through the rubber plantation. It's precisely placed trees providing a stark contrast beside the impenetrable jungle which reared up abruptly in fearful, prehensile profusion where the plantation ended, running alongside the orderly rubber trees in a menacing, 'wild wood' sort of way. I was wondered why escaping C.T's would consider heading for our defensive position further down the track? Anyone trying to make a break for freedom would invite certain death by approaching our patrol lying in wait in their prepared ambush position. Any sensible escapee would avoid our ambush position altogether and surely favour this seemingly deserted and unguarded area right here. An escaping CT's could slip right through this area and avoid our well placed ambush position. Here they could wander off at will, even a casual stroll would do. Perhaps they actually preferred to stay where they were, to remain in the smelly swamp.

There was a sudden, tremendous crashing in the solid undergrowth just opposite us. We froze. Rifles ready but our bodies still stupidly festooned in aluminium water bottles, like useless bloody mobile Christmas trees. We tried to take cover behind a rubber tree, but failed miserably for the trunks of these trees are on the slender side. This prompted a fierce grunt of frustration of, "Oh Shit," from the usually morose Charlie. We were ready with safety catches off, but exposed to whatever was heading noisily for us through the dense undergrowth, heaving and waving as if an emergency path was being urgently hacked through it by a desperate bunch of escaping C.T's.

This was the real thing, the bit when you shit yourself with fright and then die a messy death. Not much dignity there. The only thought that went through my shocked brain was "What the fuck am I doing here?" Not much comfort from the brain department really. This situation had not been covered in the 'Scouting for Boys' publication I had purchased when I joined the Boy Scouts.

There was a hell of a crackling and crashing noise as the last piece of foliage was demolished and into the clearing rushed a herd of wild hogs. A tremendous bang came from the direction of Charlie and one of the pigs fell dead at his feet. I was sweating just like a bloody pig myself for I had really expected a heavily armed bunch of C.T's to erupt from the jungle, ready to mow us down in our exposed position when they made their escape from the swamp.

The rest of the herd disappeared through the rubber trees. Charlie turned round to me, unfazed. He ejected the spent shell from his rifle breech, bent down to pocket the tell-tale empty case, and straightened up with an evil smile. 'Give us a hand wi' that, we can have a proper meal of that bugger when we get back,' he said, indicating the unlucky piggy. My frozen brain started to function again. Mentally it acknowledged Charlie's reaction. "What a cool wee bastard", I thought. It seemed the wild pigs had saved my bacon, so to speak, plus my dignity, not to mention my jungle green army issue trousers which were still unsoiled. Also saved were my drawers cellular, green, pairs one, other ranks for the use of. A general, all round 'plus situation'.

I had been convinced I was about to breath my last, and here was Charlie, cool as hell, looking forward to a decent piece of roast pork, with plenty for all of us. I mentally awarded him a medal for valour but decided I was myself still only in the 'tries hard-could do better' class. I was very impressed by Charlie's performance until I noticed my rifle was still pointing directly towards the jungle, but held by rather shaky hands. I decided it would look rather cool if I casually lowered it now. There was a lot of noise from the constant shelling, so one more rifle bang from Charlie would not have been noticed. I casually lowered my rifle and returned a conspiratorial grin with Charlie as we lifted the dead piggy between us. I could also play it cool, you know.

Here is a photo of Jock Winton and me when we returned to our wee, wooden hut at Batu Pahat. It was advisable to give us a wide berth at this point, we had not been able to wash for a few days. Pheew.

56   McNICOLLS TRIES TO WORK HIS TICKET!

Most of our guys adapted to the different qualities needed for jungle warfare. However, there was always the odd one who just seemed unable to adjust, and McNicolls was one of them. He was no hard man, just a wee guy, but there is safety in numbers. In civilian life and he used to belong to an unruly local crowd led by a constant trouble maker called Skin Pender who was always being banned or ejected from neighbouring dance halls.

McNicolls was with us during basic training and had then been allocated to one of our rifle companies. I did not see much of him after we arrived in Singapore. About a year later we meet him, this time as a Private with one of our rifle companies in Malaya. He still yapped a lot, however, as one old soldier remarked," He talks all day and says nuthin". This pretty much summed up McNicolls as a loud but empty bag of wind.

He had not adapted well to jungle warfare. There were reports of him displaying erratic behaviour when on patrol. This was not an acceptable attitude when he had other soldiers relying on him for the common safety in the jungle. There were even rumours of him being so unnerved when detailed for patrol duties that his actions were taken as signs that he was, ' Trying to work his ticket'. This is an army expression to describe making one's self undesirable for army service on the grounds of either physical or mental unsuitability for military service. This could lead to a possible discharge from the service. I eventually heard the full story of McNicolls disappearance from our ranks when I bumped into another of my Penicuik friends, Jimmy Oliver who was in the same rifle company as McNicolls.

It seemed McNicolls erratic behaviour was getting progressively worse as the days went by. He had been disciplined for breaking the silence when on jungle patrol. Apparently he would suddenly start to bark like a dog and sometimes would break into his cockerel impression. He would shout, 'Cock a doodle doo', in a strange, high pitched voice, sending shivers down the spines of his companions, goodness knows what it was doing to any C.T's who overheard him. I imagine the sound was something like the noise a banshee would make, although I have never actually heard a banshee.

His last dramatic performance came during a routine foot patrol in the jungle, scheduled to last over a five day period but, thanks to the mad chicken McNicolls, the schedule had to be revised on the first night.

I have mentioned how quickly night falls in Malaya. It appears to happen even sooner in thick jungle. As a result, jungle soldiers try to stop at a suitable spot before the light disappears to set up camp for the night. Hoping the remaining light would last long enough to enable the patrol to erect some primitive kind of shelter from the rain which descends in torrents, particularly during the monsoon season; the area is not called a 'rain forest' for nothing.

On the first night of the patrol, perimeter guards were in position, the rest of the guys had erected their individual 'bashas' made from draping one groundsheet on a makeshift roof structure of branches. Then, using the groundsheet belonging to his mate who was on guard, the 'off duty' guy would spread the other groundsheet over any kind of grasses or moss available. When pushed for time before the inky black night descended, they sometimes just laid the groundsheet on the damp earth to keep them above the wet ground. However, where possible, the lads would try to make some kind of raised bed which would hopefully keep them above ground and a bit further away from slinking snakes, sneaky spiders and stinging scorpions.

This is the thick, wet, sticky, sweaty Malayan jungle. Bad enough at the best of times but sheer hell on wet wheels during the rainy season when it is usually streaming with constant heavy rain and you are permanently soaking wet. Gazing at the stars is out of the question as the forest is so thick it makes stargazing impossible. Leeches are usually also busy sucking blood from various delicate parts of your fine young body, but you can't see that kind of shite at night when the use of artificial light is forbidden. The treat in store for the victim with these loathsome bastards already attached would have to wait till dawn and enough light to disengage them.

All your senses are engaged listening to strange rustling sounds in the pitch dark. Is that a slithering snake coming closer? Apart from the sounds of creeping things, during the dark night you can sometimes hear sounds which could come from a different, unseen, creature. This is tiger country after all. You have to hope none of your mates on guard 'stag' have dozed off. It could be a bunch of heavily armed C.T's creeping towards your wee camp, intent on bloody murder. No wonder daft McNicolls was trying to work his ticket to escape from this lunacy, perhaps McNicolls was really going daft. His faraway home town of Bonnyrigg could be a bit rough round the edges after the pubs closed on a Saturday night, but never like this.

That particular first night on patrol the guys were making use of the few minutes of daylight left to organise themselves for a long night ahead. McNicolls was busy as well - cutting very thin branches, not really suitable for constructing a basha. Nobody noticed at first, they were all busy making their own preparations. McNicolls appeared to be weaving the thin branches into a square shape, best described as a square nest, rather than building a normal basha.

When the walls of his nest reached about a foot high, he stepped into the middle of his construction, hunkered down, laid his head back and broke into a loud "Cock a doodle doo " routine in a loud, cackling, crazy voice. He really was a daft chicken, coming back to his square homemade nest to roost.

All hell broke out in the little encampment. The strictly enforced rule of silence where all commands and communications were done in mime had been suddenly shattered. McNicolls was overpowered but what to do now? With this gibbering nutter on board, he was now barking like a dog, the patrol would have to be abandoned and he would have to be escorted to the nearest road to be picked up, under heavy escort, by a truck from the base camp. Wireless silence had to be broken and a message sent back to base requesting a truck be sent to the nearest road position at first light. Roads were few and far between in this jungle covered country in the fifties, marching through the jungle to try and find the rendezvous in the pitch black would be asking for trouble. The decision was made to head out at first light.

All this mumbo jumbo was due to McNicolls. He then joined the group of 'never seen again guys'. I can only assume his erratic behaviour had progressed to a real illness, he was probably discharged, clucking quietly to himself, and sent back to the U.K.

Jock and me. These pics are only two days apart !

The previous two pictures show both Jock Winton and me carrying out our varied army duties from one day to the next. Never a dull moment in the Pipes and Drums. The following photos are of two friends from back home. 'Basher' Gillies and Jimmy Oliver.

Above is picture of Corporal Derek 'Basher' Gillies, my supposed adversary in shipboard physical training exercise, but actually good friend. He is accompanied by Jimmy Oliver, another old friend of mine, also from Penicuik.

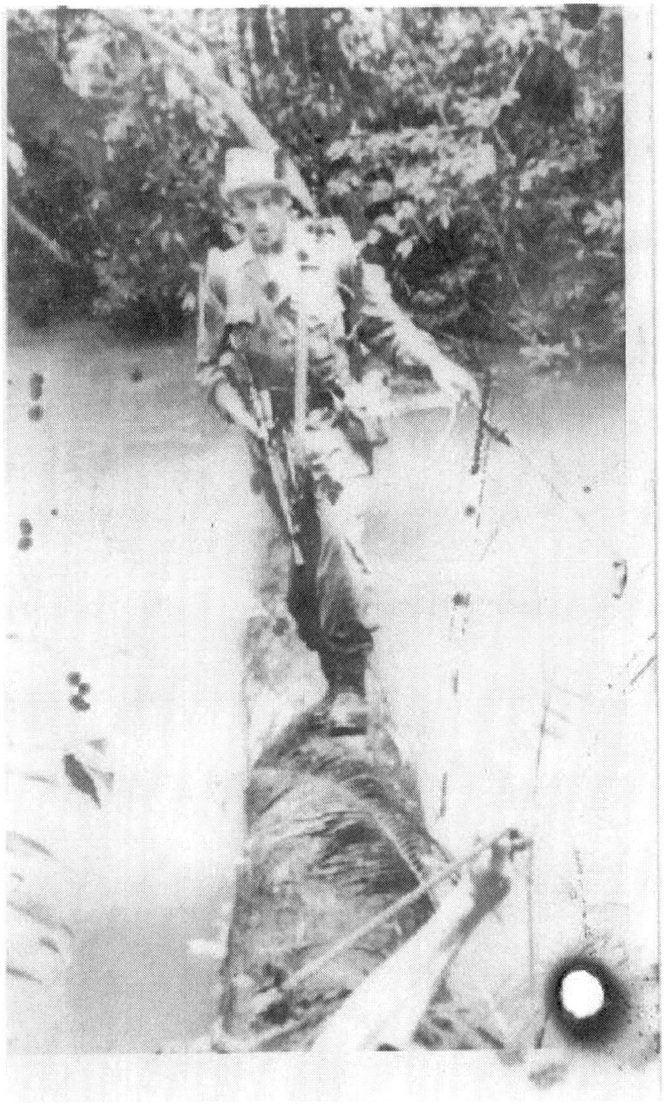

This is a much damaged picture of Ray Reid from Jedburgh. Ray was my mate and somewhat guide through life's mysteries. He claims the hole in this photo was from a round fired at him by a C.T., the photo was enclosed in a slim tin box in his shirt pocket where he kept his fags dry. He swears it saved his life but I know for a fact the hole was actually caused when one of his lit fags burned a hole in the picture, I told him I had already heard several versions of that tale.

Makes a good story though, fags were 'easy come, easy go'. We had a free issue of tins containing fifty cigarettes each week. I was a nonsmoker and used to sell mine to a smoker buddy for one Straits dollar per week. I even took a load of cigarettes with me as gifts for friends when I left for home, walked right through customs at Southampton with the lot. Good, healthy stuff! Some gift, some friend! It was all a bit different in those far away days.

My good friend Birka Bahadur Rai from the Gurkha Regiment. Birka Bahadur was loaned to us for an enjoyable while from the Gurkha Pipes and Drums. We were to meet again a year later when I was a civilian and he had arrived in Edinburgh to attend a military piping course.

Me and Piper 'Tug' Wilson from Peebles with some of our friends from the Gurkhas. Batu Pahat. Johore State, Malaya. 1956. My piper friend loved to wear borrowed 'Scottish' stuff.

57 JUNGLE SOLDIERS

What our guys feared most in the jungle was not an ambush by the CT's, but, as previously mentioned, an attack by a leech. This loathsome creature could insert its tiny self into your clothing and even through eyelets in our jungle boots with the driving instinct to reach human flesh. This is where the expression, 'Hanging on like a leech', comes from. These creepy little bastards would attach their almost invisible selves to your flesh, sometimes in the most sensitive areas of your body and take their fill of your blood unless they were detached from your person but detaching was difficult..

By that time they looked for all the world like fat, slimy slugs, (the leeches - not the guys.) My stomach never failed to lurch whenever I discovered leeches attached to my body, they would be bloated and satiated with my precious blood. You could wait till the bloody things sucked their fill then they let go and slithered away but none of us wanted them hanging from various delicate parts of the body.

The detaching operation sounds simple but was in fact a tedious and revolting, and needed to be performed as soon as we stopped to rest for the night. If the bloody thing was simply pulled off when it was feeding, its body could leave the firmly attached mouth part still in position on your skin causing the blood to continue to flow even when creature had been dealt with. The leech would already have injected its chosen feeding area on your skin with an anti-coagulating element to keep the blood flowing freely, all very horrible and messy.

The quickest way to get the bloody thing off was to bum a lit fag from a mate, but not to smoke, (wee play on words there). You applied the lit end of the cigarette to the attached leech, then you might get a little satisfaction as the creature shriveled and let go quickly. I always offered to return the still lit fag to the donor but the return was often refused depending on how many fags he had left in his damp packet. You just had to hope the shriveled horror would leave your groin or other tender parts without bursting. 'Oh the army life is the life for me'!

I believe there exists, but never saw, a species of squirrel that can fly and also a reptile called the gliding snake which can propel itself at you from the jungle canopy above. Pause here for a violent shudder.

Apart from lead, gliding snakes and suicidal squirrels flying through the air, there were other dangers. Thankfully we had been inoculated during initial basic training against the unspeakable Far Eastern horrors such as, Beriberi, black-water fever, cholera, dysentery and other ghastly diseases. That thought takes me back to the day during our initial training when our brave muscle man Nesbit passed out cold at the prospect of being injected with the powerful T.A.B. drug. . He was another guy soon to join the 'never to be seen again' club.

Malaria was dealt with when we paraded to receive and swallow our daily dose of anti-malaria tablets under supervision every morning. As far as I know, there is no injection available to guard against flying lead. You must take your chances with that problem. However, there are other delights still available in the wet and humid jungle. Ulcerated legs used to be quite common, scratch these legs at your peril.

Some light relief could be obtained when anybody developed tinea. This is a fungus which usually affects damp and sweaty parts of the body, it is similar to ringworm. It usually attacked the groin and could be cured after a fashion when the M.O. applied a bright purple ointment by painting it generously onto the affected area. This caused lots of merriment when the afflicted party hit the showers in the morning, jolly shouts of, "'Hey, Purple Balls," etc. Oh, how we laughed.

Morning showers were, of course, not available on jungle patrol, you just have to stink till you get back to base. No M.O. available in the jungle either. You had to wait to reach base at the end of your patrol where the regimental doctor is scheduled to visit about once a week. Too bad if you arrived back at camp too late and had just missed the MO's visit.

58 THE SECURITY TIDE TURNS A WEE BIT

Due to a piece of inspired thinking from a forward looking military type, a decision was made to hit the terrorists where it would really hurt, in the stomach or, as we called it, the breadbasket.

The decision had been made a couple of years before our arrival in Malaya, but results were now showing clearly in the levels of terrorism through the country.

The 'bread basket' idea was really quite simple. Since the time of the Japanese occupation, the Chinese Terrorists had obtained their food from local peasants whether the peasants were willing or not. A method for cutting or at least reducing these food supplies was implemented. This was achieved by throwing a secure fence around every rural village, called kampongs. A kind of curfew was installed in as much as all villagers had to be home by a certain time in the evening when the entrance gate was locked and patrolled by armed guards.

This method was not totally effective in cutting off all food supplies to the C.T's. A heavily armed attack would certainly overrun any small guard force guarding the village, but would cause a radio alarm to be sent off to alert the British army which was spread out over the Malay Peninsula. Results of this security action could be seen: food supplies and important medical supplies to the terrorists were much reduced. The C.T's even had to start their own vegetable gardens by clearing spaces in the middle of the jungle; these gardens were hidden as much as possible then they would have to tend them regularly to produce vegetables. I imagine this must have pissed them off as it was using precious time which they could have spent more productively by carrying out ambush actions, more their style really.

59 OH - AN ACTORS LIFE FOR ME.

Strangely enough, the trend in making the natives live in secure kampongs provided an unexpected benefit for us. I was sent with a small patrol to keep an unobtrusive eye on a kampong not too far from one of our outposts. Soldiers of the Malay Regiment now mounted a regular guard on the kampong. They were not informed of our sneaky visit, we just wanted to check and see how things were progressing.

We set up our basic little camp for another uncomfortable night; then four of us were detailed to approach the secure kampong to see what was going on. We had chosen to camp near a narrow path through the woods which was used by the local labour force at a nearby rubber plantation during the day time. It was, of course, deserted at night (we hoped so, anyway), and my well-armed foursome used the path to advance quietly to reach the outskirts of the village. We were to stay hidden, just observing, for a couple of hours to check things out for security before returning.

I am so glad I was chosen as one of the four spies. As we got closer to the kampong we could hear the distinctive Chinese music; it was pretty loud and did not seem like a radio programme. We were aware we should not get too close in case the village dogs sensed our nearby presence, they would figuratively, 'Blow the whistle', by setting up a loud racket of barking and our covert spying operation would be blown.

We found a secluded vantage position where we had a fairly clear view of the lamp-lit village, just far enough away not to alert the dogs. One area was brightly lit, the light and the loud and impressive music was coming from a travelling Chinese theatre with their own group of musicians and actors dressed in traditional style. The actors were putting on quite a show for the isolated villagers and they loved it. The villagers were not the only ones. Although I was unseen and could not understand the language, I was enjoying it as well. The acting was so dramatic and, to me, overacted, but this was their style, rather like the over acting in the old silent movies. The whole drama was being unfolded to wild, scary music accompanied by sudden cymbal crashes and wild shouts. It was great.

I was reluctant when our allocated two hours was up. We had to leave the fun and creep away along the narrow path in the dark to reach our overnight camp. What a great experience. This was the type of thing I had hoped to see.

60   WEE SPOT OF LEAVE

We returned to our happy wooden home to receive good news. We were all due to take some leave, quite a nice surprise. However, when I considered the news, it did seem to be a long time since the leave I had enjoyed way back at the end of basic training in 1955.

The British Army had decided the Pipes and Drums should all take two weeks off at the same time which made sense really, but what were we to do? We were all stuck in this bumfuck no-man's land, somewhere in Johore State, Malaya.

One bright thinking guy suggested applying for rail passes to Singapore. Easily done - the clerk who worked in the orderly office would do that for us. Better still, being military travellers, it would not cost us a penny or Straits dollar, our currency at the time.

Where to stay was the next problem? One old hand who had been round the block a time or two provided the solution. He recalled a still-existing relic from the old British Empire - we could stay at a Sandes Home for Soldiers. "What's a fuckin' Sandes Home for Soldiers?" This wail came from a profane young soldier. He was quickly reprimanded by the old hand who was, after all, a full corporal, demanding some respect. "It's a place run by fuckin' Christians you fucker, show some respect."

We learned, (not from the corporal, I had to do some checking up on this myself) Sandes Homes for Soldiers was founded in 1869. Named after its founder (bless her), Miss Elsie Sandes. During the 1800's, she started a soldier's coffee room in Tralee, County Kerry, Ireland. This country was a fertile recruiting area for the British Army at that time but has come a long way since then. There was a Sandes Home in Singapore. The Homes provided affordable bed and breakfast accommodation for the lads and were efficiently and charmingly run, as we were about to find out, by a small, very select groups of refined, elderly ladies. Rather like the sweet, slightly older and batty British ladies often depicted in the old Ealing comedy movies of the late forties and fifties.

We decided to head for Singapore to stay at Sandes Home for Soldiers, this turned out to be a very fortunate choice. The Home in Singapore had a rather imposing entrance and reception area leading to a great swimming pool which was surrounded by comfortable accommodation for up to four persons to a room. We split up into the four person groups. I shared with Pipers, Jock Winton, Lance Corporal Les McKinley and our 'old hand', Corporal Dan Grant.

Here is a photo Dan took of me, Les and Jock arriving at Sandes Home for Soldiers. The entrance looks a bit swanky. I am the good looking one, wearing unfortunately fashionably wide bottom trousers. Some followers of fashion may notice waists were a bit higher then.

These are all pics of good, clean fun. I realise we were on holiday in steamy, sweaty and hopefully wicked Singapore and you might be expecting pictures of a different kind. However, I was sending all my photos directly back home for Mummy to see, what did you expect to find here?

What a great place we had chosen to stay. True, it was (still is) a Christian establishment, but, unlike some other so called Christian establishments, nobody questioned what you did or where you did it (thank goodness). Nobody pushed unwanted literature under the door of your room. In fact, I can't recall anybody bothering us in any way. The ladies who ran the place were very sweet and kind, probably a lot like the mothers some of our guys would have gladly swapped for their own mothers. I even borrowed a pair of scissors from one dear, helpful lady, have you noticed scissors keep popping up in my memoirs?

I had purchased a pair of denim trousers in a Singapore street market. I don't think they were being called jeans at that time, probably work overalls or something. I liked to style myself as a follower of fashion then and I planned to cut the pants legs off with a pair of scissors. I would then be the proud possessor of a pair of denim shorts which I imagined would establish me as a kind of trend setter, a real dedicated fashion follower.

Alas, it was not to be. I borrowed scissors from the sweet lady but then realized I did not like the look of the new shorts I had created, even after I had jumped into the swimming pool wearing the bloody things. I was possibly not quite sober at the time but that did not improve the way they looked. Strands of material from the scissor cut area started to hang down exactly the same as the fashionable look came to be years later when worn by the trend setters in the swinging sixties.

Unfortunately, I could not see into the future, but was destined not to be a trendy fashion pioneer. I threw them into the trash bin, regretting my waste of money. The 1960s would have to wait for someone else to set the trend.

To cheer myself up I suggested a group visit to the Tiger Balm Garden. I had passed the ornate entrance but had no idea what Tiger Balm meant. Once again there was a cry of, "What's a fuckin' Tiger Balm Garden"? The four of us visited the Gardens to see what it was all about; we enjoyed the trip, the place was full of Chinese fables with actual size figures displayed in a way totally unfamiliar to us unsophisticated Jocks.

Me, posing on our visit to the Tiger Balm Gardens, Singapore City. 1956. This picture was for my mother, O.K.!

61   IT'S SATURDAY NIGHT AND I JUST GOT PAID.

On the first Saturday of our almost two weeks' leave in Singapore, Jock Winton requested an urgent meeting to discuss fiscal matters. We each dug deep into our pockets to extract what seemed to be a much dwindled cash situation. Not one of us had in excess 20 bucks. Even if we pooled all our funds, the total would not reach $100.00. I am, of course, dealing with Straits dollars, not the more valuable American dollars.

We had been paid our advance leave money but still had a full week to go, what to do? Luckily, we had paid for our two weeks accommodation up front, but we were still in a tight spot financially for our second week. We had also hoped to have a Saturday night on the town.

Fat chance. It seems financial planning was not a strong point among bagpipe players. Even if we pooled our remaining cash for food, we would be having slim pickin's for the week till we could use our rail warrants to get back to our safe, wee, wooden hut in Johore where the army would supply accommodation and food of some kind at no charge. This fiscal brush with civilian life came with a jolt which underlined how even we young, conscripted soldiers had come to rely on the military for everything. Release back to civilian life might come as a shock to some of conscripts after even only two years army life. For some regular soldiers who had served for years before finishing their stint with the secure if rather Spartan military style of life, it must have been incomprehensible. The army was a kind of mum and dad for these guys. Facing up to civilian life when eventually released by the military could be horrendous. What could the future hold for people like old Willie, the peeing monkey man? I shuddered to think.

Once again our reliable old hand Danny Grant seemed to offer a faint glimmer of hope. "We could try Housey, Housey tonight," he suggested. "What the fuck's Housey, Housey"? I bleated, already beginning to regret mixing with bloody pipers.

However, back to the matter in hand, I was still ignorant regarding the question of Housey, Housey. Luckily, Corporal Dan explained it. He was a regular soldier, he must have been all of perhaps twenty six, but we all regarded him as an 'old sweat'. If we had any problems we went straight to him for advice or guidance. He explained, 'Housey, Housey' was an army game played regularly on Thursdays and Saturdays at the Union Jack Club in, not only in Singapore, but at Union Jack clubs worldwide.

Armed with a pencil, club members would sit at tables in a hall where a committee member would call out random numbers obtained from numbered rubber balls as they spilled from a rotating drum.

The contestants would check off any number on their sheet which corresponded to a number being called out by the committee member. The contestant who managed to cross out all their numbers first would call out loudly, "House". All activity ceased as another member checked the winning numbers with the caller. If the numbers checked out, prize money would be paid out to the winner before the game started over again.

Dan reckoned the prize money could be a fair amount according to how many people were in attendance. He also reckoned Saturdays attracted a fairly big crowd. Housey, Housey seemed to be our only chance of making money. By chance, it was Saturday and 'chance' seemed to be a word full of good prospects for us. We decided to take a chance and visit the Union Jack club pronto to see if perhaps Lady Luck would favour us.

62   THE UNION JACK CLUB, SINGAPORE. 1956.

The four of us arrived at the Union Jack club in Singapore, properly prepared for action at the Housey, Housey activity with specially purchased pencils sharpened to a business like sharp point. We took our seats at a small table among a group of expectant fortune seekers, and so my experience of gambling night life commenced.

Being a beginner, I was a bit slow locating the numbers as the caller announced them. Everything was a wee bit too quick for me. Perhaps I was thinking I was no match for the regulars. I seemed to be playing 'catch up', just behind the rest, but I still managed to cross out quite a lot of the numbers on my slip.

The guy was still calling numbers when it dawned on me that I had no vacant numbers left. I turned to Jock Winton to ask what to do. He glanced at my ticket. "Shout HOUSE, ya daft wee bastard," he stage whispered. In confusion and aware that I seemed to be letting the side down, I shouted at the top of my voice, just as my occasional stammer decided to join in," H, H, H, HOUSE - YA DAFT WEE BASTARD!". There was immediate silence, but Corporal Dan saved the day, "It's his first time playing Housey, Housey", he called out to the rest of the shocked punters. This raised a few titters and I guessed my language infringement had been overlooked. I should remind you the year was 1956 and people swearing in public were frowned upon.

The checker arrived at our table, looked at my numbers and gave the caller the thumbs up. "Congratulations, soldier, you have just won $500," he announced into his mike. My table erupted in cheers, my mates were slapping my back and trying to shake my hand all at the same time, as the checker handed the winnings to me.

I had never won anything in my short life except perhaps for the Tootal tie at the spot dance during our weekly fund raising Boy Scout hootenanny. Unfortunately the awful Tootal tie is the one I was wearing when our picture of the 'raw recruits' was taken at Berwick on our first day of basic training. I had already fixed that win with the guy who picked the winner, so I don't think that counts. It's too late now if anybody reads this.

Just to prove we were not just visiting the Union Jack Club for the chance to win some money. We played one more perfunctory game before leaving with our winnings. Housey, Housey is the old army game which evolved to become the very alive, 'Bingo' of the present day. I split the winnings four ways with the guys before we stepped, flushed and happy, into the steamy Saturday night scene in Singapore.

The scene was now set for a possible orgy of spending and drinking. Unfortunately, chasing loose wimmin was out of the question as Corporal Dan was a happily married man and I think both of the others were faithfully writing to their girls back home. In spite of these restraining circumstances, we still managed to enjoy the evening, drinking in the old Scottish manner. Although, I later became beside myself with the strong drink, also in the traditional, old Scottish manner.

I blame it for my inability to remember much about that celebration evening. I recall piling into a taxi at a later point, then falling flat on my face trying to make a dignified exit from the cab when we arrived back at Sandes Home for Soldiers. I can only assume my less drunk mates trundled me to bed.

I certainly remember enjoying the next few days when we had a few bucks in our pockets and could eat and drink in style until once again we ran out of money. So great was my reputation as a provider that the lads hauled me off to the Union Jack Club the following Saturday where we used what was left of our cash to invest once again in the Housey, Housey lark. Once more I actually won the bloody thing, although for a smaller amount this time. We ate and drank well that night before boarding the Sunday train to Johore next morning. We were the only guys from the bunch of leave takers to return to the unit with some cash in our pockets. Could this be a first?

63 MERDEKA

Boredom was never a problem in our outfit. Rioting broke out in Singapore just as we were leaving the station to return to our army base. The locals had been threatening this for some time but, luckily for us, they started to burst out rioting all over town just as our train was already pulling out of the city to head back north.

These were the Merdeka riots. Merdeka being the local battle cry meaning, 'Freedom'. It was the same type of word used by the Scots long ago during our struggle against the same type of people now oppressing the locals in Singapore. This was mainly the brainchild of the majority Chinese population who had not wanted the British back after the war. Come hell or high water, they wanted the Brits to quit playing at Empire building and get the hell out of Singapore to let them get on with running the place.

Our Regiment had been preparing for some time for just such a situation. We had paraded up and down on the sacred drill square ground at Selerang barracks, rehearsing the nice, firm but friendly, British style for handling riots. This practice consisted of armed squads of us marching across the barrack square in a determined manner until being confronted by a gang of our own guys masquerading as locals. Our guys really enjoyed playing the part of wicked rioters, dressed in sarongs etc. Shouting and yelling insults was one of the most popular traits displayed by our 'rioters'. We, in turn, had a fierce white cloth banner mounted on stick supports which we unrolled when we halted smartly in front of the 'mob'. Our banner unrolled to reveal the menacing message printed in both English and Cantonese telling them to disperse. Failure to obey this command would, it was promised, surely end in tears for them or some such sporting British nonsense.

To add flavour to the affair, one of our squad was armed with a tin loud hailer which he used to warn the rioters about the possibility of some arse kicking being involved in our retaliation. This information was, of course, delivered in English with a strong Glasgow accent. It was accented with suitable unintelligible Scottish threats, probably totally incomprehensible if we had any real Chinese rioters present. Our own hooligans loved this part of the procedure, their shouting rose in volume as they joined in swearing and yelling Glasgow insults back at us. This was their chance to shout at authority with permission and no likelihood of any comeback. At the time it all sounded very realistic. How any real rioters would react was, thankfully, not my immediate problem.

We were rich and happy that day, heading back by rail towards our little wooden hut in Johore State. We had just crossed over into Malaya when a train travelling in the opposite direction sped past us at a great rate of knots towards riot stricken Singapore City. Somebody commented the train seemed to be travelling a bit fast for an early Sunday morning jaunt to Singapore. Of course, we were quite unaware that it contained nearly all of our regiment in full riot gear heading urgently towards the scene of the rioting.

Surprise! We arrived back to find our HQ a hive of activity. We were ordered to debus and wait for further instructions. Our regimental white cloth riot signs plus megaphones had been hastily unearthed from storage, and the whole regiment in full combat gear was making all haste to quell a massive uprising No more silly wee riot games for our lads. This was serious stuff.

This mass exodus of our regiment from Johore state left our rifle company camps almost unmanned. It was decreed the Pipes and Drums were to split up into a few small sections, get into combat gear, then make haste towards our now almost deserted rifle company locations scattered across Johore State. We were also instructed to gather up any available odds and sods lurking at H.Q. Company, including even the unfortunate few being held in our small, homemade regimental prison compound.

Somehow we had to man each denuded rifle company camp, from Alfa through Bravo, Charlie, Delta and Support Company compounds located across Johore State. This left us a bit thin on the ground, to put it mildly.

I was sent to man the ramparts at Bravo Company accompanied by a few other brave souls, just enough for a skeleton guard which would enable us to provide basic security for the almost deserted camp, now only protected by a few strands of barbed wire. One Regimental Sergeant Major, normally based at our fairly secure H.Q. Company base camp, was detailed to accompany us to keep some semblance of order. The 'keeping order' part actually applied to us, not the C.T's, they were the potential attackers we were being sent to repel. This particular Sergeant Major had been a bit of an old fashioned martinet type of soldier when we were stationed in Selerang barracks in Singapore. There he had a parade square on which to strut. He had a fierce reputation back there, but had not been seen very often after we moved to bandit country in Johore State.

I found out that this guy was nearing the end of his army career. He was due to leave us soon and return to the U.K. to retire. His move from the comparative safety of the base camp to what we called, the sharp end, at Bravo company camp must have given him something to think about. Bravo Company camp was now without its usual band of scruffy but reliable Jocks and must have caused him some misgivings. He only had our small, motley crew to rely on, bless him. For the next couple of weeks he could have been named Seldom Seen Sergeant Major. He secured an attap thatched hut in the centre of camp, armed himself with a bottle of whisky, leaving us more or less to our own devices which was o.k. as far as we were concerned.

I befriended Simon, a German shepherd cross, now temporarily deserted when his usual owner was urgently called to Singapore for riot duty. The dog Simon actually befriended me. We bonded quickly, possibly due to my sharing grub with him when we first met. He settled into my tent, making himself comfortable beneath the bed as if we had been buddies for years.

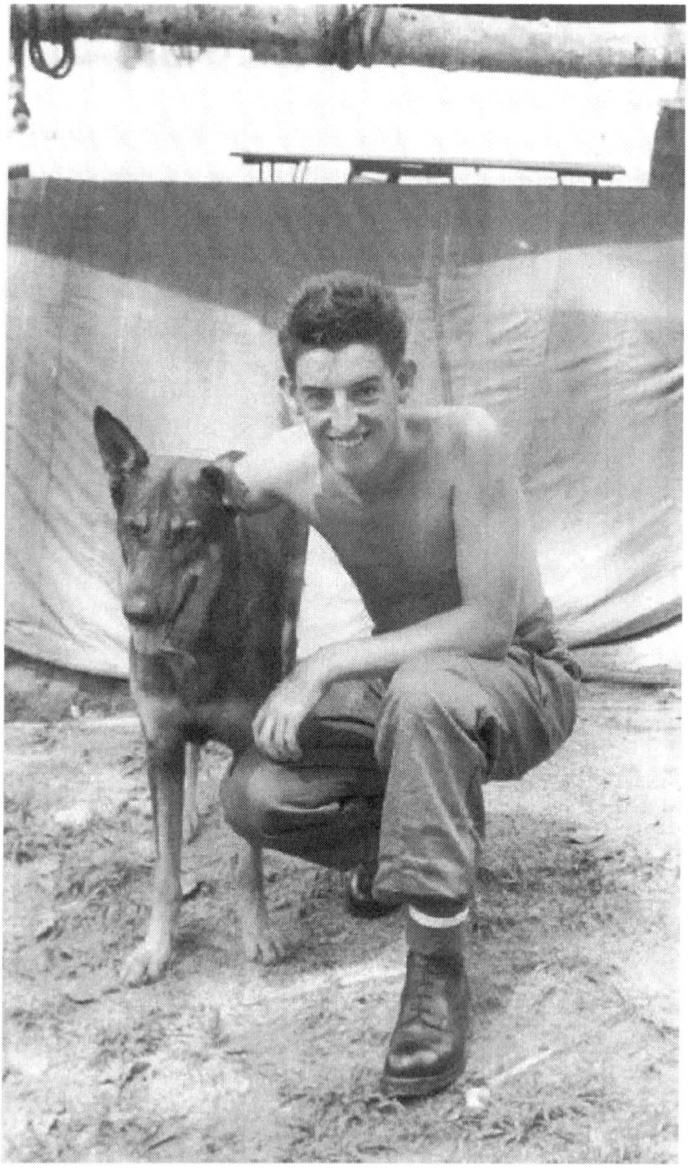

Simon and me, Bravo Company location, Johore State, Malaya 1956. The dog has obviously seen some other guy across the compound eating a sandwich and I am no longer at the centre of his wee world. Fuck doggy love and devotion. Incidentally, Simon would possibly turn up his snout if offered any sandwich made from the sliced bread issued (sounds just like issuing blankets) by our cookhouse at H.Q. Company. The bread we received always had a fair ration of active weevils scurrying through each slice!

64 BRAVO COMPANY COMPOUND (DESERTED). JOHORE STATE, MALAYA.

It must have been my day for making new friends. I found one of the prisoners released from our little regimental jail to help us guard the camp at Bravo Company was named Alex Hanratty. It turned out his brother Eddy was Drum Major with Penicuik Pipes and Drums from my home town back in Scotland.

Alex had been in our regimental jail for being A.W.O.L. from Bravo Company. I have no idea where he was heading when he went absent. I suspect he did not know either, I guess it was just habit. Apparently he seemed to disappear from the regiment on a regular basis, he was probably glad to be arrested. It was better than wandering around by himself in darkest Malaya.

"Fancy us meeting like this. Better have a wee drink to celebrate," suggested the resourceful Alex. I agreed, but could think of no way to cement the new found friendship. Alex, however, checked things out and found the solution lay in the direction of the wet canteen in the camp. This wee bar was deserted but technically still operating with a happy, wee Malay bartender in attendance, although all his usual customers had been called away on riot duty to Singapore.

Alex and I gamely attempted to step in to represent absent friends. We made such a good job of representing that we managed to keep the canteen open all that afternoon, consuming quantities of

Tiger beer, not one of my favourite pilsner beers but any port in a storm, as they say.

Before retiring to his 'safe house' in the camp with his bottle of whisky, our Seldom Seen Sergeant Major had appointed our only NCO to be in total charge. This poor guy had to organise a night guard squad near the entrance gate at around six p.m. 'Seldom Seen' promised to make an appearance to ensure the squad would be mounted for the night. I later learned the Sergeant Major was to be picked up in an armoured scout car around night fall. He had been invited to the home of a local British rubber planter for dinner and would be away overnight.

We were also staying for the night, but, unlike our Sergeant Major, we would be guarding the deserted camp against any possible attack from the C.T's who would now be aware of the absence of the entire personnel of Bravo Company, now dealing with the rioters in Singapore.

The emergency troops we had supplied to keep the camp secure in the absence of the Bravo Company soldiers were a bit thin on the ground, to put it mildly. We could only muster a total of eight reasonably fit bodies, plus Simon the dog. This would not be enough for one normal guard mounting, never mind manning the camp on twenty four hour shifts as would be the case if the entire company was here.

The total would have been nine if we counted 'Seldom Seen', but we were soon back to eight again after he appeared briefly when we gathered for guard duty. He nodded curtly at the young lance corporal who had been left in charge, then hopped smartly into the waiting armoured scout car to be driven away for dinner with the Rubber Plantation owner.

In contrast to the Sergeant Major's dinner arrangements, our food was found in the cartons of emergency rations held in the storage tent. I actually preferred the emergency stuff to the usual mess dished up by the regular cooks from The Army Catering Corpse, as we referred to them. There were no cooks left at this camp anyway. We could choose which rations we wanted, and prepare our own grub when, and where, we wanted.

There was the slight problem with mounting a security guard that night. It was really a numbers problem and a sobriety situation combined. Four of the seven available guards had spent the afternoon in the corrugated shed referred to as the wet canteen and were now pissed as rats.

It was fortunate the departing Sergeant Major had only given us a fleeting glance before making his swift exit in the scout car. In different circumstances he would probably have noticed I was actually using my rifle as an aid to balancing myself in an upright position. Simon was resting on my foot to await further instructions or perhaps awaiting food as the case may be. The dog helped with my balancing act by lying over my unsteady foot. Alex was wobbling a wee bit standing next to me using his rifle as a crutch, feeling no pain. Mercifully dusk falls rapidly in the Far East which probably covered our real condition from the rapidly departing but slightly pissed sergeant major.

The lance corporal was left in charge of us. Luckily, he had the sense to pair each of the pissed guards with a sober one. There was not the slightest possibility of mounting a normal two hours on and four hours off guard routine, we did not have enough men either drunk or sober for that. He instructed us to bugger off to patrol on the inside of the barbed wire in pairs and watch out for any sign of trouble outside the perimeter which was lit by powerful lights from our industrial strength electric generators. If anything moved outside the wire we were to shoot immediately. I gathered this was the old shoot first and ask questions later approach, I would be quite happy to work with that.

Luckily, I was the odd man out in more ways than one that night. I was paired with the doggie as I wandered off around the perimeter wire, accompanied by man's best friend. Simon could switch to being another man's best friend provided the other man possessed a beef sandwich. Fortunately for me, beef was rather like our absent Sergeant Major, very seldom seen and a rare commodity in this area.

Even in my unsteady condition I sensed, correctly, that Simon would be my best bet for emerging unscathed from night duty. He had stuck faithfully by my side since my arrival at Bravo camp. To be fair, his affection was probably largely due to sharing my food rations with him. I had drawn a full set of rations for him from our slightly confused Seldom Seen RSM who found himself in charge of the stock of emergency rations. Simon and I had bonded, and I was certain he would give early warning of approaching danger. I was carrying a loaded shotgun plus a revolver, and I was also armed with the knowledge that we were behind a robust security fence well lit by powerful perimeter lights.

My faith in Simon was well placed. After a couple of wobbly circuits of the wire, I was suddenly aware that I was really pissed and retired to my nearby tent to take a little rest. Simon made himself comfortable on the other bed. I passed out, snoring and clutching my shot gun in the true drunken soldier fashion, secure in the knowledge that my friend would keep a watchful guard until it was time for breakfast.

The following few days and nights passed pleasantly enough. Simon and I would take a stroll around the wire from time to time, breaking only for a friendly shared breakfast and then lunch. This activity was followed in the afternoon with a leisurely visit to the wet canteen where I got quietly pissed with Alex. The ever watchful Simon lay beneath my bench seat ready to receive tit bits. I still had enough beer money for both Alex and me as there was absolutely nothing else to spend it on anyway. This was more like a wee bonus holiday.

It seemed our only duty was to have a presence in the camp which was surrounded by thick jungle, possibly infiltrated by hostile C.T.'s. We may have been small in number, but we had a healthy range of fire power, enough cash for beer, virtually no discipline and, of course, the faithful Simon. I also found another plus in the shape of half a dozen Sarawak Ranger head hunter friends who were stationed with us.

I carried out my daily tasks diligently. I was never late arriving at the wet canteen every afternoon, then taking an evening stroll round the perimeter with Simon. This was the life, in this deserted camp where I was really quite happy with the almost zero discipline. I would visit with the former head hunters and, although most of the conversation included lots of mime, it was friendly. I could also still make believe in the old British Empire romantic shit I used to read about. I was now part of it, good old Kipling, I thought, happy and pissed as I took a wander round the camp at night. From a distance I was presenting a fairly accurate picture of a nineteen year old British conscript soldier on duty. I was also presenting a well illuminated target wandering along beneath the bright perimeter lights, inviting a hole to be shot in my daft head, silly bugger. Oh, the romance of it all.

65 THE TATTOOED HEAD HUNTERS FROM SARAWAK

I mentioned that we had company. There was a small band of Sarawak Rangers stationed within the camp. These were former Eban head hunters from Borneo now employed by the British Army as jungle trackers to hunt out the C.T's. They were very good at the job.

I made friends with the Ebans, found them very outgoing which, I suppose, depended on which side they were on. Probably it was not a good idea to make enemies of these guys.

The best idea was to keep a cool head on your shoulders if you know what I mean. Luckily, they liked the Brits so I was accepted as being o.k. I liked them too and was soon admiring their various exotic tattoos.

I had always avoided having a permanent tattoo. A bunch of my mates had acquired a variety of these body decorations during their various drunken visits to Singapore city. My feelings about tattoos fell into an even worse category than sending letters home expressing undying love to girls. Imagine having 'I LOVE MARY' permanently printed on your body, then receiving a letter from Mary to let you know your true love affair has suddenly ended as she had run off with a big, hairy guy from Jamaica. Not a good idea.

One of our other conscript soldiers came from Motherwell, near Glasgow. For a dare after a drinking session, he had a huge, painful tattoo plastered across his chest. In bold, blue, capital letters, the message read, 'ONCE A BORDERER - NEVER AGAIN'. This was bad enough but it was based on the Regimental motto,' ONCE A BORDERER - ALWAYS A BORDERER'. Our hero was obviously only been trying to make a statement showing his displeasure at having been bundled into the army as a conscript in the first place. However, his bold tattoo decoration was a 'bad idea'.

Our not too bright guy from Motherwell had not been given a chance to consider his actions. He was beside himself with the drink when he and his mates had discovered the tattoo parlour. I guess the notion of a permanent protest tattoo plastered across his chest must have seemed like a 'good idea' at the time. He had overlooked the fact that, come Monday morning, our usual mode of army dress for normal duties in the hot barracks was mainly only jungle green shorts with socks rolled over boot tops. In the humid heat of the Far East, this dress style is referred to as shirt sleeve order. This never made sense to me for a shirt was not being worn. As a result, his newly decorated bare chest was now visible for all to view.

His freshly printed torso was soon spotted by our Regimental Sergeant Major. With apoplectic face and raging voice he had two men fall in beside our Motherwell guy to march him up to temporary custody in the guard room. The R.S.M. then confronted our C.O. to break the news about the newly discovered chest decoration. After a hurried conference, some money was extracted from Regimental Funds and the tattooed soldier was extracted from the guard house, placed under guard escort into an army truck and transported rapidly to the tattoo shop in Singapore. A complaint was issued to the tattoo artist, who explained the offending decoration could not be erased, but (for a small fee) a compromise tattoo might be arranged. This might take care of the problem.

On muster parade next morning our painted friend was again the main attraction. His new, amended decoration still read, 'ONCE A BORDERER', but this was now followed by a row of large, blue, Scottish thistles which obliterated the previous insulting words, 'NEVER AGAIN'. Payment for the additional thistles was a cash transaction from Regimental Company Funds, such was the importance of the supposed insult to the Regiment. As far as I know, the daft bugger must still be carrying the body decoration. I imagine it does not invite much comment now that he is back in temperate climes with his offending chest covered, unseen, against the colder weather.

Having seen the exotic tattoos sported by our trackers, I was considering having a fairly small tattoo, perhaps done unobtrusively on my shoulder. Being almost nineteen, I was still striving to be seen as a bit different from the herd. I was already imagining comments being made by envious observers as I shed my shirt on the beach, preparing to take a manly dive into the sea. There would be no possibility of any potential bully kicking sand into my face if this manly, head hunter tattoo, was on display.

The more mature reader will notice our 1950's way of thinking was influenced by the old Charles Atlas adverts featured in newspapers. These ads showed a line drawing of a skinny, very pale and white male bather on the beach having sand kicked into his face by a bulky sun tanned bully. The advertising message advised any similar skinny male sea bathers to enroll in the Charles Atlas body building course. The resulting newly built muscular body now mysteriously sun tanned as well as possessing a huge new chest would make potential bullies think twice about sand kicking. The attractive girls would ignore the bully and gather around to transfer their affection to the former skinny guy. All thanks to the Charles Atlas muscle building course. That, I believe, was the theory.

My manly thoughts concerning body decoration were abruptly chased away from my thinking that evening. I had strolled round to the big tent used by our trackers, still considering which decoration to request. One of the younger Ebans was lying bare chested on a bed with one of the others applying an intricate tattoo to the young guy's throat, the light for this operation was provided by only a dim lamplight!!

The Eban tattoo artist was using a slim piece of bamboo with a needle inserted in the split end. He kept dipping the needle into the lid of a boot polish tin which contained a homemade native concoction of dye made from wild plants. This dye was applied by placing the left hand on the shoulder bone at the top of the young Eban's chest, then, holding the sliver of bamboo firmly in his right hand, he would strike the right hand quickly down against the left. This action absorbed some of the force and acted like a pivot to allow the needle to strike the skin but prevented it from actually burying itself fiercely into the young guy's throat, only breaking into the flesh at the right depth to achieve the correct penetration. This, obviously painful action, was repeated again and again, following some traditional design plan, broken only by the frequent dipping of the needle into the mess of dye. The young Eban never flinched or even so much as blinked an eye.

(Photo. Thanks to: Lai Wah Photo Studio, Batu Pahat, Johore State).

Studio photograph of some of our trackers, the former head hunters from Borneo. They are displaying their tattoos against an unfortunate background. Something a bit fierce with tigers might have been a bit more appropriate for these guys. The intricate tattoo on the throat is the one I have witnessed being applied. Not for this child, thanks.

Brave guy, I thought, comparing his composure with the performance of our hard man Nesbit. He was the guy I mentioned during our initial training when he fainted on seeing the innocent but sharp little needle presented by the medical orderly at inoculation time during our basic training..

I was told the manual tattooing made in this painful, old fashioned tribal way was a test of manhood. The Iban guys in the photo are each sporting just such a decoration of painfully acquired manhood. These guys had fathers in Borneo who had probably earned another manhood qualifying test by obtaining the head of some guy belonging to a neighbouring tribe. Still striving to be different, but not willing to strive just that much, I smiled and shook my head when it came to my turn. I tried to look cool but thoughtful, and declined.

After about a week, the news arrived from Singapore city that the riots had been subdued, probably involving a lot of broken Chinese heads. This was in the good old days of the 1950's when the British Empire could still display the effective use of 'the iron rod' to control the natives. My guess was the riots had been broken by the Brits but not forgotten by the 'natives' who got their revenge a few years later when the Brits finally gave up any pretense of being worldwide empire builders and returned to the U.K.

Our small band of outpost guards could now return to our 'little wooden home' at Batu Pahat. I said cheerio to the head hunters and bade a reluctant goodbye to Simon who probably could not follow a word I said. I laid a dish of bully beef at his paws which would keep him fed until his owner reappeared later that day. I also said farewell to Alex who was about to become absorbed once again into his returning rifle company. He could then make his own drinking and dining arrangements. Little did I realise that Alex and I would soon meet again in different circumstances.

(Photo. Thanks to the Lai Wah Photo Studio, Batu Pahat, Johore, Malaya).

I am second from left. Drum Major Tom Black is on extreme right. We also have two of our Gurkha friends visiting that day. Note our old fashioned rope tension drums. The two snare drums with rod tension belong to the Gurkhas who were way ahead of us in these matters. I seem to recall they were also ahead of us when it came to drinking dark rum!

THE PIPERS, 1st BATALLION KINGS OWN SCOTTISH BORDERS 1956.

(Photo. Thanks to: Lai Wah Photo Studio, Batu Pahat, Johore State, Malaya). John Scott, second from left, my companion for the failed S.A.S bid!

66　HOGMANAY 1956.

It's now Hogmanay 1956/7 in darkest Malaya. It's only dark because we are celebrating the bringing in of the New Year after midnight with a much depleted Pipe section of our Pipes and Drums - we could only muster seven pipers that night.

The reason for the shortage of pipers is because we had sent two pipers to each of our four rifle companies to help the guys celebrate New Year. The British Army Authorities had withdrawn the Regiment from active service for New Year celebrations. I guess the Authorities realized they could not expect or receive much sense from a Scottish Regiment hell bent on celebrating Hogmanay in the old, traditional Scottish fashion. The wet canteens would be operating as usual that night till the bartenders fell down, also in the old traditional Scottish fashion.

Our Commanding Officer had also thoughtfully appointed the fat, Irish Quartermaster (you may remember him from my disastrous guard mounting photo) as Guard Commander in charge of our small Regimental lock up jail located at our H.Q. centre. The jail at H.Q. company site contained four of our regimental bad boys who were serving a few weeks of punishment dished out by our Commanding Officer for minor offences like insubordination, AWOL etc. as these did not qualify for the more severe army punishment in the regular army glasshouse.

The C.O. reasoned the appointment of an Irish guy in charge of the prisoners over the Hogmanay period would be a 'good idea'. Our C.O. probably reckoned any Scottish NCO's left in charge of our small jail might be a 'bad idea'. A Scots N.C.O. might be tempted to have a wee drink to celebrate Hogmanay, perhaps forgetting to keep a watchful eye on the incarcerated detainees.

Unfortunately, that careful thinking on the part of our C.O went all to hell, as they say. The Irish Quartermaster decided to sample the Hogmanay activities for himself. He enthusiastically joined in early with the Scottish celebration. This quickly led him to achieving a wonderful evening of heavy drinking followed by an equally wonderful night of heavy, drunken sleeping. Around that time one of the prisoners reached through the wire, grabbed an unpopular guard by the throat and extracted the jail house keys to obtain freedom for the night.

Alex Hanratty, my newly found friend from the time spent guarding one of our camps in Johore, was now being guarded himself. Once again he had been found wandering along a lonely road through the jungle during yet another attempt at Absent Without Leave. He was brought to our H.Q. to be handed over to our 'Seldom Seen' Regimental Sergeant Major who placed him directly into our local Regimental jail. He was no sooner officially incarcerated before he was then unofficially released again when a fellow prisoner 'obtained' the key to the jail and they all unofficially walked out to freedom. Alex made good use of his temporary freedom. He realised it was almost midnight when official New Year celebrations were due to begin. He located a supply of bottled beer (probably from behind the Sergeants Mess) and made a beeline to share some New Year drinks with me. How could I refuse such hospitality?

Actually, I did not refuse, and have a photo to prove it. If you look carefully, you will see a small arrow inset in the picture below, it reveals me neglecting my drumming duties and visiting with Alex. An enlargement showing the 'crime' is enlarged below.

I had also been doing a wee bit of drinking and was well into the mood by the time Alex located me. I was so much in the mood that I had stopped playing and turned to give both Alex and his welcome beer bottle gift my full attention. I have no idea what the punishment might be for that act of insubordination but I was well past caring. It was Hogmanay, we're Scottish. Now, do you understand?

Things got a wee bit hazy after that although I remember playing at the Sergeants Mess for a while until a reasonably sober Sergeant relieved us of our instruments; then locked them away safely. Perhaps he should have locked us all away safely with the instruments but we were allowed to run free for a few more hours to celebrate in the old Scottish manner.

(Photoon previous page. Thanks to Lia Wah Photo Studio. Batu Pahat, Johore State, Malaya) .Lee Bailey and me, close to the point of no return. My tartan troosers are starting to concertina at the bottom, always a sure sign of my having taken strong drink as a 'refreshment'.

It all ended in the old traditional blootered fashion. The last thing I can remember was having an argument about music under the stars with some guy. He must have said something daft about some subject which I can't remember. I certainly do remember telling him he was a stupid bastard and I giving him a shove to make my point.

Unfortunately, for him, we were standing near one of the deep monsoon drains which ran through the camp. His alcohol intake had been similar to mine, i.e., way too much and my shove propelled him backwards for a couple of shaky steps till he disappeared into the deep drain. His luck was in. It was not the monsoon season and the drain was dry. Unfortunately, and this is the unlucky part for him, he was not completely dry himself, as the saying goes, he went to sleep lying on his back in the empty drain. I also took a couple of shaky steps to the edge of the wide monsoon drain to see if he was o.k., but managed to pull up just in time to prevent me from joining him at the bottom. He looked quite comfortable down there in the moonlight, lying on his back and snoring loudly. I decided it was time I had a wee rest as well but, rather than join him in the drain, I made it back to my own bed to sleep it off.

67 NEW YEAR'S DAY 1956. FRIENDLY FOOTBALL GAME.

Officers versus Sergeants. Sunshine brollies were very popular that day.

The football game on New Years day was a hoot; the referee kept blowing his whistle often just because he liked the sound it made! Quite a few of the players should have been sent off for trying to make a failed fashion statement. The rules of the football game were being applied in widely diverse interpretations by both sides. Some joker even introduced an extra football at the far end of the pitch because he thought it would save some of the players at that end of the field from running around too far in the mid-day heat!

Wee Charlie Jeffrey, our hero from the great pig shoot, was taken very seriously drunk that New Year.

He and several others had carried on the old Scottish tradition from the Hogmanay celebrations of the previous evening by extending their drinking into New Year's Day. A bunch of us were gathered on a grassy slope beside a deep drain to watch 'the game'. Wee Charlie, still suffering from a bad haircut, laughed so hard at the antics of the tipsy football players that it caused him to lose his footing and he tumbled into the deep but dry monsoon drain, completely pissed and unable to extricate himself. See photo #1.

#1

However, help was at hand. Unfortunately the 'help' turned out to be completely pissed also and not making too much sense either. The great rescue plan turned into a rambling discussion regarding the best way to extricate Charlie from the deep monsoon drain. The best method for the rescue was for one of us to descend into the drain to join Charlie and then assist him to climb out. This idea was put on hold after a couple of the rescuers tumbled into the deep monsoon drain and were unable to help themselves, never mind helping Charlie. Now there were three! These failed rescuers decided to seek assistance. They staggered in opposite directions along the dry monsoon drain trying to solve the now, even bigger, rescue problem, leaving Charlie to his own devices. I see he had removed one of his boots in picture #2. Exactly why he considered this act to be of any help in the rescue operation was not made clear!

First attempt has failed, in spite of heroic but useless boot removal. Plan 'B' then swings into action. Wee Charlie, full of resolve, determination and whisky, replaces right boot and tries again.

#3. Eeky Blyth, also suffering from the same bad haircut epidemic plus excess of alcohol which had afflicted Charlie, is about to complicate the situation by losing his pants when trying to offer help.

Picture #4. Second attempt having failed, wee Charlie is abandoned to a death worse than fate. Charlie's only comment, "Aw fuck".

68   THE POINT OF NO RETURN

The real point of no return came for me just after my twentieth birthday on February 10th 1957.

My two years National Service was nearing an end. However, my happy little band of brothers still had to make the journey home to the U.K. to end our service. The initial journey to Singapore from Belfast had taken us four weeks on the troopship Devonshire. This time our trip back would be six weeks on board the saucy MV Dunera. The blocking of the Suez Canal by the Egyptian President, Colonel Nasser, meant we had to sail for home by a different route.

Our paternal government dictated that former employers must keep our jobs open for a period of time when we returned after completing our National Service. However, some of us had changed quite a lot, what would happen next? Our little mixed bag of amateur soldiers gathered together at H.Q. Company in Batu Pahat for a couple of days before being loaded onto Bedford army trucks for transport to Singapore docks and home.

It was great to be with my old friends again, we had lots to talk about. We had been located with different rifle companies in the Regiment and scattered across Johore State for most of the time. We would be making the final journey home together again. Just like it used to be when we first met to start basic training at Berwick on Tweed back in early 1955 which seemed to have been years ago. Some of us had matured a bit, some less so and more or less looked the same. But there were a few thoughtful faces as we wondered about how we would fit back into civilian life again.

The guys were allocated army tents for their brief two day stay at H.Q. Ray found me at our wee, wooden hut for the Pipes and Drums. We had not seen each other since that memorable last evening in Singapore. He was the same old, daft Big Ray but seemed to be a bit more mature now, probably due to almost two years active jungle patrol service. Robbie soon surfaced although he had acquired another dimension having been shot in the chest a few months ago. He had been rushed to hospital with a collapsed lung. I also rushed to Kluang Military Hospital as soon as I heard the news of the shooting where I found him pale and a wee bit wan though recovering his old Glasgow street wise composure.

We all sat and swapped tall stories with each other for that first night, bit daft really, we were about to be together for six weeks, crowded onto a troopship with all the time in the world for yarning. There was a difference this time, we were going home.

The end of another day. Pipes and Drums 1/K.O.S.B. playing, 'The Black Bear'. This is the pipe tune to signify that the working day has ended. It is always played by, ' The Jocks' when they leave a parade. I am smack in the middle. This time it really was my last parade.

I can remember clearly the early morning of our departure from the regiment. For the first time since joining I was to be separated from the Pipes and Drums - an evocative experience for me. It was almost like being wrenched from a family. I was used to being able to ask for advice from Corporal Dan Grant about life in general, swapping stories with pipers, 'Bunny' Campbell and Jock Winton. My friend Piper John Scott was the only other National Service guy in the Pipes and Drums, he was leaving also. John and I were in the same conscript draft during training. We went through our signal platoon training together, we were involved in the volounteering for the S.A.S. debacle together, and we transferred together to the Pipes and Drums. We were now heading for home together, wearing white tape on our puttees which marked us out as members of the Pipes and Drums. It all seems a bit silly and long ago now.

Early o'clock in the morning all the departing National Service guys were herded onto the trucks, swearing and farting as usual. Silence fell as the Pipes and Drums marched towards us, wearing full parade kit of white jackets, kilt, spats and shiny black brogues. They came to a smart halt beside the trucks. Drum Major Tom Black gave the command, "By the centre, Quick March," The drums rolled; the pipes and drums broke into, 'Hey Johnie Cope, are ye wakin' yet, and are your drums still beatin' yet?' The outfit had turned out to play, 'The Long Reveille', just for us.

It's a compliment, not performed for just anybody. I now knew how the Fiji Regiment must have felt when the Pipes and Drums played for them as the Fiji ship slipped out of Singapore docks, heading for home after their period of service in Malaya.

I hoped none of the other guys would notice a wee tear in my eye, but I certainly noticed the same thing with Piper John Scott as the evocative sound of the Pipes and Drums faded away behind us. The trucks gathered speed as we hit the road through Johore State, Malaya in the direction of Singapore Island and, eventually, home.

Oh, were goin' down the track

and we'll never come back.

Sergeant Harrigan is our leader.

Oh, we know he's true but he has'nt

got a clue.

Away down in the green hell. Yes, the green hell.

Now my story must end

for I've things to attend

like packing my kit for Blighty.

To Singapore

see Malaya no more

Away down in the green hell

Yes the green hell.

 It was necessary for us to take 'the long way round' journey to the U.K. The Suez Canal had been blocked by Egypt's President Nasser because of a dispute between the President of Egypt and the Governments of both Great Britain and France. The Egyptian President decided to have a good pout. He ordered some ships to be scuttled in the Suez Canal thus effectively closing our usual way home. War was quickly declared on Egypt by both France and the U.K., the old colonial days were not quite dead yet. 'Send in the gunboats captain!'

Now the only way for us to reach Europe from the Far East by sea was to sail to Cape Town in South Africa. After rounding the Cape, we would then travel up the west side of Africa to reach home. Our total sailing time stretched from four weeks to six, I had already started to look forward to many weeks of daily sun bathing on the open deck interspersed with some sight-seeing stops here and there, not a bad experience for a young, impressionable Scottish lad.

The situation was finally resolved when the USA gave both France and the U.K. a bit of a 'ticking off' for getting involved in the now unfashionable way of dealing with international problems. Both countries backed off with heads bowed. It was clear that the US was calling the shots. The gunboat approach used in the old British Empire days was coming apart at the seams, just as we had noticed during our stay in the Far East. This was the 1950s and 'the times they were a changing'. The change came too late for us, we were already committed to sailing the altered route back round the Cape to home.

The good ship mv Dunera which took us back the long way round to the U.K.

69 NEWS FLASH

News flash from home, 'Supplies of Bananas are now quite plentiful'. Wartime rationing restrictions were lifted in 1952. Poor old Britain, the war had finished in 1945, but imports of fruit and other 'luxury' items were still scarce. 'Hurry home lads, bananas are available'. The first banana I saw was in 1946. None of my age group of kids had seen imported fruit at all during the war. Food imports were restricted to foods considered to be basic necessities. Things like sugar and tobacco! We had all seen pictures of bananas and knew what they looked like. However, the banana I received after the war was nothing like the pictures of bananas I had ever seen. It was a dehydrated one which my auntie May had managed to obtain. She heated it and placed it on a plate in front of me, steaming and hot all by its lonely self for my delight. My treat looked more like a piece of brown dog shit. I never really acquired a desire for any exotic foreign fruit after that, an attitude which has remained with me to this day. I also never did find out why the bloody thing had been heated in the first place.

70 HOMEWARD BOUND

Happily for us, the long trip home took six weeks of sunshine and comparatively lazy cruising. It was, of course, raining heavily when we reached the English Channel.

Some of the motley crew on board the Dunera. My mates Big Ray and Robbie on the left. Most of the lads seem to be smoking healthy, free issue fags.

We had soon slipped cable on the Dunera (it's started again, have you noticed the speed with which I switch from landlubber talk into the language of the salty, old, seadog?). We were now heading west, saying goodbye to the South China Sea, entering the vast Indian Ocean and Colombo was our next stop. The atmosphere on board was different from our previous seagoing trip when we had sailed with our Regiment. This time we were a small detachment of about one hundred bodies, afloat amongst groups of other returning army and air force personnel from other units. We had none of the previous regimental bullshit. There were no daily duties, physical exercises or even parades. The atmosphere was casual, it seemed as if, not only us, but the whole shipload, including the actual ship, was nearing the end of service. Discipline was visibly relaxed. What the hell were we to do for the next six weeks?

I decided to join the, 'Let's lie on the deck to work on our tans', brigade. After all, we were, with hardly any exceptions, all single men, average age was twenty years old and more than slightly randy. We had had two years of civilian life taken away from us. It made a lot of sense to develop a deep, salty old seadog suntan while on board. We were going to be away from our Regimental discipline, and free to mix with guys from all types of services for around six weeks. We had little else to do. We were due to return to the U.K. around the first week in April, at which time the locals would be emerging, pasty white, from winter. We, on the other hand, would hopefully look like sun bronzed world travellers. This, combined with our bullshit foreign army service stories, would probably knock any male competition into a cocked hat. Whatever a cocked hat is.

Every morning after breakfast, we would hang around till the sailor boys had finished their daily deck scouring duties, leaving the wooden deck gleaming. Clad in P.T. shorts and canvas shoes, bearing our green, army towels underarm, we would amble onto the nice, virgin deck to mess it up completely with our sweaty bodies. We relaxed in row after untidy row of assorted soldiery, slowly baking our way to a mahogany sun tan under the hot, foreign sun, into a possible skin cancerous early grave. This was 1957, we were twenty years old. What the hell did we know?

We were under the impression that the guys left behind in the U.K. were having a great time. We imagined them going regularly to dances, meeting and dating girls Taking girls to the cinema and all that sort of stuff. None of this had been available to us for our last two teenage years. We each had lost something, somewhere. Sure, when we were briefly stationed in Singapore, we had access to dancing of a sort. If you could classify occasional visits to the Happy World, buying a handful of tickets from the kiosk, then handing the requested number of tickets to your chosen Taxi Dancer. She would be your temporary dance partner for the time represented by the number of tickets given to her. We danced inexpertly to weird sounding swing music provided by the keen but dismally amateur band of local Chinese musicians.

When the purchased dance number finished, the girl would abruptly turn round and leave you to rejoin the groups of other, uninterested Taxi Dancers. You could then either hand more tickets to her and she would partner you for the next dance, or you could approach the kiosk once more to purchase some fresh tickets and start the imaginary relationship all over again. The wicked, naughty, excited, feeling generated by this exercise soon palled as your limited dancing time cash supply dwindled. Towards the end of the evening it was often possible to take the girl home after she had fulfilled her allocated taxi dance obligation. She would then fulfill a different kind of obligation to you.

71   THE BALLROOM DANCER.

I knew one English guy who thought he had cracked the system. Not for him was the common, earthy, soldierly way to see girls, no Taxi Dancer shit for him. This was 1955, ballroom dancing was relatively popular. The larger towns in Britain all seemed to have a 'Victor Sylvester Dance Studio' where dancing was taught. I remember seeing one in Edinburgh and understood they were all the rage in other cities. This guy had even found one in Singapore.

   I mentioned he was English. He had signed on the dotted line to be a regular soldier in a Scottish Regiment. Joining as a 'regular' entitled him to apply to enlist in any military service of his choosing, he chose our Regiment. He was nice but stood out among the rest of us like a sore thumb. He eventually told me his older brother had served with this Regiment during the war, hence his desire to join the KOSB. He was also training for the signal platoon and I got used to seeing him during the early days stationed in Singapore. I remember seeing him getting ready for his weekly trip to the dance studio, all clean and shining, glasses gleaming, wearing a nice shirt and tie. After Thursday pay day he was always keen and ready to catch the late afternoon bus to Singapore, where he would learn to ballroom dance and meet girls. Unfortunately, catching the bus to Singapore was not the only thing he caught by taking dance lessons

   A few weeks after his probing into the ballroom dancing caper, our knight in shining armour had to fall out one morning after daily muster parade. He had another appointment, but this time his appointment was with the Medical Officer where his suspicions were confirmed. The V.D. test was positive. He had caught a packet!

72 I AUDITION FOR A DANCE BAND AT SEA.

The following evening I was leaning on the ship's rail at the sharp end of the ship, my usual pastime at night. I was enjoying the solitude, watching the phosphorous glimmer as our ship ploughed through the sea, hearing the murmur of the ship's engines above the swishing sound of the Indian Ocean. No city street lights here to interfere with my stargazing.

"Where are ye, ya wee ballocks?" The voice cut through the darkness, shattering my dreaming. It was Big Ray, trying to locate me in the romantic darkness. "Have you seen the notice on the daily order board?" I had to admit reading the daily order board was not a priority. I was beginning to be 'demob happy', our expression for the state of mind which seemed to kick in when the end of our army service was looming ahead.

Ray hauled me off to read the notice. It seemed the powers that be were seeking musicians to form a dance band to entertain the shipmates. Interested personnel to report to a certain Air Force Regiment Sergeant for details, no extra payment to be expected for services rendered.

It did not require a degree in rocket science to realise there were no dance partners for the hundreds of sex starved military guys milling around on board with nothing to do. Why the daft Sergeant would advertise for dance band musicians was beyond me, where would the female dancers be found to provide a dancing audience? I was overlooking the fact that there were plenty Officer class guys on board where a small amount of women passengers was situated. This was in the 'out of bounds' area for the rest of us, but the Officers could take their pick of any young nurses and some returning Women's Air Force females on board.

The response from our shipmates was meager. Apart from the Air Force Sergeant who claimed to be able to play the alto sax, there was Ray professing to be a string bass aficionado. There was also a piano player soldier on his way back to London, and me.

"Where do you fit into the music business?" I hear you cry. I had once confided to Ray my secret ambition to be a jazz drummer. My only qualifying talent for satisfying this dream so far was my position as a snare drummer/bugler with the Pipes and Drums. My enthusiastic support for jazz music was hardly enough experience. Ray brushed aside my misgivings re my ability to play jazz or even any kind of dance band music, saying that I could obviously use drumsticks, the rest would just come naturally. Ray had this wonderful, 'can do' attitude.

Hope springs eternal, they say. What Hope did not mention, there was one more volunteer for the position of dance band drummer. My rising hopes were dashed. It was rumoured this other guy was not only good but he claimed to have had experience of playing professionally with a London band.

This seemingly fantastic applicant had only one slight problem. He was unable to apply in person for the position as he was currently incarcerated in what we called, 'The Sharp End'. This was naval slang for the lock up prison for bad boys aboard ship, situated way out above the sea in the bows of the ship, hence, the Sharp End. Information regarding his reason for being incarcerated was not forthcoming but it was enough for his application to be crumpled up and placed in the round file. I was back in the band with a shout!

I was to be the drummer, Ray, the bass player, a guy from London, the pianist, the alto sax player was, of course, the Air Force Regiment Sergeant, nominated by himself. He was, after all, in charge of forming the band. He also owned his own alto sax! I am sure he appointed himself to be the boss so he could be in charge of the band. Quick thinking on his part. This chap should go far, he is probably running Imperial Chemical Industries by now. I can imagine the help wanted column in the newspaper. 'Sharp lad wanted, good prospects, no alto sax playing necessary, good pension scheme available'.

We had a few obstacles to overcome before the band could get started. The organising Sergeant showed surprise when he learned Ray did not have his large string bass on board. The reason for this was simple, Ray did not possess a large, string bass, or even a small one, and, of course, this problem had not surfaced while he was fighting in the jungle. If it came to proof, neither Ray, the piano player, or myself, had any way to prove we could play; there were no instruments except for the sergeant's alto sax, and we were beginning to have doubts about his ability on that score. Why Ray should not require a large string bass during his jungle soldiering had never occurred to the Sergeant before now. I can only surmise the Air Force Sergeant had enjoyed a rather cushy time based somewhere on Singapore

Island with easy access to musical instruments and a nice life style. Probably the nearest he had ever been to jungle vegetation was when he sipped his long, cool drink with a piece of lemon floating on the top.

Ray took care of this bass owning problem in his own, direct, way.

We had both heard about the new craze in the U.K. called skiffle music. This was when amateur musicians created a kind of basic jazzy/folksie music played by someone strumming a cheap guitar. Another player would supply percussion on an old fashioned domestic laundry scrubbing wash board. A steady, pulsing bass rhythm could be generated from a kind of Heath Robinson affair consisting of a broom handle, a strong piece of twine and an empty tea chest.

The idea was to attach the string to one end of the broom handle, the twine was then pushed through a small hole bored in the tea chest. When the twine was stretched twixt wooden broom handle and tea chest, a strong, vibrating, booming noise was obtained from the tea chest by plucking the string in time to the music.

The ever inventive Ray established where the cooking took place on board. He located the galley, had a word with one of the cooks, and returned with an empty tea chest, plus a wooden broom handle and ball of strong twine. We were in business. Ray was definitely a guy to have around in a tight spot. The amazing thing was he could make the resulting contraption sound remarkably like a bass!

I was taken into the bowels of the ship to inspect, the ship's 'drum kit'. Poor thing, it had seen better days, but not recently. The 'kit' consisted of a battered snare drum, an elderly and unfashionable bass drum with foot pedal, a high hat stand and cymbals which needed urgent attention and one, very old, ride cymbal which could be attached to the bass drum.

There was also a set of 'skulls'. I remembered last seeing a set like this used by a 'drummer' at our Boy Scout dance which seemed like many years ago when I won that bloody awful necktie at the spot dance which was rigged in my favour.

Ray helped me to carry the old drum kit from the depths of the ship to lay it before the Sergeant for comment. He obviously had not a clue or any expectations about drumming or, as I was soon to find out, any other kind of music or instruments.

I got the impression our 'sax playing' Sergeant had expected a stronger response to his advertisement. This would have enabled him to organise things to suit himself, allowing him do lots of moving around while the other guys did the playing. This would leave him time to do a bit of conducting, just like the band leaders he had seen in Holywood movies. Better still, I privately thought, he could be employed fetching cups of tea for the other guys who were doing the playing. Our little motley band of musical brothers was obviously not what the Sergeant had in mind.

And then, there were three. The piano player from London, Big Ray with his bass contraption, and me!

73 NO ENTRY FOR OTHER RANKS BEYOND THIS POINT

The non- playing Sergeant led the way to the previously forbidden 'NO ENTRY' area to inspect the piano. It was located in the part of the ship reserved for Officers, married quarters and some young women, probably the nursing types that Ray and I used to letch after at the jazz club in the Air Force camp in Singapore, prior to losing my virginity in that naughty city at the insistence of the bold Ray.

The females on board were strictly off limits to the likes of us common soldiers. There was an imaginary line about half way along the deck where the upper class area started - this was a 'NO ENTRY' area for the lower classes after this point. We never saw any women at all.

With this in mind, we entered the forbidden area. This was my first experience of being able to freely visit previously out of bounds areas and functions, not only allowing us entry, but actually welcoming such an action. This new, unusual and sophisticated awareness was strange to wee Andy from the country. It was initially all due to my entry into the magical and previously exclusive society of privileged musicians. Since then, I have played at some posh High Society functions, Hunt Balls and various other select events. I even played once at the Coal Miners Social Institute, Whitburn, West Lothian, Scotland at a Saturday night dance, without too much melee breaking out. These were all wonderful occasions, but they are all in another, later story.

We were led to the Officers' Mess bar where we found the magic piano. Our hopes were pinned on this instrument and its player. We would be sunk if both he and the piano were going to follow our initial disappointing band experience, all would be lost and we would be cast out to descend into obscurity again.

Jim, our potential piano player was from London. He sat down at the slightly battered instrument, ran his fingers experimentally over the keys, nodded his head in approval, at least the bloody piano was in tune. He settled his arse into a more comfortable position then rocked us into a great boogie number which had Ray and I snapping our fingers and clapping with enthusiastic delight.

Our non-playing Sergeant was unaffected by this piano fireworks display. No finger clicking from this guy. Unmoved, he produced his clipboard to check potential dates with the mess waiter behind the bar, as if to prove that he was not one of us rough types. He missed the opportunity to purchase some alcoholic refreshment at the bar for the rest us. He had not earned many musical points from us so far, now his naivety at the bar and total lack of 'smarts' plummeted him right down to zero. What a prize prick!

We were allowed to practice in the mess, which was deserted when we called to inspect the piano. Ray and I went off to collect our 'instruments'. The Sergeant fetched his alto sax which he carefully positioned on its little stand at the front of the 'band' where it remained, untouched. The other three of us had a quick meeting to decide what to do with him but agreed to leave things as they were. After all, apart from his clip board, he had an alto sax which would lend a wee bit of authenticity to our claim to be some kind of a band. Even if it just sat there, silent, on its wee shiny stand during our performance.

Rehearsal was a bit superfluous. Jim the pianist was absolutely fantastic, although he did not read a note of music. This was fine with us as the only sheet of music we could find when we lifted up the hinged seat on the piano stool, was a dog eared copy of the music for, 'The Laughing Policeman', with full chorus. Not much of a repertoire there so we replaced it reverently back into its dusty grave, positioned under our piano players' unpredictable arse.

Jim either ploughed away as different numbers came into his head or responded quickly to shouted suggestions from us. Ray soon got the hang of his improvised bass and I did mysterious things with the old, basic drum kit, it all seemed to gel somehow. This was just as well as our busy, non-playing Sergeant had arranged for us to play for dancing at a party in the Officers' Mess the following evening.

He had not got a clue, and, to be fair, neither did we. We agreed to have a go to see what would happen on the night. We had nothing much to lose anyway.

74 BIG PARTY NIGHT

Musicians have an old saying at rehearsals, 'It will be alright, on the night'. The music gods must have heard us rehearse and decided we needed help. There was a good party type crowd present when we arrived, dressed in old olive green shorts with matching wrinkled army shirts, set off by rather scruffy canvas P.E. shoes, and the band did not look much better either.

After a few days at sea I imagine the other passengers on board ship were, like us, starting to get bored. The novelty of travelling by sea was wearing off, even gazing at the fantastic flying fish on display as they skipped across the Indian Ocean had probably lost their charm.

The crowd was ready for something new. They looked as if they had been rehearsing for the party already, partaking in quite a few wee refreshments from the bar by the look of them. We were more than a little inclined to help their night along with a few refreshments ourselves, but we were Private soldiers. This was an Officers' mess bar, what to do?

Ray had the bright idea of using the Sergeant to fetch some drinks. If the non commissioned Sergeant approached the officers' bar in a well pressed Air Force jacket and displaying a confident manner, he might just get away with ordering drinks for us.

I had my doubts about this plan. Our Sergeant was already sitting in front of 'his', band, apparently preparing to play by blowing experimentally into his alto sax from which came a faint sound, something like, 'a coo farting up a close' was the expression which came, uncharitably, into my mind.

Ray, Jim and I had a quick, few words before launching straight into a crazy, ambitious, (ambitious for Ray and me), boogie number featuring Jim attacking the keyboards. He was a godsend, plus he seemed able to do most of the work. Suddenly, the bored crowd came alive. They had been hoping to move the boredom a bit to the left to enable them have at least a reasonable evening for a change. They had not bargained for a crazy English boogie music piano player backed by two, very enthusiastic Scottish guys who were, it appeared, away with the fairies, and certainly not quite right in the head.

The crowd went wild as their refreshments started to take effect as well. One or two couples, not quite sure if this was either a quickstep or perhaps a foxtrot, tried to adopt a conventional ballroom dance posture, looking quite puzzled but really quite willing to enjoy themselves, come what may.

Others attempted to jive but they had never experienced dancing to anything like this, remember, it was early 1957. They just jumped up and down in time to the music in good, old Anglo Saxon style. They were having fun, probably for the first time in their hide bound, military dominated life. Jim's wild, piano music had done the trick. The entire crowd was attempting to dance on the now too-small area allocated for this purpose. Lots of the dancers broke the unmarked boundary area reserved for very reserved dancing. Rules and standards were being broken, some broken forever. I had never seen this type of thing happen before.

Bear in mind, after a long Second World War when I was growing up, followed by years of rationing, clothes coupons, no street lights, not much fun and other restrictions, Britain was broke. It was 1954 before meat rationing finally stopped, the year before I was called up for National Service.

I was seeing British people starting to throw off some of their inhibitions and to have a good time. My own memories of the wartime and following years into the early 1950s are not remembered in colour, I only remember grey-scale impressions. I recall starting to see things in colour by the late fifties. I was actually involved with this exciting music. I was part of it, I belonged. I liked it.

I also liked my first drink in the Officer's mess, somewhere which would have been out of bounds for me. I was now one of the chosen people, at least I thought I was. Imagine me having a drink in the Officers's mess? This was all new, heady stuff for wee Andy and it was an Officer who started it all.

One of the crowd was a grateful and slightly pissed, army Captain with his roving eye on an attractive, young nurse. Funnily enough, this was the same Captain who was in the bar when we had arrived to set up our gear, such as it was. He had advised us just to play nice, quiet, background music and maintain a low profile. Before he turned away to approach the bar, he admonished us to behave ourselves. Looking rather grim he reminded us that this was the Officers' Mess and some decorum was required. We should not, under any circumstances, ever start playing that dreadful new rubbish music called, "The Rock and The Roll". (his words).

We had no programme in mind at this stage, never having rehearsed, apart from hearing Jim play the piano for a few minutes when we first met. If Ray and I had planned anything musical at all, it was to follow Jim's lead to see where it took us. We would just have to try and keep up with him.

We were surrounded by an appreciative crowd as soon as we finished our first frantic number. It was then I saw the rather stern Captain shouldering his way through the crowd heading straight for us. "Oh shit," I thought, "we are for it now."

"Well done lads", he was shouting as he got closer, "Well done." He was clutching a whisky glass, it seemed the straight laced Dr Jeckyl had been pushed aside at the bar allowing a very different Mr Hyde to come gibbering out to play. He wanted to know what we would like to drink. He was all smiles and ready to have a good time. By coincidence, so were we.

Our new friend went to the bar, ordered four beers and had the barman bring them over to us with instructions to keep us supplied for the entire evening. This nice, moderately pissed man was blissfully unaware that Jim. Ray and myself were now mature, world travellers, each aged all of twenty years, who had been round the block a few times, ye know.

We had noted the four drinks being poured. Our new benefactor, the drinks provider, had obviously included the Air Force Sergeant. He, after a few tuneless, tootles on his sax before we started, had picked up his clipboard and fled in alarm, seemingly startled by Jim's furious piano pounding. He escaped through the crowd apparently making urgent notes on his clip board and remained loose till we eventually took a break. At this point he returned to lean on the piano, sipping his free drink, posing as one of the band.

The previously mentioned world travelling musicians, continued to order four, free drinks from the bar for the rest of the evening. However, we mature musician types had now switched from beer to cocktails, deemed really more suiting to our new musical life style. Ordering our drinks from the Officers mess bar was no problem as I had tipped the bartender when he delivered our first round from our friendly, half pissed, Captain.

The tipping exercise was totally foreign to us, but I had observed this rewarding habit in any American movies I had seen in the fifties. The new custom was appreciated by the bartender who made sure we were quickly supplied with booze for the rest of the evening. The actual cost was being faithfully added to our benefactor's bar bill as instructed.

The number of cocktails served remained at four but were now being consumed by just the three of us. We split the four drinks in a democratic fashion - on the basis of, two for me and one each for the other two. We swapped our turns for the extra free drink in each round and also managed to maintain fairness in the traditional, old, Scottish custom by carefully omitting the non-playing Sergeant. Did ye think we came up the river Clyde on a banana boat?

The evening was a great success. The crowd loved us and our music. Their attempted conga dance was talked about for days to come. Our music went down well, as did a few of the tipsy dancers. This was the first time I had heard the English expression, "Whoops", which was used when a wobbly dancer slid laughing helplessly to the floor. There is a first time for everything as the soldier said to the girl when he led her into the woods. Plans were laid for repeat performances by the band on a regular basis all the way back to the U.K.

We finished the night tired, sweaty and happy. We were still on a high which comes with having played music successfully, and satisfied the crowd. This was an entirely fresh new and exciting feeling for me and I liked it. At the end of the evening the three of us musical types slowly wandered back to the deserted deck at the sharp end, under a night sky which was overflowing with lights such as none of us had ever seen before. There is no light pollution in the middle of the Indian Ocean.

There was no light pollution down below deck either where we were usually incarcerated on this voyage. 'Lights out' below deck was timed for 10 p.m. when only a very dim emergency light switched on automatically for the rest of the night. Not one of us wanted to bring the evening to a close by going below, so we lingered on deck under the velvet night sky which floated with our ship above the Indian Ocean. There was no Sergeant either. We had left him, basking in a sea of admiration from our slightly pissed audience, making arrangements for future entertainment. At least he was useful for something.

We lent on the ships rail, unwilling to let the evening disappear, drinking and talking on into the night about our music and some of the vivid, daft scenes we had seen that night. Some of the time we spent just listening to the ocean whispering old secrets below us. This was the new and fascinating romantic life for us.

Ray would probably still refer to me as, "Ya wee bollocks". However, wee bollocks had now added an entirely new dimension to his character, I had tasted a new experiences and it suited me. I now knew why some successful footballers or entertainers felt different from the others. I felt that I had been accepted into the magical group of musicians. One of our magical group loosed a horrendous fart into the romantic and velvet night (I *KNOW* it was Jim !!) and we fled quickly.

And so we went to bed. I soon drifted off to sleep under the mysterious night sky, full of unexplained wonders. The other two Philistines buggered off below to their bunks, into the overcrowded region of common soldiers below deck with the overpowering aroma of unromantic farts and sweaty socks.

75 SRI LANKA (CEYLON - AS WAS).

We dropped anchor in the docks at Sri Lanka a couple of days later. We were allowed on shore for a fairly short visit of a few hours, this was fine by us as we were beginning to walk with a bit of a roll again.

I had found Sri Lanka intriguing on our outwards visit. Situated off the bottom tip of India, it contained what I imagined was as close as I was going to get to Kipling's India. It is a fascinating island. Not like the India I imagined, but I took to it and made a mental note to visit it properly as a civilian, if the occasion rose in the future. Guess I had better hurry up as the future seems to be shrinking a bit lately, and I still have not made it back to Sri Lanka yet.

During that brief few hours ashore we managed to make it to the Temple of the Tooth and saw the huge elephant there. Ray and I had been the only two to see the animal on our first visit so we had to trail the rest of our bunch to the Temple to have a look at the elephant. We had a cup of tea somewhere else and it was soon time to get back aboard. So much to see, so little time.

76 THE NIGHT TIME IS THE RIGHT TIME.

We were booked to play in the Officers' Mess again, this time it was a booking for a birthday celebration.

It was evening when the Dunera cast off to sail once again into the moonlit Indian Ocean. How romantic to be having a party in the Officers' Mess, I thought, as I watched a half naked hairy Scotsman in the next bunk cutting his toe nails. I went to the heads for a shower and got ready for our second night of entertaining.

Once again, there was a fairly well primed bunch waiting for us and, once again, our non playing band leader sergeant fled, clutching his clipboard to discuss important engagements with the mess bar tender or anybody, just as we started to play. Just as well really, as he did not fit in with us anyway.

There was a good selection of young, suntanned, good looking, women there. I noticed they seemed to be attracted more to Jim on piano than to either Ray or myself. After all, Jim was really the main attraction, most of the girls approached him with praise for his playing and requests for their favourite numbers.

I guess I had slipped into day dreaming mode again. When I eventually came crashing back onto the real world, I was barely aware that Jim was giving us a count of four beats in. This was to introduce his next musical offering which turned out to be the much requested Conga dance. The closest I had ever come to its Conga rhythm was when I saw a Hollywood (bloody Hollywood again!) movie starring Sonja Henie dancing the Conga while wearing what seemed to be a full fruit basket on her head. This was a very colourful fashion statement, but not a great deal of help for my start in my musical education.

However, the primitive rhythm we generated kicked off some hidden response in our dancers. Ray joined in with a pounding bass beat which combined with my daft idea of a Latin rhythm. Our sound was just what the dancers needed. They obviously loved it, although their dancing level was about as primitive as the music. Inhibitions were thrown aside. They were in the middle of the huge limitless Indian Ocean, some refreshment drinks had been taken, no nosy neighbours to spy on them, Wheeeeee!

We finished the evening to enthusiastic applause from the crowd. To be fair, their enthusiasm was partly due to the amount of alcohol they had consumed. However, we were convinced their enjoyment was due to our spirited and artistic interpretation of their many musical requests, even though we were a wee bit rough. Rough but Ready! We rounded off the evening up at the sharp end of the ship as usual, leaning over the ship's rail, having a last drink and already planning our musical future.

77 WE CROSS THE EQUATOR - AND YOU KNOW WHAT SAILORS ARE

The old naval tradition dictates that any sailors who have not previously crossed the equator must endure the solemn rites and rituals when entering the domain of His Royal Majesty, King Neptune.

New sailor guys, called Pollywogs, must be initiated into the royal order by learning 'The Solemn Mysteries of the Ancient Order of the Deep'. It was around this point we realised, 'The New Boys', did not refer to us army types. The Pollywogs were the uninitiated crew members in the Merchant Navy, no army types need apply.

Shit! This is beginning to read like a bloody travel guide. To be perfectly honest, we were allowed to observe the ceremonies but took no part in them. It looked a perfect shambles to me, involving the already initiated sailor boys throwing the Pollywogs into a makeshift paddling pool of water, lots of shrieking and dressing in grass skirts manufactured, I think, from combed out ship's rope. I found the so-called, crossing the line ceremony incomprehensible and a wee bit embarrassing. All that business of holding down half naked young men to give them a good soaping in the paddling pool. I moved away from the scene of the action.

I was a bit more like a cool, worldly type now. I guess I was starting to feel the effect of my own initiation into the grand order of musicians. I moved over to the starboard side of the ship, away from the madding crowd, to stare out into the vastness of the Indian Ocean. I was being rather aloof from the splashing about in the water nonsense. I was day dreaming about my new interest in becoming a musician, preferring to watch the antics of the flying fish rather than the soapy sailor boys. I must have been very full of my own importance at the time, pompous wee prat!

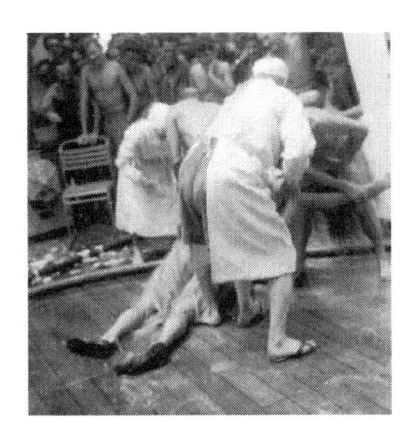

Don't ask! I have absolutely no idea what it was all about. Lots of sailors dressed up as doctors or possibly sadists in grass skirts applying gallons of soapy water to some new young guys crossing the line for the first time. The army guys were restricted to viewing only.

Me, posing in front of Table Mountain complete with fabled table cloth when we pulled into Cape Town, South Africa for the day.

78 CAPETOWN, SOUTH AFRICA.

As our ship approached Cape Town, a wireless message was received from the City Council, inviting all the ships passengers to a complimentary conducted coach tour of the area including a brief visit to the City before delivering the troops safely back to the ship. The coaches were scheduled to arrive back at the troop ship in time for our departure later that evening to continue our journey to the U.K.

The invitation was well received by the shipmates. However, only a few returning soldiers and airmen from other detachments took up the offer. Most of our guys were fed up being ordered around and moved about. The coach trip was probably a good idea but most of us opted for an unsupervised visit to Cape Town in casual style with our buddies.

It turned out later that the invitation from the Town Council really had a hidden double purpose. I am pretty certain the Cape Town Authorities were hoping to attract a greater number of us from the army contingent aboard ship to spend as much of our free time ashore under their supervision. I am also sure the actual visit to Cape Town city would be scheduled towards the end of the trip, a fairly short, supervised event. Probably a quick shufti for about half an hour or so in downtown Cape Town then herded back onto the coaches to be delivered in a safe and orderly manner right back to the ship.

I realised the Cape Town City Council must be a bit fed up playing host to crowds of restless, rowdy and thirsty British soldiers descending on their town.

I guess they were probably displeased with the unfamiliar antics of the relaxing, homeward-bound soldiers. This was a new experience for the gentle folks of Cape Town. They would be hoping the Suez Canal situation would soon be resolved and sea traffic to the U.K. could resume using the more usual way home and avoid visiting their fair city altogether.

The troop ship was dry as far as our other ranks were concerned. We were still being paid regularly but had really nowhere to spend the cash on board. A visit to a big town with plenty bars was a big temptation to most of our guys. We were footloose and fancy-free with cash to spend. Most of the troops on board were travelling in groups, quite separate from their units still stationed in either Singapore or Malaya. Nearly everybody appeared to be heading for home and de-mobilisation. There was little discipline and as we were due for release when we reached home in a couple of weeks, the city was a great temptation.

It may seem strange, but the small group I was with on the visit to Cape Town that day was not really interested in hitting the bars in town, nor were we interested in joining the free coach tour party. We were perfectly happy to spend the few hours allowed for the visit by doing just that, visiting. We wandered around town, taking in the sights and sounds, posing for a few photographs, and making observations to each other about our surroundings. Might sound a bit boring but we were a content small band of brothers who had started this adventure together. We felt easy with each other's company, making corny jokes, pointing out strange sights to each other. We were relaxed, we were heading for home.

Posing in Cape Town. Piper John Scott standing on left. I am sitting on left. Cher Smith's face is obscured by some smoke from Tosh's fag. McWilliams is holding a newspaper with a picture of a partly clothed young white lady. This picture may have been intended as a memory aid for us, it had been a long, long time since any of us had seen a girl like that.

L to R. Robbie Robertson, me in rickshaw, Dave Abernethy and Tosh. We did not actually go anywhere in the rickshaw and just used it as 'window dressing'. I gave the guy a tip for compensation.

Just me, posing again.

I took this final one before we headed back to board ship in Cape Town port. My friends, Piper John Scott, Robbie Robertson, McWilliams, Dave Abernethy and my old mate, Big Ray Reid. Where are they now?

There was one sight however, which stuck out like a sore thumb, making us realise this was indeed a foreign country. On the solid, respectable, granite steps leading up to the City Hall we noticed a small group of equally respectable looking, white ladies parading on the city steps, carrying large bill boards, hung on cords over their shoulders. When we got closer, we could see they each displayed large notices printed in black on white paper covered boards. They were holding a silent protest against the government decision to hang a number of black prisoners who had committed various misdemeanours. The hangings were scheduled to be carried out early next morning, leaving no time for a last minute reprieve as we used to see in the good old Hollywood movies.

There were no details regarding the types of crimes, no other details at all. 'Driving while black', was a possible but unlikely charge in those days when very few blacks would actually possess a vehicle at that time. They might have stolen a loaf of bread or some other heinous offence. We had no idea what the charges were. This was South Africa in 1957. A foreign and very strange country to us with its own Apartheid laws and customs.

This sight caused us a temporary bit of gloom, but it soon dissipated as our good mood reasserted itself when we got away from the depressing placards. There were plenty of other sights to be seen as we wandered around, but I have never forgotten the depressing sight that morning in Cape Town. I made a mental decision never, ever, to visit that strange country again, I never have.

As the hot afternoon waned, we made our way back to the ship which was moored close to the quay. We had been warned not to leave our return too late as we were due to set sail that evening.

On board again, we learned that some of our regiment had been involved in 'a wee bit of bother' in town where a running battle had taken place with the Cape Town police. Apparently, some of our lot had been hitting the local bars heavily, what a surprise. A wee bit of bother had broken out in one of the pubs and the police were called to straighten things out.

It seemed the cops were already expecting trouble from us. This might explain the kind invitation for the coach tour which would have kept most of the homeward bound soldiers safely away from the bars in town till it was time for the ship to leave. The city cops must have been a peeved when they learned their little diversionary coach trip ruse had largely failed and a fair amount of naughty Scottish soldiers had managed to slip through the net to descend into the bars downtown in the city.

The local cops hit the bar where the report had come from. 'Hit' was the operative word for their 'over the top' approach to a small problem. Probably some of our guys were singing songs in a bar which a lot of the guys liked to do quite often. Shock – horror! Some Scottish guys are singing songs and enjoying themselves. Must put a stop to that kind of thing.

Their singing and strange accents may have caused some concern on the part of the locals, this could probably have been dealt with easily if a tactful approach had been used. But it seemed that tact was not considered necessary when dealing with boisterous Scots. Truncheons were already drawn when the cops entered the bar and they were used on the non violent, visiting soldiers.

I may have mentioned that a fair proportion of our regiment were conscripted from in and around the Glasgow area where hitting is usually a popular pastime, especially when the pubs close early in the evening. It is usual in any of the Scottish infantry regiments to have a fairly large proportion of Glasgow born soldiers. I also mentioned previously that historically the Glasgow population contained a healthy mixture of Highland and Lowland Scots, plus a fair measure of Irish immigrant blood. The result made a population mixture believing in the right to enjoy freedom and also the right not to suffer fools gladly.

Once again, the heavily outnumbered soldiers responded vigorously to this sort of treatment, just as they had a year ago when discriminated against in the Union Jack Club in Singapore. Not only did they respond to what they considered to be an unprovoked assault, but they were also now a wee bit upset and bent on revenge. If the local cops thought they could just break a few heads with their clubs then shoo the Scots guys back to the ship with their tails between their legs, they were very, very, much mistaken.

These guys were young, fit, jungle soldiers just released from bloody active service. They were not going to stand meekly to one side when these colonial cops decided to play it hard. Our guys knew what a real hard man was and proceeded to demonstrate this in no uncertain manner. Quite a few of these cops had their first and very unforgettable, 'Glesga Kiss' that afternoon in Cape Town.

The action spilled out from the original bar as the word spread around the streets attracting other Scots guys to run forward from neighbouring bars to help even up the score a bit. This they did with a vengeance. They were rough buggers! Sure, they were rough, but they were OUR rough buggers!

The cops had started the trouble. Their action was not only unfair and unprovoked, it was also against our unwritten rules of, 'Who dares meddle with me?' Might sound a bit barbaric and primitive but these guys had seen that group of white ladies earlier that day protesting about hanging a bunch of local black men. Our guys were probably upset about the hanging. None of our business really. But they may have thought the hanging was harsh and just could not help making some kind of statement about unfair treatment from authority. They showed the Cape Town cops what was meant by barbaric and primitive, they also showed these cops a few new fighting tricks.

There was one much talked about happening. This took place as a Cape Town City Council double decker bus was passing along the main street where the running conflict was taking place. The bus conductor saw the fighting from his vantage point on the open deck of the rear platform on the bus. He recognised the badges worn by the scrapping soldiers were of the Kings Own Scottish Borderers. He yelled the Regiments' familiar call to action, "Once a Borderer - Always a Borderer", then leapt off the still moving bus. He turned round with just enough time to throw his official cap back onto the rear of the still mobile bus deck before joining in the fighting on the side of our heavily outnumbered guys.

I later heard the bus conductor was a recent immigrant to South Africa from Leith, the sea port near Edinburgh, Scotland and had served on active service with our Regiment during the earlier Korean conflict. He must have had previous experience of being well outnumbered in Korea when the

Regiment had held their ground stubbornly in spite of almost being overrun by hordes of Chinese soldiers attacking them in droves. That was when vicious hand to hand fighting took place owing to our lads running out of ammunition in various sections on the front line and being reduced to using bayonets, pick handles, shovels and anything else that came to hand. One story even mentions full beer cans being thrown at the Chinese, serious stuff indeed.

Our Cape Town brawling braves received only bruising from the cops but had a severe bollocking from a Senior Officer when they arrived back at the ship. What happened to our gallant volunteer fighting bus conductor from Leith is not recorded, it seems that common sense makes no sense on occasions like that but he would surely lose his bus conducting job. I hope he managed to survive in that strange country. Being a native of Leith, I imagine he did.

Although small in number, there were too many of our guys to be held prisoners in the small security facility aboard ship. They were severely reprimanded before they were allowed to make it back to their bunks and it was all hushed over. That was the official version. However, when the ship reached Southampton a few days later, we were besieged by newspaper reporters asking us for details about, 'The Scottish Army Riot in Cape Town', which had hit the news headlines back in the U.K.

Darkness had fallen that evening when the ship left Cape Town docks, the big engines on the ship had started to throb and cables were being cast off. I, ever the romantic, strolled along the deck in the dark to lean on the ships rail. Everything around us was quiet and still, the only sound was coming from our engines drumming from somewhere way below with the occasional verbal naval instructions being issued.

Then I heard the unmistakable sound of army booted feet running urgently across the old cobbled surface of the quay.

It was too dark to see anything. It seemed like two pairs of army boots were pounding closer and closer to the ship which was purposefully sliding away from the quay. Suddenly the boots screeched a little shower of sparks across the cobbles in a frantic effort to come to a halt and avoid their owners falling into the sea. It was then a breathless voice with a heavy Glasgow accent broke the silence, "Aw, fuck it", then all was quiet again.

The penny dropped. Two army passengers must have been celebrating the approach of home at some long shore bar in Cape Town dock area, but had left their departure a bit too late to make it to the ship in time for sailing. They would probably be picked up by the local police to be kept in jail until the next homeward bound ship visited Cape Town. They would then be transferred to the next ships' jail to continue their delayed journey home. I did not envy them their temporary stay in the local police jail, after the day's police activities in sunny Cape Town by the Sea.

79 BRIEF VISIT TO DAKAR, SENEGAL

We were allowed a few hours ashore for a brief visit to Dakar. In the hurry to get ashore I forget my camera, so no pictures of this visit.

Actually, I do have one short mental picture of one of our guys which is stuck in my head. My memory picture is of Private McCullough who had been transferred to us among a group from The Cameronians, (Scottish Rifles), to help bring our numbers up to strength before we left Northern Ireland. It seemed that McCullough was suddenly attacked by strong drink somewhere in Dakar. My mates and I nearly fell over him as we turned a street corner. He was seated on the ground, propped up against a low wall, grinning drunkenly in our direction but seemingly incapable of intelligible, or even any, speech. There was an empty red wine bottle lying on its side beside him and rocking in the morning breeze, we knew it had contained red wine because that was the colour of the vomit surrounding McCollough on the pavement.

McCullough had been with us in the Signal Platoon and I had never known him to drink any alcohol at all. Possibly he was trying to make up for previous abstinence by celebrating our pending arrival in Southampton which was now only a few days away.

I did not relish the idea of trying to get him to his feet to tidy him up. With what and how?? We would also have to cart him back to the ship in time for departure. Luckily, help was at hand, a group of his former Cameronian mates came lurching round another corner, looking for him. It appeared they too had suddenly come over a bit faint from the strong drink, but at least they were still more or less upright. My small group made a tactful withdrawal and quietly disappeared, leaving them to rescue their mate McCullough.

With the exception of the vivid mental picture of a drunken McCullough, my recollections of Dakar are pretty dim. We discovered, too late, we had missed visiting a large ancient fortress where captured slaves used to be kept till being taken by ship to the New World across the sea, God bless them.

80   LAST DANCE, GENTLEMEN, PLEASE.

Our 'band leader' RAF Sergeant was living the part of pop star musician, although the bugger had not played a single note, thank goodness. His strong point was working with his clip board organising our engagements. We were now one day out of Dakar and our last musical thrash was due. I realised it really would be my last time to pretend that I was a musician. No more fun playing drums.

The prospect of this diluted my happy feelings about returning home. What would I do about music when I returned to Scotland? Cold climate for certain and lack of both future music and female company looked like being fairly certain as well. It was all a bit of a bugger. I hit rock bottom that day, felt really despondent until Big Ray appeared beside me where I was leaning on the ship's rail.

He had just been talking with our piano player Jim, as usual Ray was looking at life from an opposite view point to mine. Of course, he had already come up with a plan for our future. "How about getting together again after we get home? I have just been talking with Jim, he thinks we could do alright if we move to London and meet up with him again. He reckons we could get plenty work down there playing the kind of stuff we are playing here, just need to rehearse a bit to tidy things up". As usual when Big Ray came on the scene, I cheered up. His London idea was heady stuff, I had only visited there once for a few days when I was younger and felt like a wee bit of a hick. This time it would be different, I would be a cool musician, able to take life by the seat of the pants. "Yes, let's do it," I boasted, already seeing the heading advertising our first gig down South. London Daze was already floating before me, daft, wee bollocks.

Next evening we headed eagerly towards the Officers Mess for our last gig (see, I'm already using musical talk). We were early and it was a quiet. We managed to buy a drink from our friendly bar steward. This was more like it. The three of us discussed our future prospects in London town, all very grown up and exciting.

The usual crowd appeared in a rush, all looking forward to having a great evening. A girl I knew as Barbara entered in dramatic fashion by cart-wheeling through the entrance door to great applause. She was no fool and would not have to buy her own drinks after that imaginative entrance.

We had already started to play when our 'band leader' made his entrance. No one paid any attention to him, which peeved him not a little. "Sod him", was our general thought, we would soon be finished with him and other authority figures like him. Fame and Freedom were beckoning.

The music went down really well as usual. I think we had to repeat our now very popular version of the Conga several times. We seemed to be the only ones in the whole crowd who were getting a bit fed up playing it. Can you detect a wee bit of blasé feeling creeping in here? Praise must already have been giving us airs. Silly prats!

The evening went with a swing and everybody had a really great time. Our 'band leader' even managed to regain face again using, I imagine, pure bullshit as all he did was pose in front of us when we were sweating like piggies playing the good music. It only goes to prove that my training N.C.O. Sergeant Fleming was right, Bullshit really *DOES* baffle brains!

After the great night ended and we had played several 'one last time' encores. We wandered back up to the sharp end of the ship to lean on the rail for the last time. We had emerged from a hot and smoke filled Officers Mess but any daft and nostalgic ideas about leaning on the ship's rail to look out to sea were quickly scrapped when we felt the chill Atlantic breeze. It was April and we were fast approaching the U.K. It was time to fold up the shorts and sort out some sensible warmer clothing. We scurried quickly below deck, my romantic nights spent sleeping beneath the stars were now finished, as the soldier said to the girl.

81 SOUTHAMPTON, ENGLAND.

A week or so had passed after leaving Cape Town till we reached Southampton. We 'met the press' which was a surprise to us. The press wanted to know the gory details of the Scottish 'riot' in Cape Town. It had been pushed to the back of our minds with the business of arriving back home after such a long time. The reporters were given short shrift, as they say. We were too busy pushing them out of the way to enable us to set our booted feet on British soil, even if it was only Southampton and raining.

Much of our army U.K. issue clothing had fallen victim to the dreaded green mould caused by undisturbed storage in the humid conditions in Malaya for a couple of years. The bags containing our heavy U.K. uniforms had only been dug out of the holds below the water line on the morning of our entering British waters where we encountered a sharp drop in temperature accompanied by heavy rain. "Welcome home mates - Bananas anyone?"

There was a frantic outburst, not only of heavy rain but also of long stored and neglected British Army uniforms. Irons appeared from somewhere, probably issued from the ship's stores and we struggled to knock our kit back into some kind of shape. Our UK gear had to be made suitable for experienced army heroes to wear when we disembarked. Medal ribbons had to be attached to our battle dress tunics. All, that is, except for Alfie, who had somehow lost his. He said he had reported it as having been stolen but managed to solve the problem by lifting a replacement from somebody else.

In the sudden rush both Ray and I had lost contact with our piano player Jim, he belonged to a separate unit on another deck. We only realized this later when we were on the train bound for London, neither one of us had an address or even a phone number for Jim. Our musical future plan was fading fast.

Our contingent of, soon to be ex, Scottish Infantry Soldiers was shepherded off the ship to much baaing again. We were herded into a large shed and suffered the indignity of questioning by the bloody Customs Officials who had set up wooden folding tables, GS, 6 foot. This was where they took their official places to examine our imported goods!! Imported goods? What an impertinence. It did not take long for these officials to realise a blunder had been made by some clod in an office somewhere.

We were loaded with every piece of gear we owned, or rather, the British Army owned. Our army possessions were normal kit bag, sea going kit bag, large back pack, small pack and pouches, all stuffed with sweaty socks, underwear and pieces of army issue clothing, some of which had not seen the cold light of day in the U.K. since we had said goodbye to the 'auld country' a couple of years ago..

The Customs Officials, wearing their important peaked hats, soon lost their air of affected, important bullshit when faced by a crowd of hard and unfriendly faces. We were all well pissed off. We just could not believe this nonsense had been set up especially to greet our troopship. Luckily, the customs men soon decided they had had enough of fumbling through our dirty socks and mouldy underwear for non existent contraband, and started to wave us through.

They noticed my wee German camera, though. I had bought it on arrival at the free port in Singapore. It was examined closely before they impounded it and took a note of my home address. About two weeks later I received an official letter from customs demanding a few pounds duty to be paid before they would return my camera, fine thanks from a grateful country! Next time they offered me a free rifle and a passport to exotic places, I would tell them exactly where they could stick it.

Memories of the next couple of days are almost blank. I recall part of the train journey from Southampton to London where we enjoyed a fine view of the seemingly interminable miles of seedy, grey looking washing hanging on clothes lines in the grey rain, on full display in the suburban back yards. I dimly recall lodging overnight at the Union Jack Club in London before catching the train to Scotland at Kings Cross Railway Station just like Harry Potter and friends did many years later when they travelled back to school.

82 HAME AGAIN

'Sailin' up the Clyde,

Sailin' up the Clyde,

Back tae Bonnie Scotland

and yer ain fireside.

Oh, a lump comes in yer throat

and a tear ye cannie hide.

Back tae Bonnie Scotland

and yer ain fireside'.

This old Scottish song would bring tears to a glass eye. Unfortunately, we had not sailed up the river Clyde to Glasgow but instead docked at Southampton in the South of England.

I and several others were sent to the army depot only a few miles from Edinburgh which housed what was then the home of The Royal Scots Regiment at Glencorse barracks, just a mile from my hometown of Penicuik to spend our last few days of National Service. However, I decided I had spent my last night sleeping on an army cot. I climbed over the depot wall, caught a passing bus and was off for home. On reaching our house, I pushed up the kitchen window to retrieve the door key which was attached to a piece of string hanging on a nail inside the window. Security levels were a bit lower in those days. I was inside the house when my mother came rushing back from shopping, having been alerted of my arrival by somebody who had recognised me on the bus. I was standing in the living room, which seemed smaller than it used to be, facing the front door, as my mother burst in all flustered and happy looking, she ran towards me. I took a couple of steps towards her and we both came to an abrupt halt, inches from, but not touching, each other.

Yes, the old Scottish reserve had kicked in for both of us. Paralysis struck. We were immobile, neither of us knowing what to do next. We broke the hesitation at the same time, together we kicked aside the old Scottish tradition. And, for the first time since my father died, we hugged, my mother sniffed through her tears. "Welcome home son".

Well, that's quite enough soft emotional shite from me. On a good day, I could bring tears to a glass eye for Scotland in an International competition.

Crossed kukries shoulder flash from the 2/10 Gurkha
Rifles and General Service Medal – Malaya.

HAME AGAIN

Here I am. Back home having travelled about the world serving in Her Majesty's Army. The Scout hut pictured here is beside the South Esk river. It lies beneath the Pentland hills, the same 'hills of home' remembered nostalgically by R.L. Stevenson, when he was sick and isolated in Samoa.

Our 'Boy Scout' rustic hut is situated just below the ruined Brunstane Castle where another Wishart, on the run from the bad guys, took refuge many years ago. The other Wishart was a Scottish Protestant of 16th century vintage. He was being pursued by the naughty Catholics and hid for a while in what is now the tumbledown ruin of Brunstane Castle. He was captured in 1546, dragged to St Andrews in Fife, and burned at the stake to teach him a lesson. It was obviously his last lesson in life, I guess being called a martyr would not compensate.

I had decided to get away from the madding crowds for a week of solitude before returning to take up my old job in the Sales Office at the local paper mill company. "What solitude"? I hear you cry. "Who took the bloody photo then"? It's none of your bloody business anyway. However, if you really need to know, I had a young lady come to visit and she helped me to break the solitude a great deal. This solitude thing is not all it's cracked up to be.

Well, that's the story of my two year's National Service with The King's Own Scottish Borderers from 1955 to 1957. We managed to cover quite a bit of ground during that time. I even succeeded in growing up a wee bit. It did not make me a bad person, as my Irish friend Kevin Mulvihill would say. (I promised you would be in my book).

I will now make a sharp turn to the right, stamp my left foot to the ground, giving a wee pause which is the Scottish Infantry way to announce this particular exercise has finished. I will then march smartly away.

I am not sure if this is a book of memoirs with some photos or a photo book with some text. It brought back a lot of memories though. "If I don't see you through the week, I'll see you through the windie".

THAT'S ALL FOLKS.

Thanks to:

Patricia O'Brien, Editor.

Andrew Brown, Design for Writers.

Matt Horner, eBook Partnership.

Special thanks to:

Kevin Mulvihill for giving me that fateful push to get on with it!

My sons Marc and Sean for support and understanding.

Laura Helen Beck from the Stroke Association for valuable advice.

My good and helpful friend Bella from Inverness.

My very special friend Sable in Colorado.

Unless where specified, all other photographs are the property of Andrew Wishart.

©Andrew Wishart. Staffordshire, England. July 2012.

THE END

I HOPE YOU ENJOYED THIS WEE STORY BOOK OF MY ARMY MEMOIRS. IF YOU LIKED THIS ONE THERE ARE SOME OTHERS WHICH I HOPE YOU WILL LIKE;

MY EARLY DAZE

MY ROCK 'N ROLL DAZE

TALES FROM THE FRONTIER DAZE PUB

ALL OF THE ABOVE BOOKS WERE WRITTEN BY

ANDREW WISHART (ME).

'MY EARLY DAZE' IS ALSO AVAILABLE IN AUDIOBOOK STYLE. RECORDED BY YOURS TRULY WITH A GREAT BIG DOLLOP OF TECHNICAL HELP FROM MY GOOD FRIEND THE MUSICIAN BILL SMITH a.k.a. BILLY THE PIK.